YORKSHIRE:
NORTH RIDING

THE KING'S ENGLAND

Edited by Arthur Mee

In 41 Volumes

THE KING'S ENGLAND

YORKSHIRE: NORTH RIDING

By
ARTHUR MEE

fully revised and edited by
FRANK BECKWITH, Jr.

Illustrated with new photographs by
A. F. KERSTING

HODDER AND STOUGHTON

COPYRIGHT © 1970 BY HODDER AND STOUGHTON LTD
AND THE EXECUTORS OF THE LATE ARTHUR MEE

ILLUSTRATIONS © 1970 BY A. F. KERSTING

FIRST PUBLISHED OCTOBER 1941

SECOND IMPRESSION 1960

NEW EDITION REVISED AND RESET 1970

ISBN 0 340 12729 5

Printed in Great Britain
for Hodder and Stoughton Limited,
St. Paul's House, Warwick Lane, London, E.C.4,
by Richard Clay (The Chaucer Press) Ltd.,
Bungay, Suffolk

INTRODUCTION TO REVISED EDITION

IN preparing the new edition of THE KING'S ENGLAND care has been taken to bring the books up to date as far as possible within the changes which have taken place since the series was originally planned. In addition the editor has made his revisions both in text and illustrations with a view to keeping the price of the books within reasonable limits, in spite of greatly increased production costs. But throughout the book, it has been the editor's special care to preserve Mr Arthur Mee's original intention of providing something more than just another guide book giving archaeological, ecclesiastical, and topographical information.

In the case of every town and village mentioned in the King's England Series it has been the intention not only to indicate its position on the map but to convey something of its atmosphere. The biographical selections about people who are ever associated with that part of the country in which they lived, or who are commemorated in the parish church—which was such a popular feature of the former edition—have been retained and in some cases supplemented.

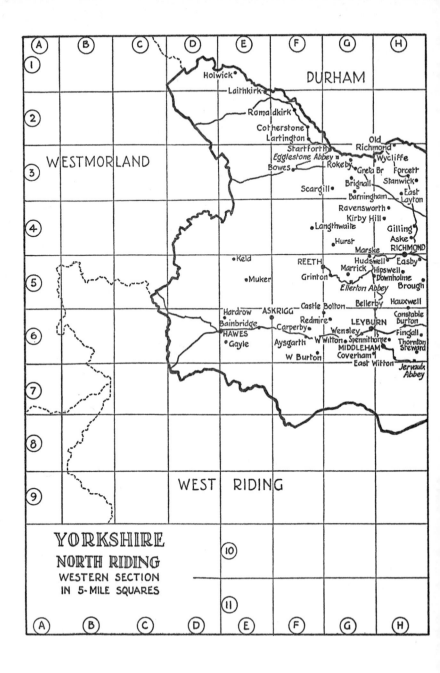

YORKSHIRE
NORTH RIDING
WESTERN SECTION
IN 5-MILE SQUARES

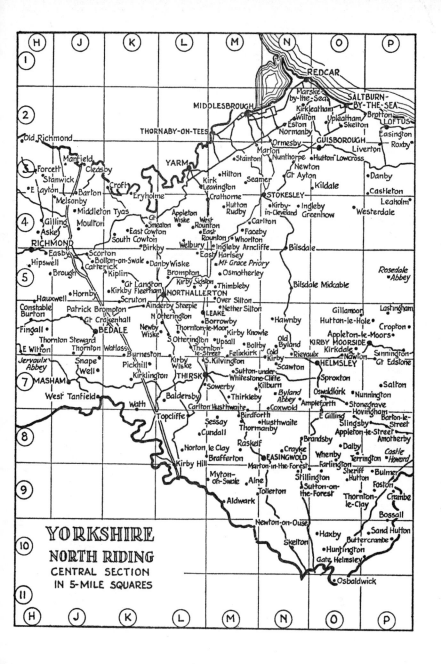

YORKSHIRE
NORTH RIDING
CENTRAL SECTION
IN 5-MILE SQUARES

Grid columns: Q R S T U V W X
Grid rows: 1 2 3 4 5 6 7 8 9 10 11

Staithes
Hinderwell
Runswick Kettleness
Lythe Sandsend
Ughthorpe WHITBY
Aislaby Ruswarp
Sneaton Hawsker
Egton Ugglebarnby
Glaisdale Grosmont Sleights Robin Hood's Bay

NORTH

SEA

Goathland

Stainfondale
Saltergate Cloughton
Scalby
Levisham Hackness
Lockton SCARBOROUGH
Middleton
Ellerburn E Ayton
Hutton W Ayton Seamer
PICKERING Buscel
Thornton Wilton Ebberston Wykeham Cayton
Dale Allerston Brompton Gristhorpe
Snainton
Kirby Misperton Yedingham

Old Malton
MALTON
Huttons Ambo

EAST RIDING

YORKSHIRE
NORTH RIDING

EASTERN SECTION
IN 5-MILE SQUARES

LIST OF ILLUSTRATIONS

LIST OF ILLUSTRATIONS

INTRODUCTION

THE North Riding of Yorkshire covers 2128 square miles, being smaller than the West Riding, but larger than the East Riding; but how vastly different it is to either of these. Apart from the Teesside area it is unmarked by industry and annually attracts many visitors for a wide variety of reasons. This is to a certain extent to be accounted for by the fact that it contains within its boundaries one complete National Park (the North Yorkshire Moors Park) and a substantial part of another (the Yorkshire Dales National Park).

These two areas suggest a useful four-fold division of the area: the Dales, comprising Wensleydale and Swaledale (and the smaller, but no less delightful dales running into them, such as Coverdale, Bishopdale, Raydale, and Arkengarthdale) and Teesdale; the agricultural plain; the North Yorkshire Moors; and the coastal area. All of these have, apart from beautiful, and occasionally dramatic scenery, history galore: one thinks of the many prehistoric settlements of the Moors; the Roman roads across the Moors and Dales, the fort at Bainbridge and the signal stations of the coastal headlands; the castles of Middleham, Castle Bolton, Pickering, Helmsley, and Richmond; the abbeys and priories of Easby, Jervaulx, Coverham, Guisborough, Byland, Mount Grace, and, finest of all, Rievaulx; the ancient crosses of the Moors, Lilla, Ralph, and Fat Betty for instance; and of the enormous number of churches which repay a visit, many of them with Norman or Saxon work. Each area has its own delights too, which deserve brief mention.

The Dales often delight with fine river scenery, and falls such as those at Aysgarth and High Force, spectacular views from such high passes as the Buttertubs, picturesque and quiet villages and small market towns such as Leyburn and Hawes where one may sample the local Wensleydale cheese and see buildings dating from ancient times to the present day, enough to keep one occupied with sightseeing for many years.

The flat plain is predominantly devoted to agriculture and has the new ultra-fast A1 road running very straight through it—although there are many intriguing byroads leading off.

The North Yorkshire Moors are a land to themselves. With many acres of wild moorland, they contain hidden valleys where one can walk, cycle or even drive for long periods without meeting others. Around the edge are many villages full of interest; to mention a few—Whorlton, with its old castle and abandoned church; Kilburn, where Robert Thompson made his "mouse" furniture, now found throughout Yorkshire and beyond; Kirkdale, whose Saxon sundial is unique in England; Hutton-le-Hole with its fascinating Ryedale Folk Museum; Lastingham, which has a Norman crypt; Egton where they hold the only gooseberry show left in Yorkshire, and Glaisdale where there is an art gallery in a converted byre—and so one might continue, but better by far to go and explore for oneself. The Moors themselves are crossed by several very ancient ways, some used in days gone by for the purposes of trade, and some, by the Romans for instance, for war; the Drovers' Road along the Hambletons springs to mind, as do the Jet Miners' track, and the ancient salt and fish roads nearer the coast. A. J. Brown describes them all in his Bible for Yorkshire walkers *Tramping in Yorkshire*; what he could not mention are the two "new" walks which traverse the Moors—the incomparable Lyke Wake Walk, 40 miles from Osmotherley to Ravenscar, and the Cleveland Way, 100 miles from Helmsley to Filey, by way of Sutton Bank, Osmotherley, and Saltburn. These are specially worked out walks for enthusiasts; for the less energetic, and less able, are several walks, or trails through the forests of the Moors. The Forestry Commission looks after over 40,000 acres of this area, and very extensive afforestation has taken place; the Commission publish a guide to the North Yorkshire Forests, where one may enjoy some peace walking in the woods, and also learn something of the work of the forester. Such walks are usually known as Forest Trails, and are described in pamphlets in three cases—Sneverdale, Silpho, and Wykeham. This is an area where one can walk all day over wild, heather-covered moor without touching civilisation—only perhaps catching a distant glimpse of the three radomes of the Early Warning Station at Fylingdales.

The Yorkshire Coast has always been popular for holiday-makers, and in addition to the larger towns, which have become inevitably scarred with the trappings of the tourist trade, amusements and the like, there are many small bays and villages such as Robin Hood's Bay, Runswick, and Staithes which have delighted artists and offer a quieter holiday. The cliffs are everywhere spectacular and one may walk along the side of them, or even on the beach under them at the correct time of day. A line of fine Youth Hostels stretches from Saltburn to Scarborough, offering cheap accommodation to the young, and making a very fine tour.

It would be a mistake not to mention in this introduction the Teesside area. It is not pretty and tourists do not go there, but if it were not for such places as Middlesbrough perhaps the National Parks would not exist. In a heavily industrialised country such as ours many people must live in towns and cities, and in uninspiring surroundings; this being so, it has been felt, quite rightly, that certain areas must be set aside and kept unspoiled for the recreation and relaxation of the city-dwellers—the National Parks. The present writer met, on a Lyke Wake walk a man who typifies the kind of city-dweller for whom the Parks were designed; this was a man who works in Middlesbrough in a bakery for many hours of each day, and who has escaped from the city to cross the Moors on the walk on many occasions. Not that the Middlesbrough area is without interest; the Transporter Bridge is unique and worth seeing; the giant steel-mills, especially at night are an impressive sight, as are the enormous ICI chemical works at Wilton. A step back into the past can be taken by visiting Kirkleatham, with its 17th and 18th century hospital and church; they are on the doorstep of Middlesbrough.

All is not history in this area; there are new developments and new problems. The coastline has suffered for centuries from erosion, and the very existence of such places as Robin Hood's Bay and Runswick are in imminent danger, unless costly schemes are rapidly embarked on. Despite the fact that the National Park exists, there is at the time of writing fierce controversy about a plan to mine potash in the Whitby area, the possible marring of the countryside being weighed against the desperate need for more employment in the area. The Parks areas indeed face the problem common to all artificially "preserved" areas, that of the places within them be-

3

coming fossilised, with little work available, especially for the young, and prices of houses mounting as the city-dwellers seek weekend cottages, and are willing to pay vast sums of money for them.

Hope, however, can be seen in various new developments. The Middlesbrough area is losing a good deal of the worst of its ugliness with the demolition of slum areas and rebuilding on the outskirts. The safety and preservation of Robin Hood's Bay would be ensured if a well-planned scheme which is in existence could be carried out, and having coped with the erosion problem in one place, planners might well save other similarly threatened places. Forestry offers not only many jobs for the inhabitants of the Moors area but a valuable source of income too.

This area has attracted the interest of many artists and writers, and many thousands have found peace and contentment and interest in the area; none more than the present writer whose researches for this book have afforded him very great pleasure, who is extremely indebted to very many people in the area who have spared him their time to talk and remedy grave lapses in his knowledge, and who hopes that this volume may help to contribute to the enjoyment by others of this incomparable part of England.

Ainderby Steeple. On a little hill in the Great Plain, it gathers round a green with noble elms and beeches, and takes its name from the church's embattled tower, a landmark all round. It is 15th century, and stands at the west end of the nave, with arches opening to the aisles. The clerestory is as old as the tower, the nave arcades are chiefly 13th century, and the aisles, the chancel, and the stone-ribbed porch are 14th. A wide arch with original painting of trailing stalks and leaves leads to the chancel, whose beauty is marred by the organ. It has three canopied sedilia, a piscina with a king and a bishop between the leafy arches, and brilliant old glass in the tracery of three windows, the Scrope shield being in one of the roundels because the Richard Scrope who was executed in 1405 was rector here before he joined Northumberland's rebellion and earned the name of the Martyr Archbishop of York. The font is 1662. The modern oak lectern has two angels holding lilies. An inscription tells of a 14th century rector, William Ealeys, and a stone in the church-yard may cover the remains of an abbot of Jervaulx.

A mediaeval chapel at Thrintoft, a mile away, is now part of a farm.

Aislaby. It is the Aislaby near Sleights (its namesake is near Pickering). The church of 1897 stands finely on the hill. It has a bright red roof, a tower whose clock is a memorial to one killed in the first battle of Ypres, and much richly coloured glass glowing in lancet windows. In the group at the west end we see the Trans-figuration.

A road by a house with a queer little bridge goes up to the quarries which gave some of the stone for London Bridge.

Aldwark. Here, on a bank of the Ouse, is a quaint little church, a captivating picture in company with trim hedges, fine trees, and a lovely avenue leading to the manor house in its small park. A mile away, near Aldwark Wood, the river is crossed by a toll bridge with a long string of arches.

The churchyard is dotted with massive trimmed yews. The church is a charming medley of herringbone brick and patches of

pebblework. Built about 1846, it has the shape of a cross, the transepts like big bay windows, the tower almost detached in the corner
between the north transept and the nave. In the east wall is a rose
window, but the striking feature of the old-fashioned interior is the
fine roof of open oak timbering, resting on pillars at the crossing.

Allerston. As we come from Pickering we see the fine grey tower
of the restored old church rising like a sentinel, guarding the pretty
cluster of red-roofed houses and the charming black-and-white inn.
The tower is 15th century, but the rest of the long aisleless church is
chiefly 600 years old, with fragments of Norman carving and old
coffin-lids built into the walls. A gravestone with a cross is over the
old entrance arch of the porch, and by the old doorway within it is
a stoup. Set in the north wall of the nave are a fragment of zigzag,
a coped coffin-lid with a cross, a child's gravestone, and some
window-tracery. There are old glass fragments in the windows, a
font probably 700 years old, and a tiny piscina in the nave.
  Not far away are many great earthworks, including the remarkable
Scamridge Dikes, and burial mounds of the Stone Age.

Alne. The big gardens of its houses all come to the road, which
makes a sharp bend on its way to the little River Kyle, flowing
among alders, willows, and beeches. There are beautiful woods
hereabouts, and a mile away is Youlton Hall, with a room where
James I is said to have slept, and a clever hiding-place in a chimney.
It is a farmhouse now, but was once the home of the Ellikers, the
family to which may have belonged the mediaeval lady lying with a
hound at her feet in the 14th century chapel of the church.
  Standing among fine trees at a charming corner, the church has
beautiful old work for us to see. The top of the tower is brick, but
the lower part has a fine tall Norman arch with heavy mouldings,
opening to a nave which has a plain arch to the chancel and a 13th
century arcade to the aisle. The chancel has a Norman window, a
Norman corbel table on each side, and a stone over the priest's
doorway with Norman carving of birds. The splendid Norman font
has a man's head set in a carved border reminding us of Saxon
knotwork.
  The glory of the church is the Norman south doorway, with no

6

Nappa Hall, near Askrigg

Higher Force, Aysgarth

Bolton Castle

The ruins at Coverham Abbey

porch to shelter it, the arch a remarkable sight with its two orders of medallions resting on shafts with beautiful capitals. The inner order has animals and birds, a holy lamb, and a man killing a pig. The birds and animals and figures in the outer order are as in the mediaeval manuscripts, some having curious interpretations. The fox feigning death so that he may catch the birds about him suggests the devil after human souls. The bird looking at a man is the white bird (found in Jerusalem) which looks at a sick man if he is to recover and turns its head away if he is to die.

The pulpit of 1626 is finely carved, and rich Kempe glass shows the Nativity and John the Baptist. A pathetic reminder of an old custom is a faded paper garland which was carried in the funeral procession of a maiden and then hung in the church; it was such a garland as this that the churlish priest objected to at Ophelia's funeral.

Amotherby. It looks across to the distant moors from its place by the Roman road along the northern slope of the Howardian Hills. Tucked away in a corner is the church, which has been rebuilt in Norman style but has still a little 16th century tower. An original Norman doorway with scalloped capitals and a beakhead on each side still lets us in, and in the piles of old stones within the porch are parts of Saxon crosses, Norman fragments, a coffin-lid with an eight-armed cross, and a woman's figure in a quatrefoil. In one of two Norman recesses in the chancel is a stone with a leafy cross and an inscription to William Bordesden of 1325; in the other lies the fine stone figure of Sir John Bordesden of 1329, a knight who fought against the Scots. His legs are crossed, and his sword is enriched with a carving of a dagger. The long-sleeved surcoat he wears with his chain armour is one of the few examples of this style in England. There is a battered Norman font in the churchyard.

Ampleforth. A long village of old grey stone, it is charmingly set on the southern slope of the Hambleton Hills which goes on climbing steeply for hundreds of feet. Into the wonderful views from the top come the Howardian Hills, across the narrow valley linking the Vale of Pickering with the Plain of York. To the north of the village is Studford Ring, an ancient encampment as old as the Bronze

Age, and a few hundred yards to the west of it is the deep ditch known as Double Dykes.

While digging under the guidance of the Yorkshire Archaeological Society, the boys of Ampleforth College came upon two ancient graves, in one of which were the bones of Bronze Age people. In a pit nearly 5 feet deep they found a food vessel, with buried bones and the body of a child, and lower in the grave were three other skeletons. The bones are thought to be about 3400 years old. Another link with the past is the Ampleforth Sword Dance, revived by Cecil Sharp and still kept up here; it is said to be a survival of a religious ceremony of 2000 years ago.

Tucked away behind the houses, the church of St Hilda was almost rebuilt last century, but it has a few things old. The 15th century low tower has a Norman arch to the nave, and built up in the north wall is a Norman doorway enriched with beakheads and signs of the Zodiac, some of the signs left unfinished by the sculptor. From the end of the 12th century comes the little south doorway with a dainty hood of leaves, and capitals carved with leaves growing from stalks. The quaint Norman font has round arcading above a projecting band, and there are windows with mediaeval tracery.

Sleeping under the tower since mediaeval days is a knight whose stone figure is still here. He wears a long-sleeved coat over his chain armour, has a long beard, and carries a sword. His head rests on the shoulder of a woman in square headdress, who seems to be leaning over him as if about to speak. It is thought he may represent a knight who fought in the Battle of Byland in 1322.

The Abbey of St Lawrence, better known as Ampleforth College, is a mile east of the village, looking out on a magnificent view. A Benedictine foundation with a tradition going back to St Edward the Confessor, it has grown into a famous Roman Catholic school with handsome buildings, a museum, and a library rich in old books, some of the 15th and 16th centuries. Some of the old wood-work and doorways from Ness Hall have found a home here. The fine new church was started in 1922 and finished in 1961. It replaces one consecrated in 1857. Sir Giles Gilbert Scott designed this church, capable of seating 800 in the nave and transepts and 85 monks in the choirstalls; it also has an extensive crypt. The interior of the new part is of beautiful green stone. There are four arches supporting a great dome, and arcades with clustered pillars and capitals exquisitely carved with foliage, from which birds, a fox, a squirrel, and many other animals are peeping out. In the richly gilded stone reredos of a vaulted chapel we see Simeon with Jesus in the Temple, Our Lord on the Road to Calvary, and the Madonna with her Son. The high altar is magnificent. Fashioned from the green stone, it has a great arch with pillars resting on dainty angels, and capitals carved with angels and scenes; there are delicate canopied niches sheltering bishops and saints, and a gilded cross hangs between two Madonnas. Among other things to see are an altar stone from Byland Abbey, the figure of an abbot who died in our own time, and beautiful woodwork by the Yorkshire craftsman Robert Thompson.

Appleton-le-Moors. This lonely spot above Sinnington has fine distant views, and a long wide street with grey houses and an ornate church designed by Mr J. L. Pearson, the architect of Truro Cathedral, in 13th century style. It is a memorial to Joseph Shepherd, a poor boy who went from the village and made a fortune by foreign trade. Its tower and spire are seen far across the moors. The chancel has an iron screen, a reredos showing the Last Supper in graffito work, and wall paintings of the Entry into Jerusalem and the Road to Calvary. Painted on the walls of the Shepherd memorial chapel are Bible scenes telling of those who go down to the sea in ships. The windows illustrate the Acts of Mercy. The school and former parsonage are also by Pearson.

Appleton-le-Street. From its green knoll on a steep bank above the old Roman road between Malton and Hovingham, the church stands like a guardian of the grey houses and the vicarage with its copper beeches, looking over beautiful country.

Sturdy and unbuttressed, its windows are all of two lights divided by shafts, the arches resting on big projecting stones. The Normans refashioned the arch to the nave, and made the doorway in its north wall, oddly sheltered by a porch like a little shed with a pantiled roof, rough rafters, and old stone seats. The niche with a headless figure above the porch of the tower may be mediaeval. The walls of the nave are as old as the tower. During the 13th century the aisles and arcades were built, and the chancel was made new. There are windows of all three mediaeval centuries, the east window being 15th century, when the chancel was probably shortened. A piscina is nearly as old as the Norman tub font, and the altar-rails are Jacobean. Near the altar lie two stone figures of unknown women who lived 600 years ago, one wearing a graceful robe caught up under her arms, and a dainty headdress with a flowered band.

Appleton Wiske. Its wide street has a green verge, and its church, tucked away behind the cottages, looks over the fields. With their stones deeply grooved as if linen-weavers had used them for grinding their shuttles, the stout old walls shelter a quaint font with an old pointed cover, a cross from Flanders, an inscription telling that a woman was churchwarden here in 1687, and a wide Norman chancel arch, though flattened and sadly out of shape. Its shafts are carved with diamond pattern in which are leaves and flowers and a quaint man in a kilt. Crude heads adorn some of the capitals, and over one capital carved with cable and scallop is a long dragon which dogs seem to be attacking.

Here Thomas Rymer spent his happiest days, and after attending the Northallerton Grammar School went up to London, where he gave 22 of the best years of his life to collecting and copying old documents relating to transactions between England and foreign countries. Long years of research he put into his 20 volumes of documents, known as *The Foedera*. What he did was of great value to later historians, but it was not work to bring him either wealth or fame. Today Thomas Rymer and his Foedera are almost forgotten. Poor he lived and poor he died, in 1713, being buried at St Clement Danes in the Strand.

Arkengarthdale. The valley of the Arkle Beck, it branches off Swaledale at Reeth, and runs up to the Tan Hill Inn, at 1732 feet above sea-level, the highest inn in England. This little known but altogether delightful valley was bought in 1656 by John Bathurst, physician to Oliver Cromwell, and the connection with the family remained until 1912, and can be seen now in the name of the C.B. Inn near Langthwaite, named after a Charles Bathurst.

Langthwaite itself is the chief village of the dale, with pleasant old houses, a friendly inn and a severe church of 1820.

The valley was much dedicated to lead mining, signs of which are all around, including the remains of the C.B. Mills, the fine Old Powder House at Langthwaite, and the extensive remains of the Old Gang Mill on the moors near by.

Aske. A mile or two from Richmond, Aske is famous for its great house, the seat of the Marquess of Zetland, in a beautiful park. There are charming gardens and a lake, and the noble stone archway at the entrance to the park has fine gates. The house has towers and projecting wings, and the views from its windows reach for nearly 30 miles. There are gorgeous rooms with superb ceilings, one of the most magnificent in the drawing-room, its walls decorated with crimson plush, the ceiling ornamented in the Adam style. The ballroom is lighted by a great dome, and the private chapel, one of the most exquisite in any Yorkshire house, has a tessellated floor, richly carved pews, and windows glowing with colour.

It is one of Yorkshire's chief art galleries, among its masterpieces being portraits of the *Duke of Buckingham* by Mytens and of *Nell Gwynn* by Kneller, a striking *Ecce Homo* believed to be Murillo's, and a charming picture of a child with a bell, one of the loveliest things Rubens ever painted—the little maid in a red robe smiling as she listens to the tinkle of the bell.

Askrigg. A tiny quaint town in Wensleydale, 800 feet above the sea, the moors and fells about it rising 1000 feet higher. Over the river is Addleborough, and from the town are charming walks across the Common to the River Swale. We may climb the heights or go down into the tunnels of the Mazeholes, deep caverns below Abbotsford Common. Half a mile away is the lovely Mill Gill Force, where the Cogill Beck makes a fine fall of about 70 feet, down a flight of limestone steps in a rocky wooded dell. Farther up the little valley is Whitfield Gill Force. The glens are famous for rare flowers, among them baneberry, wintergreen, and lady's slipper orchis. On the slopes of Whitfield Fell and on Askrigg Common grows the wild sea-pink. A mile from Askrigg the old Bow Bridge over the Sargill Beck gives us a peep of a tiny waterfall, and above is Coleby Hall (of 1655), an E-shaped old house with two rooms over the porch, a spiral stairway, and a massive door of Elizabeth I's day, hung in a doorway brought from the ancient Fors Abbey; a mediaeval window of the abbey is in a barn.

Coleby Hall (of 1655), now a farmhouse, is west of Askrigg; near by is a house of 1613 known as "Luke's House"; east of it is another old house now in a farm, Nappa Hall. Built in the 15th century, Nappa Hall has embattled towers and a handsome porch, standing in a garden with an evergreen planted in the days of the first of the Metcalfes. Generations of them lived in Wensleydale, one riding to Agincourt, another to Flodden Field. Sir Christopher went to meet the judges at York in 1556, taking with him 300 other Christophers, every man on a white horse. Tradition says that James I was a guest here and that he hunted on one of his host's white horses; and Mary Queen of Scots is said to have slept in a great four-poster bed still here.

The grey town mellowed by time was once noted for its clock-makers. The old stone for the bull-ring is still in the square, but the 17th century house with a gallery for watching the bull-baiting was burned.

Begun about 1300, the church has a 15th century tower, unbuttressed and with a roof ribbed like a bridge. The south arcade of wide sweeping arches, and the Metcalfe Chapel at its east end, are also 15th century; from the 16th century come the clerestory, the handsome panelled roof over the nave and chancel, and the north arcade of flattened arches on stout Norman columns. A battered old font stands on a millstone and a modern font has a flat cover charmingly carved. There are pewter flagons and plates in a case, a small old chest, a stoup once used as a chimney pot and still black with soot, and a panel of bright 15th century glass showing the Wise Men offering gifts to the Madonna and Child.

Aysgarth. A small village of romantic Wensleydale, it has all about it the grandeur of the moors and fells.

It is stirring to come here after a storm and see the River Ure roaring along its stony bed under the trees. Rushing impetuously in a flood hemmed in by limestone walls and overhanging woods, tumbling down rocky ledges like the steps of a giant's staircase, the water breaks into amber foam. It was a spectacle that enchanted Turner, and is one of the finest sights of the Dales, which must be seen for its enthralling beauty to be believed.

There are three main Falls, all in a reach of half a mile, the church keeping them company. Coming from the village (nearly a mile away) the road drops with surprising suddenness to a fine stone bridge of Tudor days, its single arch having a span of over 70 feet; and here we see the Upper Falls in all their glory. Oaks and beeches, great firs and little hazels, crowd to the water's edge, and a woodland path on the north bank brings us to the Lower Falls, where the splendour of the Fall down a broad flight of steps is a sight for the gods. Very lovely, too, is the wide cascade of the Middle Falls.

The church, overlooking this bridge, looks down also on an old cotton mill where yarn is said to have been spun for the red shirts of Garibaldi's army. The churchyard is reached by 45 steps. A long and spacious place, the church is almost all 19th century rebuilding, but the lower part of the tower has stood since the 13th century. Its chief interest is in its beautiful woodwork both old and new.

Its arresting possession is a 15th century screen on the south side of the chancel, magnificent with its double doors, handsome tracery, deep fan-vaulting, and a dainty cornice with fruit, birds, and grotesque animals. It is over 12 yards long and dazzling in colour. From the same 15th century are two poppyhead bench-ends set in the reading-desk, showing in their rich carving a lion, a man by a chained antelope, a staff with mitre and shield, and the letter W with a hazel tree and a tun—the picture name of William de Heslington, Abbot of Jervaulx. It is supposed that the screen and the bench-ends were brought from there. There is a curiously ornamented old cupboard, and across an arch on the north side of the chancel is an oak beam on which are carved two hooded men with long ears, the date 1536, and the initials of Abbot Adam Sedbergh.

Very beautiful is the modern pulpit with its rich tracery, vine borders, and carved panels of the holy lamb with a host of cherubs, Christ healing the blind man (his wife with her basket), and Paul in chains. There is a dainty almsbox with carved panels, and in a window with striking glass is Our Lord with the children, and again washing the Disciples' feet, squirrels eating acorns above them. On the stem of the 20th century font are three child angels and flowers.

The village has lovely old houses with creepered walls, but it has nothing more charming than a rock garden by the green-banked wayside, where the grey rocks, looking like crags of the fells, are a dazzling mosaic of colour with hundreds of ferns and flowers growing in their crannies. High on the other bank of the river is Bear Park, a 17th century house with spacious lawns and beautiful gardens with Alpine flowers. Built into a wall here is a stone from Coverham Abbey, carved with instruments of the Passion; and in the woods are rare plants, including tormentil, hawkweed, avens, and silvan loose-strife. A mile and a half from the village, 1000 feet up on Aysgarth Moor, is the ancient circular earthwork known as Castle Dyke.

Recently, a museum of horse-drawn vehicles has been established in the old corn-mill which has examples of a governess-cart, a Brougham, and a Char-a-banc. Some of the vehicles were still in use some ten years ago.

Bainbridge. The Forest of Wensleydale is no more, but the old custom of blowing a horn as a guide for travellers is still kept up here on winter nights.

It is a rare old village, with the stocks and a pair of millstones on the great green where some of the houses are perched, looking down on those in the hollow. Some of them have outside steps to upper rooms. The date on an inn tells that its story began nearly 500 years ago, and at one end of the green is the Quaker meeting-house where George Fox preached. By an old mill the little River Bain makes charming crescent-shaped falls over a limestone bed, and flows under the pretty bridge which helps to give the village its name.

On the top of Brough Hill, across the Bain, are traces of a Roman fort which was occupied from the first to the 4th century, and at Cravenholme Farm is a little museum of the relics which have come to light, including pottery, coins, ornaments, implements, bones, wood, and fragments of glass; there are willow branches the Romans found growing by the river, a tiny altar to an unknown god, and beautiful vases, one with the thumb-marks of the potter still visible.

High above the fort is Addleborough, a conspicuous hill where the Romans may have had a lookout station 1564 feet above the sea. A cairn here is thought to have been built for a British chieftain 3000 years ago. We can climb the hill from Bainbridge, seeing from the summit a grand view of Wensleydale and of Semmerwater, Yorkshire's chief lake, concerning which the people have an old legend that once upon a time it drowned the village because the people refused charity to a beggar. Covering over 100 acres at its lowest ebb, this charming lake is filled by the streams from three beautiful mountain valleys, Bardale, Raydale, and Cragdale; the River Bain carries it to the Ure. Near the lake, at Carr End, is the house where Dr Fothergill, the famous Quaker, was born in 1712. He was a great doctor, a great philanthropist (one of the founders of Ackworth School), and a diligent worker for the welfare of working people. Benjamin Franklin said of him that he could hardly conceive that a better man had ever lived.

Baldersby. The village and its handsome great house are nearly three miles apart, with the church between them, and all are between the River Swale and the A1. Hiding in its park of 200 acres, the hall is now a school. With the village school and a few houses for company, the church was the gift of Viscount Downe, who died in 1857 a week or two after he had laid its first stone. His memorial of white marble is inlaid with a brass cross. The slender tower and spire rising 160 feet above the meadows is seen for miles in this open countryside. Alabaster lines the lower walls of the sanctuary and forms the reredos, which has a band of quatrefoils. The big stone lychgate with oak arches has a high pyramid roof.

A narrow stone bridge takes us over the river to Skipton-on-Swale, where the tiny bellcote church, built in 1848, stands on the hill.

Barningham. From the top of this long village on a hillside is a fine view of the country looking out to the hills of Durham beyond the wooded valleys of the Greta and the Tees. At the other end is the beautiful park with 200 acres of woods, and the great house standing on banks of lawn. Through an archway facing its gates is an ivy-walled path to the churchyard, which has fine copper beeches and two ancient gravestones. Ancient relics within the 19th century church are the bowl of a Norman piscina on a modern shaft, and the head of a Saxon cross dug up a few years ago.

Barton. By the A1 stands the old hall made partly new, its grey walls ivied, a tower at one end, and its tiny porch sheltered by gabled wings. On the green near by are the broken shaft and steps of the old cross, and below is a quaint little bridge over the stream. On the hillside across the stream are the ivied fragments of an old chapel whose font is in the 19th century church. Other things brought from the old place to the new are a tomb (under the low tower) and an inscription to Robert Dodsworth who died in 1651 and his wife who lived on till 1703. On a huge block of stone among the lovely flower-beds round the graves of the Vaux family of Brettanby Manor is a striking bronze figure of Our Lord, holding a crown.

Barton-le-Street. All who pass along the Roman road between Malton and Hovingham know the old forge, and the wise will follow the lane leading from it to the amazing little church, with the old manor house, now a farm, near by. It is a church of old and new, all in Norman style and all fine. The saving grace of what was perhaps an unnecessary rebuilding in 1871 was the inclusion of most of the remarkable Norman sculpture in the new church, and the excellence of the new work itself.

The walls outside have a fine modern corbel table, and carved stringcourses above and below the windows. The north porch with its two doorways is an astonishing blending of old and new, with a veritable riot of carving which must be seen to be believed. Its entrance has sides enriched with foliage, beak-heads, animals, and angels; its arch is of zigzag, and in the carvings of its hood are animals, dragons, angels, figures of humans, and of Michael slaying the dragon, dragons and an animal in a tree, and two animals on their hind legs. The inner doorway was the south doorway of the old church. Its arch has a band of interlaced and trailing foliage and a marvellous medley of heads and animals and figures in beak-head style; and in the carvings at the sides are birds, dragons, a man with a horse, a man riding a wild animal, a man with a sheaf of corn, and rich conventional patterns. On the nave side of the doorway is a finely carved hood. Over the doorway, within the porch, is an array of carved stones sometimes said to be Saxon, representing the Nativity with Mary in bed, the Wise Men and the Shepherds, and the months of the year.

Extraordinary is the only word for the Norman corbel table within the porch. Richly carved with arcading and leaf-work, it rests on birds, grotesques, heads, animals, and a little man, and tucked away under the arches are heads of men and women, and an odd little animal. There is a similar table in the chancel, and old heads are in the nave, making a rare collection of the best part of a hundred old corbels in all. The beautiful chancel arch is chiefly new, its arch carved with cable and zigzag and over 80 small beak-heads, its clustered shafts with rich band-work and entwining foliage. On one shaft is a quaint animal and a face, and the capitals have original Norman carving of foliage coming from the mouths of men and animals. Other original Norman carving is in the capitals of the arch to the chancel chapel, the corbels on each side of it, and a piscina shaft; and there is fine modern woodcarving in the ends of benches, screen work, pulpit, and wall panelling.

The churchyard has an avenue of limes, and part of an old cross.

Bedale. It is one of Yorkshire's small market towns, with quaintness in its streets and all the charm of an old-world setting for one of the biggest and finest old churches in the Riding. The stream on which it stands has already had four names on its journey here from Bellerby Moor, and it leaves the town as the Bedale Beck to join the Swale.

Very charming is the picture of the wide cobbled road where the market is held, with the old cross on its flight of steps and the lines of old houses and little shops in haphazard array carrying the eye to the magnificent tower among the trees. Facing the church is the great house, with an 18th century drawing-room 60 feet long and half as wide; it stands behind a high wall in a park with lovely gardens, a fine avenue of old walnut trees, and grand old beeches, limes, and oaks. In Daniel Defoe's day Bedale was famed for its horses. A 17th century stone building in the churchyard was a grammar school in his day, but the story of the church takes us back before the Conqueror.

The tower is said to have been built as a place of refuge against the Border raiders. The three bottom stages with small windows are from about 1330, and the top storey 15th century. Unusual and charming is the little stone-ribbed porch nestling on its south side, leading us into the tower's vaulted basement, where another curious thing is to be seen. The first floor of the tower has a room with a blocked fireplace, and the doorway at the foot of the stair leading to it was guarded in the old days by a portcullis; we can see the grooves in which it moved between the two arches, and in the room above is the pulley.

The mighty arch of the tower soars almost to the roof of the nave, dwarfing the splendid arcading. The walls of the nave are thought to be part of the Saxon church, which was given a north aisle towards the close of the 12th century and a south aisle a hundred years later. Their original arcades are still standing, but the north aisle was made new 600 years ago. The north arcade (another rare feature of the church) is notable for the ribbed bosses in the hollow mouldings of its sharply-pointed arches, the hoods with carving like the edge of a saw, and the capitals carved with leaves, crowning pillars which are all different. Over the arcades are the fine windows of the clerestory, and looking down is a roof of black oak resting on ten oak angels.

The chancel begun by the Saxons was lengthened by the Normans and again in the 14th century, the time of the fine sedilia and piscina. Its east window is believed to have been brought from Jervaulx Abbey. The roof glows with gilded bosses and rests on angels. Under the sanctuary is a vaulted crypt reached by a stone stair: it has an altar stone with five crosses still plain to see, and among other fragments here are part of a Saxon cross carved with knotwork and part of a hogback.

Divided from the chancel by two mediaeval arches, the south chapel has two Tudor windows and a remarkable east window so wide that it looks like half a window, with five short lights. The north chapel was built when the north aisle was made new 600 years ago, and its great east window (copied from one in a church by the Rhine) was put here by Thomas Jackson, a merchant who died in 1529. His memorial may be the battered black stone in the floor of the aisle, richly carved with the giant-like figure of a man with long hair, two smaller figures sheltering by his legs.

The old roodstairs, a mediaeval bell, and fragments of wall painting (including a restored St George) are still here. There are two fine Jacobean chairs and a pillar almsbox; and much fine old woodwork is in the rich panelling of the chancel, with cherubs holding symbols of the Passion, and quaint Bible scenes. The oak pulpit, with a figure of St Gregory and scenes from his life, and the reredos with six saints in niches, are fine work of our own century.

The monuments are worthy of their place in this fine church. One of the best examples of mediaeval sculpture in the land is the alabaster figure of a knight wearing chain mail and a surcoat with sleeves, his curls flowing loosely, his shield bearing his arms. He is Sir Brian Fitzalan, Lord Lieutenant of Scotland, the last of his line, and beside him is his wife, a battered figure holding a scroll like a broad ribbon falling almost to her feet. They are from the very beginning of the 14th century. The older of two unknown knights lying side by side in the nave is interesting for showing the beginning of plate armour. On a broken tomb enriched with tracery and shields lies the battered figure of a priest; his face and his hands are gone, but his Crucifix is still here. He is perhaps Thomas Fitzbrian, rector in the time of Henry III. On the wall on each side of the 14th century recess behind his tomb are quaint angels. Westmacott was the sculptor of the marble monument of Henry Peirse, showing him with his hand on his wife's shoulder, and near by are many memorials to members of the Beresford-Peirse family, owners of Bedale Manor.

Bellerby. Through this small place a stream meanders by the village green, flowing under little bridges, by the cottages or through their gardens, and in front of the gabled old hall, which has a porch with two rooms climbing as high as the house. It stands in friendly fashion by its humbler neighbours, facing a solitary sycamore growing from two high steps on the green. The old manor house is on the edge of the village, a farmhouse now. The church, with a quaint turret and spire between the nave and the porch, is 19th century.

Bilsdale. Here are scattered farms, a few cottages, a bridge over the stream, and magnificent views from the church high on the hill. Hiding in a square of trees and reached through the farmyard of what was the hall, it was made new last century and keeps a battered old font. The valley which gives the village its name is like a green furrow across the moors between the Cleveland Hills and the Vale of Pickering. It is watered by the River Seph which joins the Rye not far from Hawnby, and through it runs a good valley road. In autumn the hills are purple and russet, and in daffodil time the valley is a rare sight. On the moors are the graves and entrenchments of the Stone Age men, some of them over 1400 feet above the sea.

From Chop Gate (a mile from Bilsdale church) we may climb over the hills to Carlton, the highest point giving us one of the most impressive views in Yorkshire.

Bilsdale Midcable. If we come over the moors from Helmsley to this place in the heart of Bilsdale, we have wonderful scenes for our reward. Where the road bends sharply above the meeting of the Seph and the Rye in the valley below, we look up the Rye valley where Hawnby is perched on the steep hillside, and ride on with the River Seph through the green dale to the neat, trim church which Temple Moore designed for Bilsdale Midcable, giving it beautiful arches, and a fine panelled roof over the continuous nave and aisle.

Birdforth. On the old road from London to Edinburgh, it has only a few scattered farms, a few cottages, a small bridge over a stream, tall trees, an Old Hall shaped like the letter H, and a tiny church with a turret rising from walls mantled in evergreen. Like the Old Hall, the church has a pantiled roof, and at its east end is a fine weeping beech. Partly rebuilt in 1585, the church has a restored Norman doorway, and a low Norman arch dividing the nave and chancel, its stone showing up against the white walls. The Norman font has a modern base, there is an ancient gravestone, and the carving on the pulpit is three centuries old.

Birkby. It has a few houses by the River Wiske, and a small brick church with ivied walls hiding in trees on the hill. Built on an ancient site in the 18th century, and altered in the 19th, it has a dignified simplicity, the nave and chancel an oblong with a black-and-white roof, and an arch over the altar. The fine old panelled pews have bobbin ends, and the bowl of a mediaeval font lies on the floor, a modern one being used. A third font serves as a bird bath outside, and in the west wall is a fragment of a Saxon cross.

Boltby. Its glory is its approach from Felixkirk, the lovely ride giving us magnificent views of the Vale of York. After passing the stone gatehouse of Mount St John (the great house supposed to be on the site of a preceptory of the Knights Hospitallers) we soon face the splendour of the Hambleton Hills, where, deep in a valley through which flows the Gurtof Beck from Boltby Moor, the village lies. Its cottages are of stone and brick, and the tiny modern church, in 13th century style, has a bellcote. Just below it a pretty humped bridge crosses the stream, which runs under the road in fair weather and floods it when it races down after a storm.

Bolton-on-Swale. Red-roofed and charming, with rosemary, hollyhocks, and Canterbury bells in the gardens, it has pleasant peeps of green country by the river. There is an attractive well shaded by a tree, and the church has a 16th century tower with a brave array of leafy pinnacles, three shields upside down on the battlements, and a west window with odd tracery. The strikingly low arcade leading to the south aisle, with massive arches on pillars 4 feet high, seems to be old, but the rest of the structure is much restored. There is a fine Jacobean carved chest.

The loveliest part of the church is the tiny north chapel, its window glowing with figures of St Michael and St Nicholas, its walls adorned with a band of sculpture in low relief, showing men going to their work in the woods, reapers in a cornfield, and a sailing ship coming to port. A medallion has Christ stilling the waves, and in the middle of the chapel is an unusual and lovely thing, a white marble pedestal on the top of which lies the beautiful head and shoulders of a woman, resting on a pillow.

In the churchyard is a stone which asks us to believe that Henry Jenkins, who carried a load of arrows for the soldiers at Flodden Field when he was a boy, grew up and lived to be 169!

Borrowby. A village of steep streets and narrow lanes, it has a wide view from its little hilltop between the Hambleton Hills and the great Plain of York. Standing by the old cross on the green (its shaft worn by the sharpening of shuttles and knives), we look for miles over the Plain, so richly wooded and dotted with towns and villages that an ambassador at Henry the VIII's Court once declared the view to be without parallel in Europe.

Bossall. Reached by winding lanes, it has the lovely Buttercrambe Woods between it and the River Derwent. The fine old hall has noble trees and traces of a moat, facing a beautiful aisleless church in the shape of a simple cross. The nave, the transepts, and the central tower come chiefly from the close of the 12th century and are adorned with a corbel table of heads, human and grotesque. The charming chancel of rose and grey stone is about a hundred years younger than the rest. We see the passing of the Norman style to the English in the nave's two doorways, one simple, one having rich mouldings so deeply recessed that it seems to come to meet us. It is tilting now, with some of its shafts battered and missing, but is beautiful still.

All the walls are leaning outward. The glory within lies in the tower's pointed arches on clusters of tilting shafts. Years ago the north arch was built up and the transept used as a stable, the cattle interrupting the service, so that Sydney Smith once preached here from the text, What meaneth the lowing of the oxen which I hear?

The Norman font has a 17th century cover. A beautiful altar cup is 1630, and on the flagon is an engraving of the Wise Men. The oak reredos is of our own time, with traceried canopies, a scene of the Entombment, and two bishops seated, one with a fine model of York Minster on his knee, the other with a simple church at his feet; it is all beautiful.

Sleeping in the chancel are Sir Robert Belt, twice Lord Mayor of York in the 17th century, and Robert Constable, Chancellor of Durham, fragments of brass showing him in armour. A copy of Robert's will is in the vestry, and we read that he left a red cloth for the altar and a gold ring to the Earl of Salisbury. To his son he left his horse, his armour, and the possession he had treasured most, his diary, written day by day in secret and carried in his sleeve. Robert's day was over in 1454, but what would we not give to see the diary of this 15th century Pepys, and to read his story of the days when Joan of Arc was driving the English out of France?

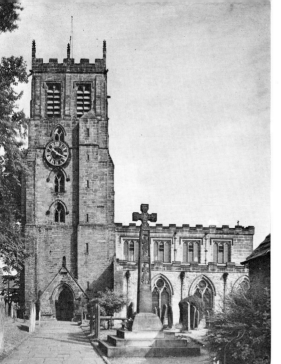

Bedale Church

The squire's pew
in Croft Church

Byland Abbey

The parish register records the marriage here in 1632 of Thomas Shepard with Margaret Tutvile; he went to America and helped to found Harvard University.

Bowes. Braving the winds that blow 1000 feet above the sea, it is on the gentle eastern slopes of Stainmore, a wild depression of the Pennine Chain with miles of grassy moor whose western slopes drop sharply down to the lovely Vale of Eden. Here life goes on in a Roman camp.

The Roman road ran by the highway which cuts across the county boundary in a neighbourhood full of interest. Just in Yorkshire is the Rey Camp of the Romans, its four sides, about 300 yards long, facing the four points of the compass; and in the camp are the remains of the famous Rey Cross which is said to have marked the boundary of the old kingdoms of England and Scotland. Hereabouts the road and the remarkable railway over Stainmore are 1400 feet up. The River Greta comes to life a mile over the Westmorland border, and road and rail and river are never far apart on their way to Bowes. Two miles before it reaches the village the Greta flows under God's Bridge, a curious natural limestone arch over which carts pass. Bowes was the Roman Lavatrae, and the highway continues on the line of the Roman road to Greta Bridge and Scotch Corner.

Climbing the long hill are the grey and ivied houses in colourful gardens, the old inn, and the church, near which stands the keep the Normans built within the Roman camp. One of the far-flung outposts of the empire, the camp was garrisoned by a legion famous for their Spanish horses; and though the soldiers can have had few comforts here they had the luxury of a bath 27 feet long and 18 feet wide, of which traces are still to be seen in a field south of the church. Known as Bowes Castle, the keep was completed by 1187. Gleaming in the sun and dominating this wonderful countryside, its defiant walls are now about 50 feet high, and so thick that chambers are built within them. Inside the keep the jagged walls rise like cliffs of rough masonry; and there are traces of the moat which once protected it.

The remains of the old village cross are in a cottage garden by the church, which stands in the area of the camp. The church has the shape of a simple cross with a Norman nave, a 13th century chancel, and 14th century transepts, though it has been much rebuilt. Two Norman doorways are sheltered by porches, one modern and one of about 1400, with a worn sculpture over its entrance showing the Crucifixion with Mary and John. One of two fonts has a 13th century bowl carved with leaf pattern upside down, resting on what may be a Roman altar with an inscription; it is thought its original stem may be that which now supports the Norman bowl of the other font. A bowl on the floor is quaintly carved; a coffin-lid has a cross and a sword, and another is rare for having a dog at the foot of a cross. There is a huge stone coffin in which a Roman was probably buried, and a millstone which may have ground flour for the Roman garrison. A stone found in the vicarage garden has an inscription to Marcus Aurelius, and the Emperor Severus who is spoken of as the Conqueror of Arabia.

On the west wall outside is a stone with an inscription to Rodger Wrightson and Martha Railton, who were buried in 1715 in one grave, after he had died of fever and she *of a broken heart*. They are said to be the Edwin and Emma of David Mallet's ballad, and old prints showing scenes in the story hang in the vestry.

North of the chancel is a grave all travellers will want to see. It is under a stricken tree and has a stone to a boy of 19 who died at William Shaw's academy here in 1822. He was George Ashton Taylor, of whom the world would never have heard had not Charles Dickens come to Bowes. Having heard of the Yorkshire boy-farms where unwanted sons and nephews were sent to schools run by ignorant bullies, Dickens came to Bowes to see for himself. Some of the buildings are here still, gaunt houses where wretched bits of humanity dragged out hopeless years, and standing back from the long street is what is believed to have been the original Dotheboys Hall where Dickens came face to face with Mr Shaw, who had a grey-green eye like the fan-light of a street door. Though unable to see over the school, Dickens saw enough in Mr Shaw's face to tell him all he wished to know, and Shaw lives on for all time as Squeers. Coming to the churchyard, Dickens stood by Taylor's grave one winter's day when the snow had drifted over the mound. He knew the sad story of the boy's life. "The first gravestone I stumbled on that dreary afternoon (he wrote), was over a boy who had died suddenly. I suppose his heart broke. He died in this wretched place, and I think his ghost put Smike into my mind on the spot."

When Dickens left Bowes it was to wage war on these horrible schools, exposing them in Nicholas Nickleby, where we read of the immortal Smike born in a country churchyard.

Dickens called at William Shaw's Academy in the interests of an imaginary pupil, thinking this the best way to discover the facts for himself. Mr Shaw's advertisements declared that he instructed young gentlemen in living and dead languages together with mathematics and orthography, use of the globe, and astronomy, trigonometry, algebra, and classical literature, all for 20 guineas a year, and out of the warmth of his heart he threw in an unparalleled diet, with beef from consumptive cows once or twice a week. Dickens knocked at the door, but somehow Mr Shaw was suspicious and regretted that he had no vacancy and was sorry it was impossible to show him over the establishment. Today we can still see what Dickens failed to see—Dotheboys Hall with the stables where the boys and animals were housed, the cobbled courtyard, the pump where Nicholas Nickleby and the little boys washed themselves shivering on a winter's day; and we can all read the book the angry Dickens wrote on reaching home again, the book that gradually closed these schools by rousing the anger of all thinking people.

Brafferton-with-Helperby. They make a big village by the River Swale, in which Paulinus is said to have baptised many people 1300 years ago. Today income from land here is given to a society sending out missionaries to far countries.

There are many old and new houses along the wide street, and from the high bank above the river the imposing church has a fine view over the wooded countryside. Under a magnificent beech shading the churchyard path sleeps a vicar, Norman McNeile, who preached here 52 years. In the churchyard lies also a coachman who served Helperby Hall for four generations. The tower and the chancel are 15th century. The two chapels have inscriptions to Ralph Nevill who built them in early Tudor days, and a bell in the tower was the gift of a Nevill of Elizabeth I's day.

The old part of the church is in the shadows, but the 19th century nave is full of light. Much wider than it is long, it has a remarkable effect inside, with its great roof running from north to south, and has a line of three fine arches leading to the chancel and the chapels. The rich modern screenwork between the nave and chapels has trumpeting angels, and rich glass shows Our Lord's Agony, scenes after the Resurrection, and Mary washing His feet. There is a little old glass, the font has an ancient bowl, and a mediaeval coffin-lid engraved with a staff may belong to a prior of Newburgh.

Brafferton Hall is near the church. Helperby Hall is in a fine park with delightful gardens bounded by the Swale. Its older part has domed turrets, the newer has Dutch gables and a tower with a cupola, and carved in stone over the porch are lines in French suggesting that our lives are like the marionette's—which play a little while and then are gone.

Brandsby. A lane with a noble avenue of stately trees leads to the ivied church. Shaped like the letter L, the rectory has a charming old wing with small 15th century windows and a pantiled roof. The big stone Hall is 18th century, and some of the wonderful trees of its 60-acre park shade the formal little church, built in Italian style about 1770.

From the middle of the church's pantiled roof rises a cupola, supported within by the vaulted crossing between the nave and chancel. Under the west gallery is a big doorway with fine gates made by a village blacksmith; they open to the nave and are sheltered by a vestibule. The fine two-decker pulpit has a richly carved desk and canopy, and round the nave is a dado of fine oak panelling, the little mouse proclaiming it the work of Mr Thompson of Kilburn. Adding to the attraction of the interior are five charming brass candelabra from which 66 electric lights shine. The oldest thing here is a curious small sculpture of the Crucifixion.

Brignall. Its farms and cottages, the rectory and the 19th century church, are on the hillside, looking far into Durham over the lovely wooded valley of the Tees, and over the Greta to the moors and fells in the south. Below the village the Greta flows through Brignall Banks on its way to Greta Bridge at the gates of

Rokeby Park, its journey so enchanting that Sir Walter Scott wrote of it:

> *O, Brignall banks are wild and fair,*
> *And Greta Woods are green,*
> *And you may gather garlands there*
> *Would grace a summer queen.*

In a green hollow by the river are the ruins of the ancient church, now roofless and desolate and alone, in a setting so beautiful that both Turner and Scott have immortalised it. The modern church among the trees is tiny and trim. Its fine panelled roof has bosses of roses and leaves, and packed into little space is much richly carved oak—in screens, poppyhead stalls, reredos, and tiny altar-rails. With many fragments of mediaeval coffin-lids (one with a sword and one with shears) is a small millstone, but something more notable than all these has this place, for here is an altar from a Roman temple, a pagan monument in a Christian church.

Brompton. One of several Bromptons in this Riding, it is eight miles on the road from Scarborough to Pickering. Its great house, set among noble trees, has an imposing gateway and is now a hotel, but on its beautiful lawns the Cayleys have walked since Stuart times. Their memorials are in the church on the little road behind the house.

Most of the church is 14th and 15th century. Its striking but-tressed tower, with a broached spire, is about 600 years old, and a worn but still beautiful traceried door of the 15th century has its old strap hinges with fleur-de-lys ends, and the clasp of its vanished ring. It opens to an interior which is spacious, lofty, and light, sheltering among its possessions a massive font 700 years old, a bracket made of two Norman capitals, a chest and a pillar almsbox both old, and a beautiful brass candelabra holding 40 candles.

One of the monuments shows Anne Harland of 1844 on a bed, her hand in her husband's, and her friends standing round. There is an inscription to James Westrop, who went to sleep with a grievance in the 16th century, for we read that he served one king and two queens with due obedience but without recompense. In the churchyard lies

Anne Waterhouse, who was 99 when she died in 1855, after serving one family here for over 60 years.

One autumn day in 1802 William Wordsworth and Mary Hutchinson were married in this old church. Mary, "the perfect woman, nobly planned", lived at Gallows Hill Farm near the Scarborough road. The house was almost destroyed by fire some years ago, but the farm buildings are little changed.

It is believed that John Brompton, Abbot of Jervaulx five centuries ago, may have been born in the village. He is reputed to have been the author of an old Chronicle from the coming of St Augustine to Richard I.

Sir George Cayley, Squire of Brompton, should be remembered as one of the pioneers of the Flying Age. He was thinking it out in the early years of last century, for he was a boy of 10 when the world was talking of the gas balloon of the Montgolfiers, and Cayley, who had a mathematical mind, devoted it to working out a plan for flying.

He actually began to experiment on the Yorkshire moors with gliding planes, and he found theoretically that the old idea of flapping wings was of no use, but that there must be a flat plane, the progress of which depended on wind pressure and the angle of the plane's surface. He never trusted himself to his own gliding planes, but it is still remembered that he insisted on the family coachman going up.

Brompton. Through it runs a moorland stream on its way to join the River Wiske below Northallerton, and on an island site near the green the church stands in a ring of trees, raised above the road. Much of it is rebuilt, but the south tower (forming the porch) is chiefly 15th century, with an 18th century weathervane and a 12th century arcade leading to the aisle, its Norman arches on round and octagonal pillars. The carved oak chest was probably here when John Kettlewell knew the church. A benefactor of this village, where he was born in 1653, he crowded much good into a short life of 42 years, was a notable preacher, and was described by Bishop Ken as the most saint-like man he knew. We see his portrait in a window with four Old Testament figures, including Abraham and Moses.

The magnet drawing us to Brompton is its rare collection of Saxon hogbacks, which, with six others now at Durham, were found here in 1867, and are perhaps the finest group of their kind in the land, thought to be nearly 1000 years old. Two by the chancel arch are wonderfully preserved, having at each end a bear which stretches out its great paws along the sides and holds in its mouth the enriched strap running along the top. With them is a hogback which has lost one of its bears, and a splendid one in the aisle has the bears lying on their backs, feet in the air, and the strap in their mouths.

Older still are the Saxon crosses treasured here. A fine one by the pulpit is covered with knotwork, another has the head almost complete, and the shaft of a third is carved with birds and men. On windowsills we found three fragments of Saxon cross-heads, and two coffin-lids. In the chancel wall is a Saxon stone with knotwork.

A modern metal Last Supper behind the altar arrests the eye.

Brotton. In the deep valley below the village are the great smoking ironworks of Skinningrove, but from the forlorn old church on the hilltop (rebuilt in the 18th century) there is a fine panorama of hills and dales and the sea, with a view into Durham. On a high bank on the hillside the fine church of St Margaret has stood for half a century, impressive with its arcades and chancel arch soaring to beautiful roofs, deeply panelled and enriched with leaves and flowers. The stone reredos has handsome carving, and fine paintings of Bede and St Hilda and other figures in charming scenes.

A walk over the hills brings us to Kilton Castle, tucked away in a delightful glen which we should see when the forget-me-nots make a carpet below the walls. Protected by an army of trees, the ruins of the towers and turrets, the gatehouse, barbican, and curtain wall stand finely on a little spur of rock. It has recently been excavated. Tradition says that Sir Robert Thweng, a lord of Kilton 700 years ago, was known as the Robin Hood of Cleveland for his daring raids on the monasteries and his custom of giving their treasures to the poor.

Brough. It is the Brough near Catterick, with some of the fairest English meadows round it, and proud trees standing where Roman sentries kept watch. The site of a Roman road is less than a mile away, and nearer still is a fragment of a Roman wall.

A turn from the shady road to Hipswell brings us to the striking

Roman Catholic church in the park of Brough Hall. Built a hundred years ago in the style of the 13th century, it has a west front with five great windows and is entered by a vestibule from which two flights of steps mount to the interior. Here groups of lancets are framed by rich arcading in the walls, the arches resting on slender shafts with fine capitals of foliage from which quaint grotesques peep out. Dividing the north chapel from the nave are two arches with elaborate ornament, and over a smaller arch between them is the sculpture of a curly-headed boy with a shield hanging round his neck. Under the altar are supposed to lie the bones of St Innocent, which were given by the Pope to the builder of the church, Sir William Lawson. One of the stained windows is a tribute to Henry Lawson, who lost his life in New Zealand in 1857 while trying to rescue a shepherd from drowning.

A stream flows towards the Swale between the church and the hall, a noble house with something of all the centuries from Elizabethan days; but in the gardens are fragments of Roman columns and two stone lions from Caesar's day. The handsome entrance has a lovely 16th century ceiling, and among the treasures is a marvellous little marble of a Madonna and Child. The private chapel has a wonderful old painting of the Crucifixion by an unknown artist; there are alabaster panels showing the Descent and Burial, and windows with 17th century Swiss glass; but the greatest treasure of all is a huge metal cauldron made by a Roman craftsman, ringing today as true as a bell.

Bulmer. It lies in pleasant wooded country on a road as straight as a ruler, a village of stone cottages, red roofs, and an ancient church. On Bulmer Hill, between the village and the River Derwent, is a monument to the seventh Earl of Carlisle. The oldest chapter of its story is in the outside walls of the nave (plastered within), for here is herringbone masonry from the second half of the Conqueror's century, as well as a slit in each of the side walls, and a blocked north doorway with a Norman arch above a lintel of a single stone. The simple south doorway from Norman days has lost its shafts, but the modern door hangs on the old hinges.

Some of the nave windows are 15th century; others of later time are set under two arches of a vanished arcade built into the north wall. The chancel has modern windows and a simple screen with some 15th century tracery. The font is Norman, and on a bracket stands the fine wheel-head of a Saxon cross. Built into a wall of the nave are a coffin-lid with a fine leafy cross and a sword, and the stone figure of a 13th century knight in chain mail, with his sword and his hands at prayer, but his legs cut off.

In our own time have been found here fragments of the Roman Empire, traces of a camp of 6 acres and of a pottery with bowls and vases, some decorated with sea-horses and dolphins.

Burneston. A tranquil spot just off the straight highway between Boroughbridge and Catterick, it has cottages lining its spacious road, almshouses founded in the 17th century, and with three stone arches leading to the churchyard. Attractive outside with battlements and a striking array of pinnacles, the church was built between 1390 and 1550. The oldest part is the chancel, with a stringcourse round the walls, a great east window between fine canopied niches with angels on the brackets, and lovely sedilia with leafy canopies, tall pinnacles, and two splendid faces. The sturdy tower and stumpy stone spire (unusual in this part of Yorkshire) were raised during the first ten years of the 15th century, perhaps at the expense of the big families whose arms are on the buttresses—Boyntons, Fitzhughs, Nevilles, and Nortons. From the 17th century come the splendid pews with carved panels and poppyheads like bobbins. Over the spacious three-decker pew for the squire is a carved oak tablet, with an inscription telling that in 1627 Thomas Robinson gave £50 for the seats. One of the bells is mediaeval.

There is rich modern woodwork in the screen and panelling of the chancel, the pulpit, and the traceried door through which we come and go. The fine roofs are 19th century, their beams carved and embattled; rich borders of tracery and foliage add to the beauty of the chancel roof, which rests on a gallery of quaint stone heads.

Buttercrambe. A Roman is thought to have had a house here in what is now Aldby Park, and in a Saxon palace built on its foundations King Edwin is said to have been attacked by a man with a poisoned dagger. Harold Hardrada, who in 1066 marched this way to Stamford Bridge, may have spent his last night here.

It is a delightful spot. The Derwent flows round two sides of a beautiful park of 200 acres, and, making an island in front of the great house which looks out to the Wolds, is crossed by two bridges. Close by is the mill which grinds corn, pumps water, and makes electric light.

Behind the cottages stands the charming little church of grey stone. The nave is down four steps and the chancel is up two, and rising between them is an unusual bellcote, shaped like a cross and crowned with a tiny spire. The church is much restored, but the chancel arch, and remains of an arcade in the nave wall, are 13th century, several windows are mediaeval, and an ancient stone with a cross is in the wall outside. The traceried screens and the wagon roofs with rich borders are fine modern work.

One of three little mourners is perched dangerously on the ledge of an 18th century monument with busts of three Darleys of Aldby Park, Richard and two of his sons.

Byland Abbey. Its story takes us back to the early days of Furness Abbey, from where in 1134 Abbot Gerold and 12 monks set out for Calder in Cumberland, the beginning of 43 years of wandering. In the end they came here. Driven from Calder by the Scots, they returned to Furness, but found little welcome, and went in 1143 to Old Byland, where Roger de Mowbray granted them land. This proved to be too near to Rievaulx Abbey on the other bank of the Rye, each monastery hearing the bells of the other, so the community set out for Stocking, where they stayed for 30 years, building a church and a cloister. It was in 1177 that they moved to their final home under the beautiful wooded ridge of the Hambleton Hills; and here, reclaiming the swampy land, the community set to work to build the splendid abbey whose ruins we see outlined on the velvet lawns.

The chief remnant is the shell of what is said to have been the biggest church of the Cistercian Order in England, 330 feet long and 140 wide across the transepts. Its size and majesty are still inspiring, though the walls are broken and battered. There was an aisled nave of 12 bays, a central tower, a presbytery with side aisles and five eastern chapels, and the transepts had two western aisles and two eastern chapels. The seven western bays of the nave served as the church of the lay brothers, whose numbers often exceeded those of the monks. The next five bays were for the choirs.

Of the arcades and the crossing only the bases of the piers are now left. The wall of the north aisle of the nave has a splendid line of windows. There are fragments of the north transept, and a portion of the south transept, the oldest part of the church (1225), stands like a great soaring pinnacle, tilting at a dangerous angle, and is interesting for showing the triforium and the clerestory. Typical of the 12th century work in the church are the round heads of some of the windows, and of the early 13th century style the west front, the chief fragment left of the church, is a magnificent though much battered example. The beautiful doorway has rich mouldings in its trefoiled head, and above it are the corbels which supported the roof of the vanished Galilee. The second storey has three lancets set in a line of blind arcading, and above these is the lower half of the frame of a great round window, with a diameter of 26 feet. At one side of it a buttress climbs to a turret. Flanking the front are remains of the west ends of the aisles, one having a pointed doorway and the other a doorway almost as round-headed as the window above it.

From a stone lying at the crossing has disappeared the fine brass portrait of an abbot with his pastoral staff. The north aisle has traces of mediaeval wall-painting showing the Madonna, and in the transepts and the presbytery are patches of old tiles. Many more of the tiles which once paved the church are in a small museum, with a fine collection of Norman and 13th century fragments, carved capitals with traces of painting, gargoyles, and bosses with iron rings from which lamps used to hang.

The buildings extended from the south side of the church, grouped round three sides of a cloister 145 feet square, and were rebuilt in the 15th century. We enter the court from the south aisle by a charming flight of round steps, near which, in the wall of the transept, are traces of the recesses where books were kept. The lay brothers were on the west side of the cloister, separated from it by a passage which served them as a cloister, and has still in its east wall 35 stone seats. Their wing was 275 feet long, its upper storey serving as the dormitory, and the ground floor partly as their dining-hall and infirmary. This wing is the oldest part of the monastery.

The refectory of the monks, 100 feet long and 31 feet wide, was on the south of the cloister, raised on a vaulted basement where we still see the bases of the pillars and the springers. At one side of the refectory was the kitchen, still with remains of the old fireplaces, and on the other was the warming house, where we see red stones reminding us of the old fireside.

On the east side of the cloister was the library. The chapter house still has two tiers of seats showing round the walls, and a gravestone (engraved with a crozier), which probably covered the bones of an abbot. Here was the parlour (the only place where the monks were allowed to talk), and a passage by which is a fine flight of winding steps which led to the dormitory. In line with the east end of the church was the abbot's lodging, and bounding this end of the site was the cemetery. At the south-east corner, detached from the rest of the buildings, was the infirmary, an L-shaped building of the 14th century, with remains of a fireplace and a central hearth, and a vaulted structure at one end which may have been the crypt of the infirmary chapel. All that is left of the abbey gatehouse is a fine Norman archway crossing the road to Oldstead.

The Battle of Byland, which must have excited this peaceful neighbourhood one day in 1322, is believed to have been fought at Shaw's Moor, to the north of Oldstead and Scots Corner. While Edward II was dining either at Byland Abbey or Rievaulx (on his return from an unsuccessful invasion of Scotland), the Scots made a surprise attack and routed the English who were encamped hereabouts. The king was the first to run away, and the Scots went off with his jewels, ransacked both abbeys, and scattered the monks. On the site of the battle stands a chapel, a rebuilt farmhouse, memorial to three former pupils of Ampleforth College who died in the Second World War.

Carlton Husthwaite. Charming companions in this tranquil place are its old houses, the small church in a green bay of the roadside, and the beautiful trees—two stately poplars, a great beech, and a magnificent chestnut. Near the church is the Hall, facing a lovely black-and-white house with a thatched roof and the manor house with creepered walls of old brick, like the Old Hall across the way. The church is a simple oblong of rich amber stone, its windows hooded, its tiny tower with a pyramid cap just peeping over the nave. The canopied pulpit and the bobbin-ended pews are 17th century, and there are old oak beams in the roof.

Carlton-in-Cleveland. From the high bank above the road along which the stream runs, the small modern church has a fine view of the hills with rocky spurs, rising grandly behind the village which shelters among lovely trees. There are gardens with old yews, and one with a magnificent cedar. Fine trees are round Busby Hall near by.

In a trim churchyard where part of the old cross still stands, the church is charming, built of warm-tinted stone in 14th century style, and lighted, when daylight is done, by electric candles. The sturdy tower, standing half in and half out of the nave, has a vaulted roof, and a curious arch which is really two in one, open to the nave and to the ringers' gallery. There is no dividing arch between the nave and chancel, and the panelled barrel roof has tiebeams enriched with carved bosses.

A strange story is told of George Sangar, who was parson here last century. He found a derelict church and determined to build a new one. He raised money, took off his coat, and toiled day and night chiselling stone to give the village a church of which it might be proud. By 1881 the work was complete, but one night a tongue of flame shot up, and in the morning the church was gone. Carlton Bank leads steeply up on to the moors, on the edge of which is the Wainstones, a good practice-ground for rock-climbers.

Carperby. Its grey houses are by a long narrow green where a fine 17th century cross stands on a noble flight of steps. We go down the hill to Aysgarth a mile or so away, and up the moorside to St Matthew's Well, seeing from the road the bold grey walls of Bolton Castle, and the crags crowning the hill.

Thoresby, close by, is said to have given us John Thoresby, a notable Archbishop of York in the 14th century. A great peace-maker in his day and the builder of the magnificent choir of York Minster, he is said to have pulled down his house to provide stone.

Castle Bolton. Here is the grim prison of Mary Queen of Scots, a great pile of masonry hobnobbing with a few houses, the small church by the green, and the fine beeches near a stream which once ran into the moat. Commanding half Wensleydale, it stands four-square, over 180 feet long and 130 wide, with huge corner towers nearly 100 feet high. Much of it is in ruin, but it is one of our best preserved castles, grey and forbidding, venerable with all the centuries since Lord Richard Scrope spent nearly 20 years and £200,000 in building it in the time of Richard II.

Few castles of its period are more impressive than this fortress of the powerful Scropes, and for sheer strength it has perhaps no equal in England. It is built round a courtyard 96 feet long and 52 feet wide, entered by a gateway under a great arch. In the basement are the army quarters, the armoury, the stables, and the kitchens, the kitchens having huge ovens and a speaking tube to the banqueting hall. There is a well with a sluice to a great stone trough, and one of the dungeons, 13 feet long and 9 feet wide, and hewn out of the solid rock, has neither door nor window, but only a small opening at the top. An arm-bone with an iron ring round was found here some years ago.

We come by a massive stair to the spacious rooms built by Richard Scrope. There is a chapel with priests' rooms near, and a balcony for the women; and rooms with huge roof timbers brought from Inglewood Forest in Cumberland. The great hall, lighted by fine windows, is now a museum, and here we may see the old Bainbridge horn, a collection of curious things found in the castle well, Roman remains from a camp a few miles off, a 15th century bed, and a magnificent treasure chest said to have come from one of the Spanish galleons destroyed in the Armada.

A builder apparently for all time was Richard Scrope, who gave himself a palace-fortress second to none. He fought at Crecy, was knighted at Neville's Cross, and rode against the Scots for 40 years. There were Scropes at Bolton Castle till 1630, when the estate passed to the Orde-Powletts. A Scrope defended the castle for the king in the Civil War; another was at Flodden Field; Stephen Scrope comes into Shakespeare; and Henry had charge of Mary Queen of Scots who was brought here as a prisoner one summer's day in 1568. Her bedroom is in one of the towers, and her drawing-room is lighted by two oriels. The big fireplace has an odd little warming-box built into the chimney, and we may still see the heavy door opened by her friends and enemies. She had a retinue of 40 servants, and among those who kept guard over her was Sir Francis Knollys, whom she nicknamed her good schoolmaster for teaching her English. Here she wrote in secret to the Duke of Norfolk, little dreaming that Lord Burleigh was reading her letters before sending them on. It was the beginning of a romance which ended abruptly when the duke lost his head.

Here we may think of all her plottings to escape—of how she sat knitting in the window seat and would ask conspirators to hold the wool for her, exchanging scraps of conversation with them even while Sir Francis Knollys, who watched her as a cat watches a mouse, stood by. It was all in vain, and when she rode off after six months at the castle it was to exchange one prison for another on the way to the block on Tower Hill.

The church is chiefly 14th century, with a low tower, a continuous nave and chancel, three sedilia, two piscinas, and an old font.

Castle Howard. There is no village; it is the great house that is on the map. A stately palace surrounded by lawns and woodlands, Castle Howard is the most magnificent of the homes of Yorkshire, if not, indeed, of England. The home of the Earls of Carlisle, it is the masterpiece of Sir John Vanbrugh, the poet and courtier who built Blenheim Palace.

Even Elizabeth I would have been amazed at the grandeur of this place, for it was and remains the supreme example in our land of that Italian style of architecture which architects call Palladian. Sir Horace Walpole declared it to be a palace, a fortified city, temples in high places, and the noblest lawn in the world fenced by half the horizon.

There have been many changes since then, but Castle Howard has lost little of its grandeur. Vanbrugh designed a south front of 300 feet and a north front more than twice as long, and the building is equally impressive from north or south. The vast dome dominates both views. The garden front has a pediment rising 60 feet above the array of stone steps leading to the tall doorway. Ten pilasters with carved capitals rise to support an open balustrade on which are set urns and colossal statues. Cherubs and winged monsters form a frieze above the nine great windows of the upper storey of this central pile, while the lower windows carry the eye along the wings on each

37

side, 27 noble windows in a symmetrical row, all set between pilasters.

The north front of the grand pile, with the projecting wings on either side, looks down on the great court from which wide steps lead to a doorway flanked by columns supporting a richly carved lintel. Above this is a window with cherubs seated amid foliage on each side of its arch. Pilasters rise to the full height of this central design with colossal statues in niches between. Above is an elaborate frieze, and a balustrade with even bigger statues; and behind rises the dome, with busts above eight capitals from which the arches spring to support a graceful lantern.

The windows of the dome light the Great Hall, which is 35 feet square and paved with marble. Fluted pillars support 50-foot arches, on whose spandrels are paintings symbolising the Elements. Standing under the dome we see high above us *Phaeton with the Horses of the Sun*, painted by the Italian artist, Antonio Pellegrini. Next to the architecture and paintings of this amazing interior, which in many ways reminds us of St Paul's Cathedral, is the richness of the ironwork. The first floor balcony, which faces us as we enter, is superb, and so is the balcony round the dome gallery. The staircases east and west of the hall have bolder balustrades of iron, worthy of Jean Tijou and probably the work of his pupils.

East and west from the corners of the Great Hall run arched corridors with vistas seeming almost endless, a feature Vanbrugh delighted in. From one corridor we enter the rooms which look out on the garden, the Garden Room being in the centre, entered from the hall itself. The room has gods painted on the ceiling and works by Marc and Sebastian Ricci on the walls. One of the rooms to the east has paintings of Venice by Canaletto; others are rich in treasures of art and decoration, the Tapestry Room with work from Brussels looms showing a Dutch housewife milking her cows and a quayside on which men land fish and despatch it in barrels. The Reynolds Room is named from the portraits of its owners by Sir Joshua. The Music Room has lovely woodwork of the early 18th century, a superb frieze, and paintings by Tintoretto and Caracci, while above the chimney-piece is Francis Clouet's painting of Catherine Medici and her four sons.

The west wing of Castle Howard was built by Sir Thomas Robin-

From the south-west

Castle Howard

The Temple of the Winds

The gallery at Castle Howard

son late in the 18th century, and contains the chapel. Eighty feet long to the end apses, it has a great array of massive pillars and a sanctuary in which the marble altar and screen rises like a temple, its canopy resting on beautiful shafts—all a frame for a painting of Christ with bound hands. The windows have scenes by Burne-Jones. In this wing, too, is a picture gallery with Charles I on Horseback to greet us. Among other masterpieces are Van Dyck's portrait of *Frans Snyders*, Gerard Honthorst's *Finding of Moses*, *Henry VIII* as a young man by Holbein, and *Thomas Howard, Earl of Arundel*, by Rubens. There is a sad little girl by Gainsborough, and another girl in a blue hat by Yorkshire's own artist, John Jackson of Lastingham. Here, too, is a rare collection of miniatures, including a portrait of Cromwell and one of the ill-fated Essex.

Wherever we go in this great house we come upon treasures of all ages. There is a marble altar from the Temple of Apollo at Delphi, Greek vases, urns, and bronzes. Busts and statues are a striking feature indoors, yet out of doors they are more striking still. As in most 18th century parks, statues and buildings in the classical style abound. On magnificent plinths stand Hercules, a cymbal player, and a hunter, while on another sits the Boy with the Thorn. These monuments lead to a domed temple raised on terraces and enriched by stately columns. There is a Gothic tower in walls built as defences to the park, an obelisk in memory of the Duke of Marlborough, a bridge, a series of gateways notable for the richness of the stone and iron; and, best of all, a mausoleum designed by Hawksmoor, the famous architect who had a hand in the construction of the great house itself, for he carried on the work of Vanbrugh after him. This mausoleum is something unique in this country. From afar it looks like a temple on a hill, approached through iron gates bringing us to flights of steps; and within ramparts of stone we mount more and more steps till we stand on a platform from which rise columns surrounding the circular building and supporting its massive stone roof, capped by a low stone dome. Within is a panelled floor, pilasters dividing the tall windows, and a richly carved and panelled interior to the dome. Horace Walpole declared that he was almost tempted to be buried alive here, and we do not wonder, for who that sees it does not covet this exquisite estate?

The house is frequently open to the public.

Castleton. The road comes north from Rosedale along Castleton Rigg, a lofty hill-ridge with wonderful views of the heather moors and the upper reaches of the Esk winding far below.

Small though it is, Castleton under the Rigg has a market. It has a tree-shaded knoll where the Yorkshire Bruces had a castle in Norman days, an inn with a Robin Hood sign, and a church of rich amber-coloured stone built in memory of the men who fell in the Great War. Its tower is low and massive, and the interior is enriched with much oak showing the marks of the adze, in the style of the old craftsmen. The screens across the tower and chancel arches have tracery and iron grilles. On the sturdy benches, the organ screen, and the panelling at each side of the altar are the mice with which Robert Thompson of Kilburn signs his work.

The moors hereabouts are rich in entrenchments and burial mounds of forgotten ages. At Loose Howe (five miles away as the crow flies, to the east of Rosedale) excavations in 1937 revealed a body, with a bronze dagger, buried 1400 feet above the sea in a coffin formed by two dug-out boats made 3000 years ago from the trunk of a tree. It is said to represent the most important Bronze Age coffin-burial found in Northern England.

Catterick. It was a military camp nearly 20 centuries ago and is a military camp today. The Romans marched along the Great North Road which comes through the village, and by this road is the modern camp, stretching from Catterick to Richmond. It is the Aldershot of the North, disfiguring some of the loveliest scenery in England. The word of command which rings out hereabouts is like the echo of the command the Roman legions heard in Cataractonium, which lay north-west of the village and was 240 yards long and 170 wide; a length of its wall is still seen. It was still one of the most important towns in the North in the Saxon days before the Norman Conquest. The Northumbrian kings are said to have had a palace here, and here came Paulinus preaching Christianity and baptising in the River Swale. Here the terrible Scots came pouring down from the hills.

Near the site of the Roman camp the Great North Road crosses the river by a stone bridge of four arches, built by men who may have fought at Agincourt; the contract-note for the bridge is still at

Brough a mile away. It is a fine sight, when the river is high, to see the water rushing over the stones and under the trees. Over this bridge have come the travellers of five centuries, pedlar and peasant on foot, royal processions from York to Scotland, mail-coach passengers, and travellers in our own swift cars. Today it is a small place proud of its past. It has many old houses, a war memorial on one of half a dozen little greens, and old inns where coaches pulled up years ago after the dangerous miles near Leeming Lane, the notorious haunt of highwaymen.

The vicarage among the trees was once the home of a man who saw Nelson die, Alexander Scott. He was on board the Victory at Trafalgar, and it was to him that Nelson spoke his last words. "Doctor, I have not been a *great* sinner," he said; and then, "Remember that I leave Lady Hamilton and my daughter Horatia as a legacy to my country—never forget Horatia." Dr Scott tried to ease the pain and the dying admiral made his last effort to speak, saying, "Thank God I have done my duty," and with his last breath "God and my country."

The church where the people gathered to listen to the man who saw the Battle of Trafalgar is high and lifted up, in a churchyard not unlike the courtyard of a castle, and reached by narrow ways between the houses. The chancel, nave, and aisles were built by Catherine de Burgh and her son about 1415, and the contract for the work, still kept at Brough Hall, tells us that the mason, Richard Crakehall, was to receive about £1000 and a mason's gown. The tower and the chapels are a few years later than the rest. Parts of an earlier church are the 13th century pillars of the nave, and the 14th century south doorway. The quatrefoil windows of the clerestory come from last century.

There are three coats-of-arms on the old porch, and other shields of North of England families are on the 15th century marble font. The gables of the piscina and sedilia have flame-like crockets, the chapels have 15th century screens, and the chest is old. One of the windows shows Paulinus preaching to King Edwin, and another shows him baptising in the Swale. There are brasses of William de Burgh, who died in 1442, and his son, and of another William, who died in 1492, with his wife Helen, a graceful figure in falling headdress. Her husband, who founded a chantry here, has a short body and long legs. In a canopied recess lies the broken figure of Walter Urswick, wearing 14th century armour and a richly ornamented belt.

One of many inscriptions to heroes is to Arthur Brook, who fell while covering the retreat of mounted infantry during a black hour of the Boer War; and another tells of a 17th century poet who lies in the chancel, Richard Braithwaite, Lord of the Manor here in Charles I's day.

Cayton. Over a mile from Cayton Bay, which visitors love for its cliffs and woods, Cayton's lowly church hides behind the houses. Its squat little tower of diminishing stages is 15th century, but within the tiny porch is a charming Norman doorway with shafts and cushion capitals and a captivating arch, the rich zigzag of its three orders having a surprisingly fine effect.

Through the low windows in the cream walls we look out on the countryside. From the close of Norman days comes the north arcade with its two huge arches resting on a low pillar with a great capital, and the font has a Norman bowl looking as if it is about to fall off its pedestal. The long chancel has a 15th century entrance arch, and the tower a door two centuries younger. There is an old chest and an old handbell.

Cleasby. A small neighbour of Darlington, it is near the River Tees, dividing Yorkshire and Durham, and has fine views of both counties from the ridge of little hills rising sharply above it. Old dwellings gather about the spacious green, which has seats shaded by trees. The cream-walled old vicarage, with a shield and a mitre carved over the door, is said to have been built by the most famous son of the village, John Robinson, who was born here in 1650, travelled abroad, became an influential diplomat at the Swedish Court, and was of great service to the Duke of Marlborough in appeasing the Swedish king. On returning to England Robinson became Bishop of Bristol and Dean of Windsor, and George I made him a Privy Councillor. He never forgot his native village, though he became Bishop of London, for he built not only a vicarage but a school for Cleasby, and often in his days of fame he returned to visit his father's cottage. There is a window in his memory in the modern church, with glass which was once in his cathedral at Bristol. His brother Christopher, probably born here, went out to Virginia and became Secretary of the Colony, his son John becoming President.

Cloughton. It lies on the road from Scarborough to Whitby, and less than a mile from the pretty inlet of the coast known as Cloughton Wyke. Farther north is Hayburn Wyke, a charming little bay with grand cliffs and beautiful woods above a waterfall. Amid the miles of heather on the moors hereabouts are entrenchments and burial mounds which were old when the Romans came this way to their look-out station at Ravenscar.

Pleasant with its many old stone houses, the village has a modern church facing the smithy and the old inn. Standing in 100 acres of grounds near the sea, Cober Hill is now a guest house, but it was last century the home of Sir Frank Lockwood, one of the most delightful men known to the Law Courts of the last generation. He is remembered as a tall handsome man with white hair and twinkling eyes; and Lord Rosebery once said that his cheerfulness would dispel a London fog.

In the church is a window in memory of this much-loved man, showing the Judgment of Solomon; it is linked with an incident of Sir Frank's early days when a girl at York Assizes was accused of murder, the judge asking if there was anyone who would defend her. Sir Frank became her advocate.

An old inscription is to William Bower and his wife, who *lived together, lovingly and comfortably, for* 73 *years*, William (at 96) dying in 1698, only a year before his wife.

Cold Kirby. As bleak as its name, this windswept village of the Hambleton Hills is often snowed up for weeks together, but it has a magnificent prospect of line on line of moors. Its grey cottages with pantiled roofs are strung along the wide road, and the neat little church, made new a hundred years ago, has an old font.

Constable Burton. In the lovely gardens of a walled park of 150 acres Burton Hall, designed by John Carr, rises from lawns shaded by cedars, a fine house with a colonnaded front, reached by a stately flight of steps. It has taken the place of a house said to have been built by Inigo Jones, and is still a home of the Wyvills, descendants of a Wyvill who fought for the Conqueror, and one of Yorkshire's oldest families.

The stream flowing through the park is an aristocrat, for during its journey to the Swale it takes to itself the names of half a dozen places through which it passes. Here it is the Burton Beck, and among the fine trees shading it are noble beeches where an old bridge crosses a charming glen.

Cotherstone. Its long winding road is near the River Tees, and beyond are the green hills and purple moors of Durham. Time has not destroyed the memories of the Vikings hereabouts. At Woden Croft Richard Cobden went to school, spending in this lovely spot what he remembered as the blackest days of his life, so grim and desolate that he could never bring himself to speak of them afterwards. He had the misfortune to find himself, after a happy beginning of school life at Midhurst in Sussex, banished for five years to one of the wretched schools which Dickens was to pillory for ever under the name of Dotheboys Hall.

Above the meeting of the Balder with the Tees are the broken walls of a castle of the Fitzhughs; built about 1200 and destroyed a century or two later, it was shown by John Morritt to his great friend Sir Walter Scott. A mile along the road to Bowes is the Butter Stone, where people bought and sold when plague made havoc here.

In the neat 19th century church is a book with the names of men who fell in the Great War, the wooden cover richly illuminated.

Coverham. Here the river is nearing the end of its 12-mile journey from the heights above the Wharfe to the Ure below East Witton. Near the head of the dale Great and Little Whernside tower above the rapid mountain stream; and where Coverham lies in a deep hollow the river comes swirling and splashing to a lovely bow bridge at the foot of a hill. It is a charming ride from East Witton along the narrow road.

Miles Coverdale began his life in this pastoral dale. He would know the village and its lost monastery. He would hear the singing of the monks, and something of their music seems to have found its way into his psalms as we sing them, and into his translation of the Bible, which appeared about the time the last Amen was sung at Coverham.

They were dangerous times in which he lived, and from here he went to his hiding-place on the Continent, working in secret there to write the Bible for the common people.

Coverdale was not of the heroic mould of martyrs, and in a dangerous age he fled to the Continent, where during the next three years he produced and published the first of all complete English translations of the Bible. It was printed in Paris and licensed in London, but was full of blunders, and Thomas Cromwell sent Coverdale back to Paris to superintend another English edition. The King of France granted a licence, but before the work was complete issued an edict against it, and as much as possible of the printed matter was burned. Zealous effort secured the remainder, and this, with the precious presses and types, were smuggled in safety to London, where Coverdale produced the *Great Bible* in 1538. A second edition was called *Cranmer's Bible*.

Coverdale had married while abroad, but in spite of this Cranmer secured his appointment as Bishop of Exeter. Under Mary Tudor he was deposed and imprisoned, but was released, and lived on the Continent until the end of Mary's reign. His growing Puritanism made it impossible for him to return to Exeter, but he was given a living in London, and preached until he died in 1568.

Little is left of the old abbey, founded in the 12th century by Helewisia de Glanville who lies here. The place where it stood can only have grown more lovely with time, and its remains are in the house known as Coverham Abbey, where on the lawn, bordered with stately beeches, are two impressive arches, a fragment of a transept with two lancet windows, and three coffin-lids, one with a pastoral staff and a chalice, another with a shield on the stem of a cross and with unusual tracery at the base.

Set up against a wall are two stone knights who should be lying down, both with crossed legs, both wearing chain armour with belts and sword; one has lost his arms, the other (a giant of seven feet) is at prayer. They may represent Helewisia's son and his heir, both having been buried here.

Not far from the one remaining arch of the abbey gatehouse, the

45

village church stands on a steep bank in a churchyard with a water-fall and avenues of limes. Some rebuilding was done last century, but the tower is 15th century, the nave arcade is 14th, and there are windows from all three mediaeval centuries. The arches are without capitals. There are two piscinas, and among shields of old glass is one of the famous Scrope of Masham. On the side of the doorway is a coffin-lid with a cross, and serving as the lintel is a Saxon stone on which are carved three little men with uplifted hands.

Coxwold. It has a beautiful setting in the narrow valley between the green slopes of the Hambleton and Howardian Hills. The broad village street has green verges, and facing the inn is the stump of a great elm, a shapely tree beside it now. There are old houses and yellow cottages, some of them half hidden by evergreen fire-thorn. There are quaint almshouses of Charles II's day, and a grammar school of 1603 which is now a delightful house, wistaria draping its walls, and windows peeping from its stone roof. Colville Hall, with memories of days gone by, is by the church, which stands on a bank at the top of the road.

We may come here for memories of two immortal Englishmen. Here lived Laurence Sterne, and here, it is believed by many, lies the body of Oliver Cromwell.

In a trim formal garden beyond the church is a lovely old gabled house with creepered walls and a huge chimney with a tiny window which was once a hole through which fuel was thrown on the fire. It was the home for the last eight years of his life of Laurence Sterne, who gave it the name of Shandy Hall. Here he finished *Tristram Shandy*, and wrote *The Sentimental Journey* and the *Journal to Eliza*. Very narrow is the old staircase he went up and down, and very quaint the bedrooms, with old rafters and uneven floors, one with a wheel used for raising water from a well. The tiny parlour is much as it was in his day, when he would sit and write at its window. It is shortly to be restored and opened to the public.

The greatest humorist of his age, he was content to be a village parson, fiddling away his evenings and spending his days writing and shooting. It is said that the villagers never quite understood their eccentric parson, whose books had set the world laughing, and they would tell stories of his hurrying down the hill, stopping in the middle of the road when a thought struck him, and making a note of it.

The striking church where Laurence Sterne preached is chiefly 15th century, but the chancel was made new a few years after his death in 1768. Standing where the Norman church stood, it is an arresting structure with its great nave, its narrow chancel, its spacious porch, a rare octagonal tower, and an array of beautiful windows, pierced battlements, leafy pinnacles, flying buttresses, and queer gargoyles of men and animals.

Enriching the fine old roof of the nave are gaily painted bosses with carvings of animals, heads of men, a bishop, and a man opening his mouth wide. A coloured boss in the porch has the bust of a man, and those in the chancel have flowers and shields. The door is still barred with a heavy beam. The nave has a west gallery, low pews with little doors, and the fine three-decker pulpit from which Sterne preached. The chancel has curious old rails enclosing the altar, and coming far down in the shape of a capital T. An odd possession is a short Spanish sword thought to have been made at Toledo in the 16th century. A copy of the *Geneva Bible* printed in 1601 (*the Breeches Bible*) is in a case on which we see the mouse carved by the Yorkshire craftsman Robert Thompson. A great possession is the 15th century glass in the tracery of the nave windows, a gallery of small figures of angels and saints.

The oldest memorial in the church is a brass inscription on the floor of the nave, to John Manston of 1464. The chancel is like a museum of monuments of the family of Belasyse—barons, viscounts, and earls of Fauconberg. On a canopied tomb on the north side, rich and elaborate in ornament and heraldic display, lies Sir William Belasyse with one of his two wives, small Tudor ruffs round their stiff necks, and crests at their feet. On the front of the tomb are three figures in Elizabethan armour, and between the pillars kneel a man and a woman, the woman wearing an extraordinary black headdress. An odd inscription says that *John Brown did carve this stone alone*. Sir William, who wears armour, was the nephew of Anthony Belasyse, one of the Commissioners for the Dissolution of the monasteries, to whom Henry VIII granted Newburgh Priory, which became their home and is still the home of their descendants.

The huge white marble monument next to Sir William's is shared by his great-grandson Henry and his son Thomas, their lifesize figures showing Henry in Roman dress and Thomas in his Parliamentary robes, a coronet in his hand. Thomas, who was created Earl Fauconberg, married for his second wife Mary Cromwell, Oliver's daughter, who is said to have brought her father's body secretly to Newburgh Priory.

On the south side of the chancel is the monument erected by Viscount Fauconberg in memory of his wife, who died in 1618. They kneel under a classical canopy, the viscount in a rich fur-lined robe and his wife in a gown with ruff and slashed sleeves, and headdress with long drapery. Looking at the monument to Henry, the second earl, we remember that it was through his daughter's marriage that the Newburgh estates came to the Wombwells. There are portrait plaques of two soldiers of the family who died abroad on active service—George Wombwell at Meerut in 1889 and Stephen in the South African War. The gallant Sir George Wombwell who died in 1913 is remembered by his bust; he too was a soldier, one of the 600 of the immortal charge of the Light Brigade. He married a granddaughter of Sir Robert Peel. A son of William IV, Admiral Lord Fitzclarence, has a tablet in the chancel, and he died when on a visit to Newburgh, sleeping in the vault under the chancel.

The road to Crayke runs by the park where Newburgh Priory stands at the head of a drive with lawns, herbaceous borders, and two yews trimmed like low roofs with pinnacles. The road itself is charming here, with fine iron gates, velvet lawns, splendid yew hedges, majestic trees, the sight of the lake with swans gliding, and a pretty row of cottages. The house comes chiefly from Elizabethan and later days and has a Jacobean porch, but has remains of still earlier buildings, for the house is on the site of a monastery founded 800 years ago. There are walls of the 14th and 15th centuries, kitchens with massive oak beams resting on carved corbels, doorways where the monks came in and out, and stones carved in the earliest days of the priory, among them one with the Madonna and Child and another with a figure holding a dish.

It is in this great house with its magnificent panelled rooms and galleries, with an alabaster fireplace brought from Italy, that the memory of Oliver Cromwell is wrapt in mystery. We found a bust of him here, with another of Sir Robert Peel, and one of the treasured possessions we saw in the house was a small silver pen with Cromwell's initials. It has a screw cap, so that he may have carried it about, and we may imagine that he would write many of his famous letters with it; it may have written *God made them as stubble in our hands.* We saw also a crimson saddle which may have belonged to Oliver or to Lord Fauconberg, his son-in-law.

The present owner of the Priory, Captain Wombwell, has a fine collection of paintings and watercolours, including a scene from the Charge of the Light Brigade, showing among many others Sir George Wombwell. The house has been extensively renovated recently and is soon to be open occasionally to the public.

But amid all the splendour of this fine house is a little bare room near the roof which transcends in human interest all the beauty about us. It is a plain attic, the end near the window bricked-up about 4 feet high with a sort of coped roof of rough planks. There is a hole in one of the planks, and we understand that it was made by a carpenter in the presence of Edward VII when he was Prince of Wales, the prince being curious to know the secret of this room. It is believed that this little bricked-up place encloses the body of Oliver Cromwell.

When Charles II, by an act of incredible vengeance, dug up the bodies of Cromwell and Admiral Blake in the Abbey, flinging Blake to the dust outside and hanging Cromwell on Tyburn, Lady Fauconberg is believed to have obtained the body after the head had been cut off, and to have brought it away to Newburgh and walled it up in what is still called Cromwell's room. The tomb has never been opened, and we cannot be sure of the truth of this tradition, but there are many who hope to live to see the head and the body of the foremost man who has ruled in England brought together again and buried once more in the tiny chapel across the road from Parliament, a yard or two away from the bones of the man who flung him out.

Crambe. As it makes its way through the little hills the Derwent makes a big sweep round this village. Over the river is Kirkham Abbey, in a lovely green setting.

Crambe's cottages and farms are dotted about the fine aisleless church, which has come from Norman days, with a Norman chancel arch. Very long and narrow, with sloping walls, it has an odd array of windows of all sizes and at all levels. One of the Norman windows was made pointed in the 13th century. The tower is 15th century, and at the sides of its round arch are a man on all fours and a weird face showing teeth and a tongue. Under the tower is a 12th century pedestal stoup; and a little older is the splendid font, whose square bowl, enriched with arcading, rests on a fine cluster of pillars with foliage capitals. The pulpit and a chalice are 17th century. The almsdish has exquisite Italian filigree work. In the walling outside are fragments of coffin-lids, a frightful face with bared teeth, and a stone, which may be Saxon, with crude carving of scrolls and a cross.

Crathorne. Lovely trees, copper beeches and firs among them, are a feature of this charming village where the River Leven flows by a watermill, and the grey church at a pretty corner has houses with white walls and red roofs for company. Even the smithy is white.

It is a fine little church with a 14th century nave, and a chancel and sturdy tower (with a pyramid top) refashioned half a century ago. The lintel of the doorway through which we enter is its great possession; finely carved with a band of spirals and an interlacing design, it covered a Saxon grave a thousand years ago. The new door below it has the old 14th century ironwork and ring. Other Saxon stones and a splendid collection of ancient coffin-lids are treasured here; many of them are built into the walls of the tower, and part of a Saxon cross is on the sill of a nave window. There are a few pieces of old glass, an old piscina, a small bell of about 1300 in the peal of four, and two stone figures of men who knew this place long ago. The very worn figure in robes, lying near a blocked door-way, represents a deacon.

The battered knight in a new recess near the altar is William de Crathorne, who died fighting at Neville's Cross in 1346. His broken sword hangs from an ornamented belt, and his hands are at prayer. The arms of this family who lived in the neighbourhood for many generations are on the nave wall outside. A stone coffin and the socket of an old cross are by the porch.

Crayke. A village that cannot be hid, Crayke is a fine sight from the Plain of York, its houses climbing the hill to the church and castle at the top; the sight of the fertile Plain from the village is charming.

It is supposed that there was a fortress here in Saxon days. Of the Norman castle only traces of foundations remain. The battlemented house we see, standing behind the church among great trees, is the tower-house known as the Great Chamber, built early in the 15th century and restored in modern days; it has a beautiful garden, and a splendid view from its new windows. By it are the remains of a 15th century house called the New Tower, now ruined fragments of walls mantled in green.

The church is said to mark the place where St Cuthbert's body rested during its long wanderings, hence the name of the inn here, The Durham Ox. Made new in the 15th century, it has fine battlements, an imposing tower, and a spacious simplicity within, an air of Jacobean days given by the bobbin-ended pews filling the nave, the splendid canopied pulpit of 1637, two chairs, and the cover of the font. The 15th century chancel screen is restored, and has a cross in memory of those who fell in the Great War. There are three fine old chests, two dug-outs and one elaborately carved, a panelled reading-desk, a great altar stone on the wall of the aisle, and stone figures thought to be Sir John Gibson and his wife, who lived here-abouts in Elizabeth I's time. Dean Inge of St Paul's was born in the village.

Croft. Long famous for its wells, it lies on the old Great North Road, here carried across the Tees into Durham on a fine old bridge with a string of ribbed arches. A striking picture by the bridge are two old companions, the church and the rambling inn, and behind the houses is an old mill where a wheel has been turning since the Conqueror's Domesday Book was made. In a fine park a mile across the meadows is Clervaux Castle, a handsome house of many towers, keeping green the name of a family who had land here for 300 years. Two miles farther south stood Hanlaby Hall, where Byron spent part of his honeymoon with the Milbankes.

Extraordinary within and quaint without, the church has much for us to see. Most of it is 14th century, but there is Norman masonry in the west end, the south arcade and the south doorway are 13th century, and the tower is 15th. The odd little porch has stone seats coming right to the entrance arch, which rests on corbels. The arcades and the walls of the aisles are leaning, and the chancel is almost as big as the wide and lofty nave, the great round arch between them (over 700 years old) soaring to the roof.

A fine example of its time, the 14th century chancel has buttresses adorned with niches, an aumbry under a hood with four-leaved flowers and heads, a piscina with shafts and heads, and three stepped sedilia with an amazing wealth of carving in which are men in long tunics, a man kneeling, one man standing on another, a lion, a ram, a bear, an imp, a dragon, a dog, faces of men, and a pig eating acorns; by the shafts with foliage capitals on which the arches rest are strings of ballflower ornament.

The fine roof of the chancel is modern, but has old bosses richly carved with flowers and emblems. There are handsome old altar-rails, a splendid old chest with three locks, restored screenwork round the south aisle chapel, and an hourglass in a metal stand. The most astonishing thing here is the Milbanke pew; raised far above our heads on oak pillars, it is about 15 feet long, and reminds us of a small wooden house on stilts, reached by a stairway imposing enough for a mansion. It was in this lofty place that Byron and his bride are said to have sat one Sunday morning while spending their honeymoon at Hanlaby Hall; and in the days when George Hudson (the Railway King) was one of the richest men in Yorkshire he and his wife sat here in fine style. The story goes that George always turned his back on the parson when he sang, and that his wife put up her parasol during the sermon!

There are two astonishing tombs in the aisles. One, a 17th century memorial to Sir Mark Milbanke, is ostentatiously ornate and has lion heads at the corners; the other, a massive tomb about 10 feet long, is of Sir Richard Clervaux, who with Richard Place probably built the tower. Splendid in itself and in its preservation, the tomb is notable for the excellence of its carving and the lettering of its inscription, which tells us that Sir Richard was related to two kings, Edward IV and Richard III, the Nevilles being the connecting link.

Older than all else here are three carved stones. Two in the north aisle are parts of crosses from Saxon England, one showing rough knotwork, the other in a charming fragment with foliage, birds, and dragons. The stone in the south aisle wall has a battered figure looking like a phoenix, and is probably from Roman England.

In this church we think of the boy who was to grow up to give us *Alice in Wonderland*, for his father was rector here, and the boy, whose mind was full of comical thoughts even then, must have seen the nobility who went up the broad stair to the Milbanke pew like a Punch and Judy show. The rectory, begun in Elizabeth I's day, is across the road almost hidden by tall trees, and we may be sure that it was in its charming garden that young Charles Lutwidge Dodgson (as he was in those days) played some of his queer games.

Cropton. A pleasant upland village at the edge of the Pickering Moors, it has old houses, a wide trim street, a little green shaded by a shapely sycamore, and a modern church in Norman style, perched on a hillock. Within it are three fine brass candelabra made in the fashion of three centuries ago, and a tub font looking old enough to have been shaped by the Normans. Outside is a fragment of the old cross, and we remember the rhyme which says that on Cropton cross there is a cup, and in the cup there is a sup. The cup used to be placed on the cross, filled with water for thirsty travellers.

Two yews make an arch over the churchyard gate, from where is an exceedingly fine outlook over the deep valley of the River Seven to the swelling lines of the purple moors, with Appleton-le-Moors and its church on the opposite ridge, and the chimney conspicuous in the view up Rosedale. To the west of the churchyard is a mound on the edge of a steep bank, marking the site of the castle built about the close of the 11th century by Robert de Stuteville.

Between here and Newton are the famous Cawthorn Camps—four of the most interesting Roman enclosures in the land, standing on the Roman road known as Wade's Causeway which runs over the moors to the North, and is perhaps best seen near Goathland. Three are roughly square, one rather like a coffin. Covering in all about 25 acres, they are almost lost among heather and pines, but the embankments can still be traced, and there is a mound believed to have been used as a platform from which the General could address his troops. The oldest is said to have been built in Agricola's day, the others about the time Hadrian was building his wall across Northumberland.

In this village were born the famous William Scoresbys, father and son. The father was born on a farm and made his name as one of the boldest and most skilful navigators of the Arctic; the younger sailed with his father to the North when he was only eleven, and lived to share the father's fame. Born in 1760, the father tired of the farm at 19, and joined a ship for Gibraltar, being captured and thrown into a Spanish prison. He escaped and returned home, and in the prime of life he made a famous voyage which brought him within 510 miles of the North Pole. His men began to murmur at the foolhardiness of the captain, but Scoresby went on, and on May 25, 1806, stood nearer the Pole than any man before him had ever been. The son developed rather as a scientist than as an explorer, inventing an apparatus which revealed the temperature of the Arctic Ocean bed, and writing the best work on the Arctic till then. Deeply religious, he gave up the sea and entered the church, sacrificing £800 a year for a poor curacy.

Cundall. The small church hides in the fields, looking to the old hall (now a farmhouse) near the Swale. The 19th century church has an old chest with three locks and a treasure from Saxon England leaning sadly in a corner of the tower. It is the shaft of a cross, over 5 feet high, carved with knotwork, and dragons and birds in inter-lacing branchwork. It may be 8th century, and has one corner cut away.

Dalby. Remote and beautiful, tucked into the southern slope of the Howardian Hills and looking down on a magnificent view of the Plain of York, it is a charming spot to find. On one side of a field (in which is a glorious avenue of trees) the small bellcote church stands buried in trees, sandwiched between the rectory and a farm. The Norman building was made almost new in the 15th century, but we still enter by a simple Norman doorway in a porch of oak and stone (draped with roses when we called); and a tall Norman arch divides the nave and chancel. Dim and quaint is the chancel—curious inside, where walls of tremendous thickness curve inwards to form the simple barrel-vault, and looking outside like a low embattled tower. The nave has four big tie-beams in its old roof. The font is

Anglo-Saxon sculpture
on the north front of
Newburgh Priory, Coxwold

Hogback tombstones in
Brompton-in-Allertonshire
Church

Constable Burton Hall

Coxwold

ancient, and an inscription tells of Alan Ascough and his wife who sleep here after living together for 63 years of the 17th century.

Danby-in-Cleveland. Its name covers a lovely district of moorland hills and valleys, stretching between Danby Low Moor to the north and Danby High Moor to the south, with the River Esk winding through it from west to east. On the north side of the valley Danby Beacon rises nearly 1000 feet above the sea. The village itself, known as Danby End, lies on the road crossing the river.

At Danby Head, 5 miles away as the crow flies, a stream comes to life at 1300 feet up, and flows north to the Esk. It is in the great loneliness of this Danby Dale that we find the church, 2 miles from the village, with farmhouses dotted here and there under the heathery moors. It has a 15th century tower, a nave of the 18th century, and a chancel made new. There are a few old fragments in the arcades soaring to the roof, and some old stones in the wall above the chancel arch, two carved with zigzag. Under the tower are several old gravestones (one with a star of interlacing pattern) and an old piscina. Some of the windows are frames for Nature's pictures of the moors; others have rich glass, the east window bright with Our Lord in Glory and figures of St Oswald, St Aidan, and the Madonna. Another shows Christ sending His disciples into the world, and below are St Hilda, St Wilfrid, Bede, Caedmon, and Bishop Colman. To Paddy Higham, who was eight when she died, there is a window showing St Bride standing by Ireland's rocky shore and mountains, and the face of the saint is the face of the child.

An old wheel-head cross stands in the churchyard, and a simple cross marks the place where lies the man who immortalised Danby. He was John Christopher Atkinson, who sleeps amid the men and women he loved.

He walked 70,000 miles over the moors and through the dales. Born in Essex in 1814, he was author of a bird book known to three generations of boys. A lover of outdoor life, happy among his books, he put into his *Forty Years in a Moorland Parish* all the knowledge, humour, and experience of a parson who had known this place for half a lifetime. He wrote of its folklore and superstitions, and of the antiquities abounding on the moors. His was one of the widest and wildest parishes in England, but he knew everyone in it, and watched

55

TO21158

its natural life unfolding in every season. After being vicar for 53 years, he died in 1900.

At the end of the high ridge rising between Danby Dale and Little Fryup Dale the Latimers built a castle when the 14th century was young. Now part ruin and part farmhouse, it has little of its ancient splendour, though some of the walls still rise almost to their full height. The courtyard, about 50 feet long and half as wide, is shadowed by two towers set diagonally, and there are walls with fireplaces and broken windows. A dungeon keeps its vaulted roof and small doorway above dark steps, and there is a room with a long roof resting on old beams. A curious wooden seat has a panelled back, and in a panelled room is a handsome oak chest. A spiral stair remains, part of it resting on a stone figure as old as the castle.

The castle looks down on the Esk, which is here crossed by a mediaeval packhorse bridge on which are the arms of the Nevilles, who followed the Latimers about 1380.

Danby Wiske. The inn and a few cottages are by the little green, and the old moated rectory is where the church stands apart by the river. We pass the old manor house on the way to the church, and over the stream is Lazenby Hall, which has become a farmhouse but keeps its fine plaster ceilings.

A massive 15th century tower with a vaulted roof rises at the west end of the small embattled church, and a porch with old stone seats shelters a crude Norman doorway which is rare in this part of Yorkshire for having its carved tympanum still in place. Its curious sculpture shows a woman wearing long hanging sleeves and a tall figure giving what seems to be a book to a smaller figure. There is Norman masonry in the stout leaning walls of the nave; the aisle and arcade are mediaeval, and an extraordinary arch, out of shape and resting on sloping sides, leads to the chancel, which was made new in the 14th century. There is an old piscina, the font is Norman, and the effigy of a woman is 600 years old. From the 17th century come two chairs, carved panels in the reredos and in some of the chancel seats, and a fine set of carved pews.

Downholme. Its few stone houses are on the slope of a little valley going down to the Swale. From the churchyard in the hollow (at the foot of the cone-shaped How Hill) is a lovely view of the dale, with line on line of hills coming sharply down.

Steps like three sides of a well bring us to the old sunken porch of the stout-walled church ringed with great firs; and a fine Norman doorway, tall and massive, opens to an interior wearing the gracious air of age. The nave has Norman walls, and dividing it from the aisle is a 13th century arcade with stout arches and short pillars, their capitals like table-tops. A wide 13th century arch with low capitals leads to the 600-year-old chancel, which has an arch leading to a north chapel. The font and the piscina are old, a coffin-lid with a cross and shears is in the wall of the porch, and in the churchyard is the base of the old cross and a stone coffin with a lid.

Over a mile along the road between Stainton Moor and Hipswell Moor is the fine old Walburn Hall, an Elizabethan house with gables and clustered chimneys, projecting bays, a flagged courtyard, and fragments of an old chapel. A farmhouse now, it was once a home of the great Scropes, and was garrisoned for Charles in the Civil War.

Easby. We know few more beautiful riverside walks in Yorkshire than the mile from Richmond to Easby, the path by the Swale bringing us to the small village in a perfect setting of water and meadow and wood. Its houses are few, but it has great possessions, and is a place of pilgrimage for all who love old stones. Here are the remains of an abbey where for nearly four centuries the White Canons lived in a green world, till Henry VIII's destroying hand fell upon their house; and keeping the ruins company is a rare little church with a story older than the monastery's. Splendid trees are in abundance, one a huge chestnut with a double trunk over 20 feet round, another the Abbot's Elm, with a girth of 24 feet.

The abbey builders left the parish church where they found it, setting their gatehouse to one side of it, and their own church and domestic buildings to the other side. The aisleless church of the Normans was refashioned in the 13th century, but the chancel still has some of the original windows, and a round-arched recess sheltering a fine stone coffin. The two eastern bays of the south aisle were built as a chapel in the 13th century and altered two centuries later; the two western bays and the porch are 14th century. The arms of the Scropes, the Askes, and the Conyers are on this porch, which has stone seats, an unusual aumbry, and old doors to the nave and aisle, and is like a tunnel with its arched roof supporting an upper room. Enclosing the south chapel are restored old screens, and in it is a lovely trefoiled piscina. The north chapel of the nave, and old glass in the east window of the chancel showing two figures and an angel, are 600 years old. A century older are two low windows, three trefoiled stone seats and a big piscina in the chancel, and fragments of coffin-lids in the outside wall. The splendid font is Norman, and the battered sculpture of a seated figure in a niche on an outside wall is probably from the same time.

The chief treasures of the church are its wonderful 13th century wall paintings, surpassed in Yorkshire only at Pickering, and a cross which is a copy of one set up probably 1200 years ago. Now in the Victoria and Albert Museum, the original cross was reassembled a few years ago after having been in pieces for nobody knows how long, part of the shaft having been in private hands in the village, and three fragments embedded in the walls of the church. Its sides are richly carved with interlacing and knotwork; in the trailing foliage on the back are birds and animals eating berries, and on the front is Our Lord in Majesty, with the Disciples below.

The nave arcade is covered with painting of chevron and leaves, and worn patches of painting and later lettering are in the aisle; but it was in the chancel that the artist painted his pictures 700 years ago. On the sedilia are portraits of archbishops, and on the splays of the north windows are spring and winter scenes, with men sowing and pruning, digging and hawking; the sower has a pert little rook following close at his heel, one of the drollest and most alert mediaeval birds we have seen. The series of pictures on the walls are concerned with man's sin and God's love, telling the story of Adam and Eve on one wall, and of Jesus on the other. One of the best pictures on the north side is of Adam and Eve spinning, both earning their bread with the sweat of their brow; the artist has painted an angel as if to comfort them with the promise of forgiveness. In the first of the south wall pictures we see Gabriel with a scroll and the Madonna with lilies, followed by a quaint Nativity scene in which Joseph is snatching forty winks, and two men are walking on their toes, led by an angel. Then comes the Adoration of the Wise Men, and in the row below are the Descent from the Cross, the Entombment, and the Resurrection.

Of our own day is a fine portrait plaque of Robert Pulleine, who died at 19; beside it is the wooden cross from his grave in Flanders.

Like the church, the abbey was dedicated to St Agatha, the Sicilian saint martyred for her faith in the 3rd century. The abbey was founded about the middle of the 12th century by Roald, Constable of Richmond Castle, and in the time of Edward III it came into the possession of the Scropes, lords of Bolton. Its splendour has gone, but there is still a rare beauty in the ragged pile of walls, high and low, and some with lovely windows and arches. The little mill-race still flows through on its way to meet the Swale under a green roof, though now it is making electric light for the great house on the slope above. From its fine lawn there is a view far down the dale, the river shining by the ruins.

Separated by a little road from the church and the ruins, the abbey gatehouse stands almost as when it was refashioned in the 14th century, a beautiful building with a stone staircase on the wall outside climbing to the upper room in which the abbot held his court. Owing to its cramped site the abbey itself is of unusual plan, with the church set in the middle, and the domestic buildings extending from its north and south sides. Some of them are at odd angles, for the cloister, on the south side of the nave, is a quadrangle of irregular shape, with no parallel sides. Another unusual thing is that, though there are considerable remains of the other buildings, the church has almost disappeared. Begun soon after the foundation, and completed early in the 13th century, the original church had the shape of a cross, with a short aisleless presbytery, transepts with eastern chapels, and a nave with aisles. About 600 years ago the presbytery was lengthened eastward and given a sacristy, and a chapel (which still has part of its altar) was built on to the north aisle of the nave. The canopied stalls which once adorned the church are now in the parish church at Richmond.

Occupying the eastern range of the cloister buildings, the sacristy and the chapter house were rebuilt 700 years ago, and altered two centuries later when an upper floor was added. Of the splendid refectory and its vaulted basement the roofless walls still stand on the south side of the cloister. The dining-hall itself, over 100 feet long, was rebuilt about 1300 and has a fine array of big windows with fragments of tracery, and its old pulpit remains in a recess.

The two-storeyed range joining the west side of the cloister and extending beyond the end of the dining-hall had a vaulted ground floor serving as warming house, cellars, and guest hall, and above them were the dormitory and probably the prior's lodging. We still see the doorway which stood at the foot of the stairway leading from the cloister to the dormitory, its Norman arch carved with a double row of worn beak-heads, and resting on later sides. The three-storeyed block extending towards the river was the guest house, still keeping two fine windows; the one in its south wall is seen as part of beautiful arcading in the outside wall.

Grouped on the north side of the church are the infirmary buildings, and the abbot's lodging on their upper floor. His gallery was over the passage connecting the block with the north transept of the church. The passage opens into the infirmary hall, with a 15th century chapel at its south-east corner.

The abbey owed much of its splendour to a family famous in our history, the Scropes. The founder of the House lies on the site of the vanished presbytery, where they laid him to rest 600 years ago.

Easington. Crowning the hill between Staithes and Loftus, it has stone houses with thatched porches, an old church rebuilt last century, the stump of an ancient cross outside the churchyard wall, and Grinkle Park, a great house two miles away in 200 acres with beautiful trees. In the thickly wooded valley below the village two streams are flowing to the sea.

Many Saxon and Norman stones found when the old church was pulled down are now in the new one, which is attractive with its imposing tower, soaring arches, and pleasing windows showing the first Christmas morning and saints. Very fine is a coffin-lid near the altar, carved with a cross which has a leafy head, and a stem enriched with oak leaves and acorns. It comes from about 1300, and has a Norman-French inscription to Robert Bushell, many of the letters being filled with the original lead. The beautiful woodwork of the north chapel (the enclosing screens, the chairs, and the altar with its candlesticks and cross) is the work of Mr Thompson of Kilburn.

Very charming is a monument in the porch, where little Katheran

Conyers sleeps in her stone cradle under a stone coverlet. She had had one month of life when she died in 1621, and here she lies with her head on a tiny hand.

Easingwold. Those who rush through its long street on the way from York to Thirsk do not know how quaint and old-fashioned this small market town is, yet it is only a step to the old creepered houses, inns, and shops gathered round the greens and the cobbled market-place. Here too is the bull-ring, and the steps and base of the old cross under a huge shelter, and on the way to Uppleby is a timbered house on which we read "God with us 1666", perhaps put here by a man who remembered the rallying cry at Marston Moor.

A road with a fine avenue of beeches brings us to the big clerestoried church, with windows high in the walls. Much of it is 14th century, though most of the windows are a century younger.

The arcades are without capitals, and the wide chancel arch springs from the walls. There are fine old roofs, an old chest, an old pillar almsbox, a chained Testament, and a parish coffin—a grim relic of the days when poor folk were carried to the churchyard in a coffin and buried in a shroud. Leaning pillars, a gallery dropping at one end, and a chancel with walls bulging, give the dim interior a rather curious aspect.

Linking Easingwold with Alne was one of England's few private railways, its permanent way so short that the journey from end to end was completed in 10 minutes. There was only one train, its old-fashioned engine having a tall smoke-stack and a big boiler.

East Ayton. West Ayton across the Derwent has the ruined castle. East Ayton has the weatherworn little church, charming and quaint. Much of it is 13th century, including the slender tower, but there is a Norman chancel arch, and a low Norman doorway (enriched with beak-heads) has a door with the old bar fastening. At each side of the tiny sheltering porch of 1634 is an Irish yew. Odd indeed is the interior with its cream walls sloping, the chancel arch tilting and touching the roof, and the tower (half in and half out of the church) opening to the nave with a low and sharply pointed arch, its capitals only 4 feet from the floor. Under the arch is the big Norman font, shaped like a cheese and carved with arcading.

An avenue of fine trees brings us to the Forge Valley, through which the river winds under magnificent beeches, chestnuts, and pines, and steep banks which are a wonderful sight to see in bluebell time. The whole ride through the valley indeed, from the Aytons to Hackness, is one of Yorkshire's great delights.

East Cowton. It is off the beaten track, but in its neat little 20th century church, with a quaint spire growing from the roof between the nave and chancel, is a treasure worth finding. There are two Jacobean chairs, an old pulpit with carved panels and a canopy, and four golden angels guarding the altar; but the great possession is the splendid Norman font, shaped like a tub and covered with zigzag. Its cover comes from the 17th century. The font was brought here from the older church half a mile from the village, a forlorn building with a brick tower and a 14th century east window. Near by lies Ralph Alcock, on whose stone we read that he lived 99 years in the house where he was born.

East Gilling. Charming in itself and in its setting, it lies in the narrow valley between the Hambleton and Howardian Hills, where many little streams are flowing to the Rye. It has noble pines and chestnuts, a spacious green where an Indian rajah loved to play cricket, a church with a 16th century tower gleaming in the sun, and Gilling Castle hiding in the thick woods on the hillside.

The rajah was the famous Prince Ranjitsinhji, one of the best batsmen of our time. When the Great War came he raised an Indian troop, led his men into the firing line, and was given a place on the League of Nations Council. He lived at the rectory with the tutor he had met at Cambridge, loving the fine garden with its view of the village and the valley, and the glimpse of the castle from the mound close by. It was Ranji who gave the church tower its clock.

Fortress, great house, and now a Roman Catholic school, preparatory department for Ampleforth College, Gilling Castle has beautiful grounds and terraced gardens, and is reached by a noble beech avenue nearly a mile long. Much of the house is Tudor, but the west front was probably designed by Sir John Vanbrugh a century later, and the remarkable tower, about 80 feet square and 70 high, has a 14th century basement built by Thomas de Etton. After the Ettons

came the Fairfaxes, whom they had married, and when the last
Fairfax son died in 1793 their successors carried on the old
name.

Sir Nicholas Fairfax escaped execution by a miracle, keeping his
head in Henry VIII's day and dying quietly in his bed in 1572. His
son William has no place in history, but is said to have given Gilling
Castle its Elizabethan dining-room, which was unsurpassed for its
time. With its wonderful ceiling and wainscot, its windows brilliant
with heraldry showing the shields of hundreds of Yorkshire families
in the branches of trees, it was one of the great possessions of Yorkshire till stripped of its splendour. Fortunately, the building itself
was saved from demolition, Ampleforth College purchasing it in
1929.

The last of all the Fairfaxes sleeps in the churchyard below the
hill. She was Lavinia, who married the rector, forsook her castle for
the rectory, went up the hill again after the rector died, and was
carried down for the last time in 1885. There are windows to her
and her husband in the church, where the memory of other Fairfaxes
is kept green.

A gate in memory of those who fell in the Great War brings us to
the church, which is chiefly 14th and 15th century; but the lofty
nave arcades were built just after the Normans, and the chancel arch
is new. There are fragments of a Norman font and some mediaeval
glass, a peephole, coffin-lids carved in high relief, and a rich recess
in the south aisle with battered arms.

To an unknown knight of the 14th century there is one of the rare
monuments found here and there in our churches, combining some
of the features of a coffin-lid with those of a sculptured figure. In the
quatrefoiled head of a cross are the head and shoulders and hands
(which seem to be holding a heart), and the feet are shown in the
trefoiled base. By the stem of the cross are the shield of arms and a
sword, and his crest of a deer's head.

Sir Nicholas Fairfax of 1572 lies with his two wives on a great
tomb under a bay of the south arcade, their figures notable only for
their clumsy style. Sir Nicholas wears armour and has a lion at his
feet. One of the wives has a dress like a funnel, with balloon-topped
sleeves and a frill round the neck. The other lady's dress is similar,
but more elaborate. It is pleasant to turn to Joseph Gott's lovely

monument of Thomas Fairfax of 1828, showing a woman in fine drapery mourning over two urns.

Dragons are carved on a Jacobean chest, and fine modern carving is in the strapwork screen of the tower, and on the traceried chancel screen and reredos, which are touched with gold. In the vestry is a 16th century carved crucifix. Older than anything else in the church is one stone in the tower, for its carving of two quaint little figures by the Cross is thought to be Saxon. The ancient cross is in the church-yard, having been dug up there.

East Harsley. Its long street, with new and old houses and a fine village hall with a pillared loggia, looks out to the Cleveland Hills beyond the hanging woods of Ingleby Arncliffe, and the Hambleton Hills to the south, with Black Hambleton rising 1257 feet above the sea. At one end of the street is the forge. At the other an avenue leads to the great house with ivied walls and the little bellcote church which keeps it company above a deep glen. It is a charming setting. The north aisle is modern, but the rest of the church has much of its mediaeval work. One of its treasures is a great coffin-lid which is rare for having on it two crosses, perhaps memorials of a man and his wife; on one cross are a sword and a shield, on the other a book and shears. A little coffin-lid has an inscription and a book by the stem of a cross.

In the sanctuary lies a fine stone figure of a knight with long curl-ing hair, hands at prayer and feet on a lion. Wearing chain armour and cloak, with gauntlets, sword, and shield, he is probably Sir Geoffrey Hotham who died about 1326. He was at the siege of Scarborough and fought the Scots, but a kindly soldier he looks as he lies here.

East Layton. A mile from the Roman road between Scotch Corner and Barnard Castle, this small place near Sorrowful Hill has a surprisingly charming little church, with roads about it like tunnels of greenery. Built in 1895, it is shaped like a cross and is like a lantern of light with about a score of beautiful windows, the capitals of their shafts delicately carved. The fine clustered columns of the central tower are crowned with wreaths of rich flowers, and there is a handsome font.

East Rounton. A neighbour of West Rounton, it will for ever be linked with the Bells, one of the most famous families of the north. The Grange, their great house, is in a spacious park. The war memorial cross stands in front of the hall they gave the village, and in the simple church they refashioned in 1884 are their memorials. Its nave and chancel are under one roof. The font is an ancient bowl on a new base, and sheltering two ebony chairs wonderfully inlaid with ivory are shallow old wooden canopies in classical style, with festoons of flowers and Corinthian columns with fine capitals.

The east window's lovely glass by Christopher Whall is a memorial to Sir Isaac Lowthian Bell and his wife Margaret, in whose name their old home at Washington in Durham is now open to waifs and strays. In the window we see St Lawrence kneeling before the Madonna, St Margaret on a purple dragon (a book in her hand), and St Nicholas with a little boy, a ship in the background. One of the great builders of the iron industry by the Tees, Sir Isaac lies in the churchyard. He was a man of remarkable abilities, and of unrivalled knowledge in his world of chemical metallurgy. A Liberal in politics and in nature, he promoted social welfare and education in Newcastle, of which he was twice mayor.

A stone panel with a border of English flowers is to Sir Hugh Bell, whose daughter Gertrude was that famous woman who understood the Arab mind better than any other English man or woman, with the single exception of Lawrence of Arabia. Her Arab friendships were of great value to England in the war, but it was her work in peace that pleased her most. She built up a national museum at Bagdad, and there is a bust of her in it as a memorial of her devotion to the Arab peoples. She was ten years in the country with only three brief visits to England, and she wore herself out in service for others. This remarkable woman has been sleeping in Bagdad since 1926, but the glass in the 15th century window in the north wall of the nave is her memorial in this little place, together with the inscription, the Arabic characters, and the verses cut in the white stone of its frame and splays.

East Witton. The village is captivating, between Witton Moor and a lovely stretch of the River Ure, crossed by a fine bridge not far from its meeting with the Cover. From the church (of 1809), we see

65

Danby Hall in its beautiful park across the dale. From the Moor, with its pines outlined against the sky, we look from over 1000 feet up to the Vale of York. On the Fell behind the village is a delightful waterfall in the little ravine known as Deep Gill. The fine green, long and sloping, is dotted with trees; and the old grey dwellings, some with red roofs and some with ivied walls, mount each side in flights of shallow steps. At one end of the green is a huge boulder with the date 1857.

Ebberston. Lined by trim stone houses with flowered walls and gay gardens, the village street bridges the triangle made by the roads at this part of the journey from Pickering to Scarborough. Half a mile off the long creepered church is charmingly tucked away by a thickly wooded little valley, and behind it is Ebberston Hall, built in 1718 by Campbell, with a baluster parapet and flight of steps to its entrance.

The church fits into the hillside; the roofs of the chancel and nave and tower go up in steps, but the floor is a gradual slope from east to west. The Norman nave and chancel have been partly rebuilt, but the chancel still has a Norman window, with others of the 13th and 14th centuries. The sturdy arcade with pointed arches was built when the aisle was added at the close of the 12th century. From the 14th century come the tower and the big arch (now in the south wall of the nave) which once led to a chapel.

The font and the south doorway are Norman, though the spirally-carved shafts of the doorway are renewed. A rare and precious possession is the ironwork on the modern door, for this too was most probably the work of the Normans; the hinges are enriched with curious scrollwork in haphazard fashion, and over the top hinge is the dove with the olive leaf, a fascinating touch. Built into the walls are fragments of old coffin-lids with crosses and a sword. The churchyard has a noble Wellingtonia, an old cross with its head and part of the shaft renewed, and a glorious outlook over the Vale.

There are tracks leading to the moors north of the village, where there are great dykes and entrenchments and ancient burial mounds. Hereabouts is Ilfrid's Cave, where King Aldfrith of Northumbria is said to have sheltered after fighting with Oswin.

Egglestone Abbey. On a green knoll rising majestically above the River Tees flowing between Startforth and Rokeby is the ruin

of a once stately abbey founded in the 12th century. Its great days
are gone, but its setting can only have grown more perfect with the
years. The river scenery is superb, with the stream flowing amid a
wealth of trees and greenery, foaming in amber-coloured cataracts,
and dashing tumultuously into a gorge. From the abbey lawns we
have a glimpse of the Thorsgill Beck, which runs under a charming
packhorse bridge to meet the Tees not far from Abbey Bridge,
where we cross the river to Durham. This lovely bridge with a
single arch, its battlements 76 feet above the Tees, was built in
1773.

Three centuries saw the building of the monastery, and four have
seen it crumbling away since its seizure by Henry VIII. There are
a few fragments of the monastic buildings, and their plan can be
followed in outline and in high and low walling, but the chief
remains are of the church, which had the shape of a simple cross
with an aisleless nave and chancel, transepts with eastern chapels,
and a central tower of which there is still part of a pillar to be seen.
The greater part of the nave and chancel walls still stand, but the
north transept fell half a century ago, and of the south transept there
is only the west wall, its two windows with fragments of lovely
tracery telling of its rebuilding in the 14th century. In the angle
between this wall and the nave is a stair turret which led to the
tower.

Something of the church built in the last quarter of the 12th century survives at the west end of the nave with its flat buttresses, and
in the north wall. The south side of the nave, with the simplest of
tracery in its line of three-light windows, is about 1300. The
beautiful lancets grouped in the walls of the 13th century chancel are
framed in shafted arches; and the curious east window, 22 feet wide
and only 26 feet high, has four mullions like bars, each 4 feet thick,
which go from the sill to the arch without tracery.

There are two piscinas and two aumbries, and old gravestones,
one of an abbot rare for its carving of a hand clasping a pastoral
staff. Other memorials are the figure of a priest, and the 14th
century tomb of Sir Ralph Bowes, enriched round the sides with
shields and leafy niches, but now without a top. This tomb has
come back to the abbey after having been taken many years ago to
be set up near Mortham Tower. It was there that Scott saw it

between two great elms, as he tells us in *Rokeby*, the last scene of which is laid among these ruins.

Egton. To antiquarians the neighbourhood is of great interest for its ancient graves, and the wealth of bronze and jet ornaments which have been brought to light.

Sheltering in trees halfway down the hill, the church was built last century with the materials of an ancient one which stood about a mile away. Most of it is in Norman style, with a saddleback tower, and the simple arches of the fine arcade are as the Normans built them. The bowl of an old stoup lies on the floor. Two of the bells are old, and the almsbox was fashioned from timber which came from Nelson's flagship, the *Victory*.

Egton Bridge, a hamlet in the wooded valley, has a stone bridge over the river, and an imposing Roman Catholic church whose striking feature is a great ribbed roof like the inside of a ship, painted blue and dotted with golden stars. The great annual event at Egton Bridge is the Show of the Old Gooseberry Society, which was established in 1800. We talked to the treasurer of the Society, Tom Ventriss, who is 77 and lives at the Old Mass House, so called because the Roman Catholics held mass here when they were being persecuted; a bag of old coins was unearthed when the place was renovated, and they are now in the Roman Catholic church at Egton Bridge. Mr Ventriss, who grew the largest gooseberry ever recorded, showed us records of gooseberry shows dating back to 1843, when there were nearly 150 shows in England; now there are eight and the Egton Bridge one is the sole survivor in Yorkshire.

Higher up the very steep hill, in Egton, we found Donald Dean, an artist of some repute, working in his studio. His work is worth travelling some distance to see.

Ellerburn. It lies off the beaten track and hides in a deep green valley. The way to it from Thornton Dale is charming, for the road runs under hanging woods, with the Beck winding through the meadows. Charming also is the picture we see as we open the last gate and come to the end of the road; with the stream flowing by and the handful of cottages standing with the captivating little church, it is a tranquil place.

And a rare little place for its simplicity and its gracious old age is

68

the church itself. Built by the Normans or the Saxons, much of it stands as in their day, though remains of some of the ancient windows and doorways are now built up in the walls. The west window is almost hidden by two massive buttresses supporting a bell-turret only just higher than the nave. In the south wall of the nave outside are traces of an arch which is seen as a big recess within, where the light pours through clear glass, and the warm-tinted stone left exposed contrasts pleasingly with the neat white plaster.

The big pointed arch leading to the chancel was made new in the 13th century, but it rests on older stones with crude carving. Still to be seen are a 13th century lancet, a Norman font, an ancient altar stone, and parts of Saxon crosses built into the nave and the modern porch. There is old woodwork in the pews (attractive with acorn-topped ends), a Jacobean chair, the fine pulpit with a star inlaid in its canopy, and the studded door through which we come and go.

Ellerton Abbey. In a beautiful open stretch of Swaledale are the ruins of the small church of a priory. The slender 15th century tower still stands bravely above the shattered walls, and a few trees look down on the nave. Near by is its only companion, a fine old creepered house.

Eryholme. Hereabouts the River Tees seems to be trying to make a jig-saw puzzle with the county boundary, twisting and turning for nearly a score of miles while the road goes four. Eryholme, by one of its loops, looks over two others to Hurworth a mile away in Durham. Charming is the Tees below the village, flowing between deep wooded banks and crossed by a dainty iron bridge.

There are cottages in bright gardens, a gabled Old Hall, and a small church of red sandstone, coming chiefly from Norman and 13th century days. The low roof of the nave reaches the battlements of the tiniest of towers, which has round belfry windows and a modern arch. The porch is like a museum of old stones—tops of mediaeval windows, tiny coffin-lids, part of a lid with trailing leaves by a cross stem, and a recessed stone with a quaint little figure. The narrow doorway within the porch has a round arch, and on its modern door are hinges looking old enough to be Norman. Massive for so small a place is the Norman arcade to the narrow aisle, one

capital carved with simple overhanging foliage. The chancel arch is
13th century, and the font is Norman. In the striking modern glass
of the mediaeval east window we see Our Lord in Glory, a shepherd
and sheep, a ploughman, and harvest scenes. The oak pulpit has a
bronze panel with a charming Madonna, turned from us as she
holds the Holy Child above her head.

Eston. It lies under Eston Nab, a bold promontory of Eston
Moor where the Ancient Britons had a fortress. There is a watch-
tower on the Nab, and here are magnificent views of the North Sea,
the River Tees, and the Durham hills. Eston itself is an ironstone
centre not far from Middlesbrough. It has a war memorial with the
statue of a soldier, an old church used now as a burial chapel in the
cemetery, and Normanby Hall in a park of 40 acres with a rich array
of fine beeches.

Faceby. A mole hereabouts brought to light a bit of the Roman
Empire which had lain in the earth nearly a score of centuries. He
found a beautiful bracelet and left it on his molehill till a ploughman
picked it up.

The natural glory of the village is its place on the eastern slope
of Whorl Hill—the oddly shaped, detached, and wooded hill rising
sharply to 773 feet. The church, trim and sturdy, has been made
new in the lancet style, but over the south doorway, inside the
church, is a fine Norman arch with zigzag and a carved hood. The
curious tapering font looks as if it too belonged to the old church,
and the vestry window is a frame for a lovely peep of the countryside.

Charity loaves are still given every week to six poor folk, according
to Anthony Lazenby's will of 1634. His bequest is recorded on a
board in the crypt under the chancel.

Farlington. Its few houses are on the banks of a stream running
to the River Foss, crossed by a tiny bridge. The lowly church looking down on the rest is only a room with a porch and a bellcote, but it
has come down from the 12th century. The doorway, with fine deep
mouldings, was built by the last of the Normans, and in the east wall
are three Norman windows, one altered.

70

The south front

Newburgh Priory, Coxwold

The gateway

Easby Abbey

Easby Church

Felixkirk. Looking over the Vale from its lovely setting on the Hambleton Hills, the village is delightful with its winding roads, green banks shaded by trees, and a fine little church. Standing in a crook of the road, it is one of very few churches dedicated to St Felix. Compact with its dim and lofty nave, its bright narrow aisles, its beautiful chancel and embattled tower, it was begun by the Normans and given its sturdy arcades and aisles at the close of their century. The top of the tower is 400 years old. The apse is partly rebuilt, and many of the windows are new, but restoration has not robbed the building of its charm.

The apse has original work in some of its masonry outside, the flat buttresses, the stringcourse, and grotesque heads in the corbel table. Traces of the old are in the lovely modern arcading of its walls inside, and two of its windows are 14th century. The chancel has two Norman windows and a filled-up Norman doorway. The splendid arches of the chancel and the apse are made new (one carved with zigzag and beak-heads and the other with bobbin pattern), but they rest on their old piers with capitals richly carved.

In the old window on the north of the apse is a medley of 14th century glass, with fragments, a tiny Crucifixion, and shields; and below it lies the splendid figure of a knight wearing chain mail and surcoat, with crossed legs, a sword and a shield, his hands at prayer, and a lion at his feet. Almost as perfect as when he left the sculptor's hands, he is probably William Cantilupe of 1321. A graceful lady in a wimple, with angels at her head, lies on the other side of the sanctuary. The mouse carved at the foot of the lectern is the sign of a Kilburn craftsman of our time, Robert Thompson.

Finghall. It is like a fragrant garden on a hill. The road has splendid trees and green verges with flowers; the cottages have roses and creeper on their walls. At the foot of the hill a track by the Leeming Beck leads to the charming little church, alone in the meadows. The stone roof covering the nave and aisle is modern but the bellcote may be over 500 years old. Dividing the nave and aisle is a fine Norman arcade with traces of old painting on one of the arches. The massive pointed chancel arch is a little later, and there are fragments of old glass.

A mediaeval treasure is a splendid coffin-lid with a leafy cross, a rose in the middle of the head, tiny shears and a book by the stem. The worn head of a Saxon cross is among old stones, and a Saxon fragment is in the wall of the porch. The head of a cross is in the wall of the churchyard, where there is an old coped tombstone.

Forcett. Hereabouts came the Scots Dike, the ancient embankment which can still be traced between the Swale near Easby and the Tees at Barforth. Part of an entrenchment is in Forcett's beautiful 200-acre park, which has old yews and a grand cedar, a fine lake, and is encircled by road. Near its gates is a row of Scots firs behind red-roofed cottages; and here too is the church, made new, though the porch, entered by a 13th century doorway and sheltering one of Norman days, is a treasure house of old stones.

Some of the stones are Norman, some Saxon; and there are Norman and mediaeval coffin-lids and the figure of a 14th century priest lying in a recess. On three Saxon fragments carved with knotwork we see three animals round the top of a cross, two quaint men side by side, and a little man sitting on a bench, his arm sheltering an animal. In the wall outside are part of the head of a Saxon cross and a stone carved with two animals. The chancel has some of its old walling, but the rich carving of its panelling, stalls, and altar-rails is modern. The brass portrait of Anne Shuttleworth, who died in 1637, is in the nave.

Foston. By one side of the thickly wooded park a stream flows on its way from the Howardian Hills to the Derwent; at the other side are a few cottages and farms, and the small bellcote church. Yews make a tunnel over the cobbled path from the gate to the pretty black-and-white porch, which shelters a remarkable Norman doorway with a scratch dial beside it. It is the chief possession of this 800-year-old church which has been restored in our century.

Resting on scalloped capitals and two shafts, the arch of the doorway has a dainty string of roses in its mouldings and a wonderful hood with 11 sculptured panels. On each end panel is a dragon-like creature. In the middle, serving as the keystone of the arch, is the Last Supper, with Our Lord, Peter, and Judas among the seven figures by the table. The rest of the panels show two quaint animals and the head of another with big ears; a man bowing before a figure playing a harp; a knight on a horse which has a man's head under it, and a dragon clawing its leg; a holy lamb and an angel; a man kneeling before a seated figure whose shoulder is touched by a demon; a figure with bow and arrow, shooting at a beast; the head of a man peeping over a cauldron, while Satan pulls back a retreating figure; and two people who seem to be embracing. The old door still has its original ironwork.

A fine feature of the interior is the Norman arch to the chancel, its rich mouldings continued on the under side of the arch, the capitals scalloped. The chancel has a Norman slit, the nave a 14th century window, the new aisle a Norman doorway and a pointed arch, both blocked. The dainty little shaft piscina, carved all over, and the quaint round font with a tapering stem, are also Norman. Of our time is the pleasing arcade in 15th century style, the neat oak benches, the hat pegs on the nave wall, and the reading-desk with a beautiful pelican on her nest.

For twenty years of last century Sydney Smith preached in this church, and lived in the house he built near Thornton-le-Clay a mile away. He came to church in a green coach he christened Immortality because it grew younger instead of older. This astonishing parson is remembered in this church by an inscription saying of him:

He was a faithful friend and counsellor, a seeker of peace, a wit who used his powers to delight and not to wound.

Gate Helmsley. Strung along one side of the Roman road which divides it from the East Riding, it looks over cornfields and Derwent meadows to the blue line of the Wolds. In the long line of old houses stands the dainty church with trim ivied walls—a church in miniature, with aisles and chapels to the nave and chancel, and a tiny yet sturdy 15th century tower. The chancel and the windows are almost new, but the nave arcades (with round arches and curious base mouldings) are mostly over 700 years old. The font looks mediaeval, the head of a piscina in the porch is Norman.

Gayle. Its old stone houses and barns are in Wensleydale, below the fells, and if we come after heavy rains there is a sight to amaze us—a mountain torrent roaring down innumerable rocky steps by the village street and flowing under an old bridge, the tumult and the thunder something to remember.

Gillamoor. The surprise view for which Gillamoor is famed bursts upon the sight as we come to a turn of the road, and is entrancing from the east end of the churchyard. Beyond the River Dove, flowing through the green valley of Farndale deep below; in spring the valley is covered with thousands of wild daffodils, and for a short time, the otherwise lonely place is crowded with visitors from all over the North.

Keeping watch over the few old houses and a pillar-sundial with three faces, the little church is sturdy and strong to withstand the raging storms. It has a nave and chancel under one roof (bare of windows on the east and north sides), and a bell-turret crowned with a spire which has a fish turning in the wind. The church was rebuilt in 1802 by James Smith, entirely with his own hands; he was a sound workman, we read on a stone. There is old woodwork with twisted balusters at the west end. The altar table is Jacobean. The enormous font looks old enough to have been made by the Normans. St Aidan and St Hilda are in the lovely glass of the west window, and another has St Catherine on her wheel and St Elizabeth with a basket of bread and a lapful of flowers. On some of the gravestones outside are copper plates engraved by an 18th century craftsman.

Gilling. It is the Gilling near Richmond, set in the beauty of the wooded hills. It has a bridge over the beck flowing to the Swale, and a church among stately trees just withdrawn from the road, its walls, charmingly draped with ivy, making a pretty picture by the green court of an 18th century house. East of the village are the 150 acres of Sedbury Park.

Gilling was a Saxon capital long before the Normans founded Richmond, and it comes into our early history as the scene of a tragic event 13 centuries ago. Oswin was then the last King of Deira, one of the small Saxon kingdoms absorbed by Northumbria. We read in Bede that he governed for seven years in very great prosperity, and was beloved by all men—except by the neighbouring King Oswy of Bernicia, whose jealousy led him to challenge Oswin in battle. Oswin raised his army, but, wisely perceiving that he could not win against a stronger foe, ordered his soldiers to go home and himself withdrew to the house of an earl who claimed to be his greatest friend. But the earl betrayed him to Oswy, and Oswin was slain at what is now called Gilling and was then called Ingethlingum.

It was one of the most pitiful crimes in the long history of Saxon tragedy, for Oswin was a man of great humility and piety. Bede tells us that he gave "an extraordinary fine horse" to Bishop Aidan, though he himself would travel on foot. Bishop Aidan declared that the king would not live long because his nation was not worthy of him, and it happened in fact that soon after this Oswin was slain, and the good bishop followed him to his rest in 12 days more.

For many years monks prayed for Oswin's soul in the monastery at Gilling, and it is believed that the fragments of Saxon stone in the porch come from that ancient place. The stone seats in the porch are made from mediaeval coffin-lids.

The church has an extraordinary appearance, with a second north aisle making it wider than it is long. The tower, half in and half out of the nave, has a Norman base (with the original plain round arch) and a 15th century top. The Norman chancel has been refashioned, but the arcades and the vaulted vestry are 14th century. There is an old piscina, and a gravestone with a cross.

Deeply carved on a huge black stone on the nave wall are the Tudor figures of Sir Henry Boynton of Sedbury and his wife, he in armour with an antelope at his feet, she in netted headdress with a dog at her feet. A memorial of the Great War is to Admiral Sir Christopher Cradock, who went down with his ship in the lonely South Atlantic in 1914, his ship the *Good Hope* having been engaged with a much superior force, the squadron of Admiral von Spee. It is a tablet enriched with vine and grape, a bronze sword, and an anchor in a wreath. Born at Hartforth Hall a mile away, he is honoured as one of England's great seamen, one who followed in the line of Collingwood, and Nelson, and Blake.

In the churchyard, which has the base of an old cross, is the gravestone of a man who was waylaid by a highwayman as he was coming home from market in 1715.

Glaisdale. It is the name of a dale shut off from the world by the moors, and of a village with old and new houses dotted on the hillside climbing to Glaisdale Moor. The River Esk winds through its lovely valley, and Arncliff Woods are close by; we do not wonder that artists find inspiration here for a hundred pictures.

Limber Hill, so well known to motorists, is on the other side of the river, here crossed by three bridges, of which the oldest has a single stone arch. Too narrow for traffic today, it has unusually low parapets, and a stone with the initials of Thomas Ferris, who is said to have built it about 1620. The story of Thomas and his Beggar's Bridge has been sung in verse.

An admirably enterprising landlord here is Mr Walker of the Anglers Rest. He has converted an old outbuilding into the Byre Art Gallery and has shows there frequently; he also has a whippet track, and thus caters for various tastes, in addition to serving excellent food.

Glaisdale's church, standing on a natural ledge with sheep-trimmed banks about it, has been made new. It has an east window aglow with figures of a radiant Christ, the Madonna, and St Luke, and a Jacobean cover for an oddly shaped font, like a square capstan set on four short pillars.

Goathland. Thrilling rides over the heather bring us to Goath-land—this most delightful place to find, in a countryside abounding in interest. A spacious village befitting its place among wide moors, it has sheep-trimmed greens along its rambling road, grey stone houses dotted here and there, and a beautiful church with which the top of the hill was crowned at the end of last century. The ancient Plough Stotts or sword dancers have been revived and perform ancient dances.

Standing more than 500 feet above the sea, the church is impressive in its rugged strength. It has stone roofs, a squat and massive tower rising between the nave and chancel, windows of saints (St Hilda, St Aidan, and St Cuthbert), and an east window with scenes from Our Lord's Life. From the earlier church come a crude font, a 17th century pulpit, a massive altar stone thought to have been used by Osmond who had a hermitage here in the 12th century, and a silver chalice of 1450, said to be one of only two of its kind in England.

Sleeping in the churchyard are William Jefferson and his wife, who were 80 and 79 when they died within a few days of each other in 1923. Their unusual memorial is a huge anchor.

From the pretty ivied inn facing the church a path leads down to the West Beck in a charming setting of rocks and trees. Here is Mallyan Spout, a waterfall 70 feet high, looking like a gossamer veil when it glistens in the sun. It is one of several little waterfalls we come upon in these moorland glens. Farther up the valley is Nelly Ayre Force on the Wheeldale Beck; it is only a few feet high, but the walk to it is delightful. High on the moor to the east of it is the site of an ancient village known as Killing Pits. North of the village is Thomason Force, in very lovely setting on the Eller Beck, and near it is Water Ark Fall. Walking down with the stream we are soon at Beck Hole, a tiny hamlet as lovely as its situation, noted for rare flowers. On the moors near by is a magnificent stretch of Roman road.

Great Ayton. It is Captain Cook's village, a big and pleasant place with the River Leven flowing down its long street. It has old houses and cottages, one or two inns, an old church and a new one, a Quaker school founded a century ago, and a precious association with one of the greatest of all Yorkshiremen, who was born a few miles away at Martin-in-Cleveland but came to Great Ayton at the age of eight when his father became bailiff to the Lord of the Manor, Mr Skottowe.

Great Ayton was proud until a few years ago to keep what had long been known as Captain Cook's cottage.

In 1934 the Cook cottage, with its precious memories, was taken down brick by brick and rebuilt in Australia; it was one of the emigrations of which Yorkshire can hardly be proud. An obelisk stands on the site of the house, a replica of one at Point Hicks, the first bit of the Australian coast sighted by Captain Cook. Hewn from the rocks near Point Hicks, the obelisk is Australia's gift to England in return for the cottage, but it is a sorry bargain.

From the spot where the little house stood it is only a few minutes' walk to the old school which has grown up from the school where James did his lessons. An unpretentious building by the river, and close to the green where he must often have played, the school has a

77

stone telling us that Michael Postgate built it in 1704, and that it was made new 80 years after. There are stone steps to the upper room, now a museum, with rows of hat-pegs, and an old ceiling and fireplace. We see the bench at which he sat, and the desk he leaned on as he pored over his copybook, writing in the wonderfully neat hand in which his journals and accounts were kept. Here are the bellows he may have used to blow the fire, the iron lantern by which he worked on dark winter afternoons, a horn cup he used. It stirs us to recall the day when this boy of 13 went out at the door for the last time. Saying goodbye to his old schoolmaster, he set out, as everyone thought, to learn grocery and drapery at Staithes, but actually he was beginning the career of his dreams.

Near the stone bridge over the river are the two churches of Great Ayton, new and old. The new Christ Church has a tower and spire, and one of its possessions is a New Testament of 1601. The old church of All Saints is a charming building among trees. Like many of the Cleveland churches, it was altered in the 18th century, and its tower was pulled down in 1880 (soon after Christ Church was built), but we see in the nave and chancel something of the church the Normans built. A mediaeval porch with a modern roof shelters a fine Norman doorway with roll and zigzag mouldings, four shafts, and a tympanum; and other Norman remains are the blocked north doorway, a deeply splayed window, the misshapen arch to the chancel, the corbels on each side of the nave, and the font with a shallow round bowl. There are fragments of Saxon crosses and old coffin-lids, quaint pews with candles ready for lighting in the old metal holders, and a fine three-decker pulpit with a canopy. There is a sundial of 1702.

In the churchyard sleeps good Mr Skottowe, who lived at the manor house and gave young James Cook reason to remember him with gratitude, for when he found the boy was quick and intelligent it was he who paid for Cook's schooling. Happily he lived to hear the name of James Cook ringing through the land.

Here too sleeps the best friend Captain Cook ever had, his mother. Though old James Cook lies above the sea at Marske, she has with her five of their children, their names and the cherubs on the gravestone supposed to have been carved by their father. Four of Captain Cook's brothers and sisters were less than five years old when they were buried here, and James must have stood by this grave more than once in after years.

Above Great Ayton rises Easby Moor, crowned with an obelisk in memory of the Yorkshireman who gave England a new dominion in uncharted seas. Near by is Roseberry Topping, the conical hill which may be climbed from this village.

Great Crakehall. Lovelier than its name, it is one of Yorkshire's spacious villages, standing on a stream flowing under an old bridge and over a weir, eventually reaching the River Swale. The old houses and trees are in delightful haphazard array round the great green—a splendid sycamore among the trees, and a big creepered house with its humbler neighbours. The green is crossed by roads, and on it stands the simple church, built a hundred years ago. Fine glass in one of the windows shows St Peter in green, the Madonna in blue and white, Christ as King, the shepherds in Bethlehem, and Christ and the disciples by the sea.

Great Edstone. From its hilltop we look down on the Vale of Pickering and the red roofs of Kirbymoorside, and find by the village pond the small church with 13th century walls and two treasures older still. One is a Norman font with a tub-shaped bowl on a base with crude arcading; the other is a Saxon sundial over the south door, divided into the eight hours of the Saxon day. Its inscription says, *Time-teller for wayfarers: Lothan made me.* There is an old stoup by the font.

Great Langton. In spite of its name, it is only a small place by the River Swale, with a lowly bellcote church near the park of Little Langton Hall. The nave and chancel have stout old walls, and we come in by one of two Norman doorways, the other being blocked. The font is also Norman. A wide pointed arch leads to the chancel, which has a 14th century east window, a group of lancets a century older, and a recess with the stone figure of a priest holding a chalice. Built into the west wall are two old coffin-lids with crosses, one having a sword and the other a chalice and a book.

Great Smeaton. The fine manor house with red walls and pantiled roof is seen through the trees of the park. Between the green and a pretty row of creepered cottages stands the church, a Georgian house behind it; and from the churchyard is a fine peep between the houses of the distant fells. The low pillars and wide arches of the nave arcade are 14th century, and the chancel arch is perhaps as old, but the rest of this simple place is made new in mediaeval style. Its treasure is a splendid Norman font, crudely carved with lattice and diamond pattern which the sculptor did not complete. The unique distinction of the church is its dedication to St Eloy, for there is said to be no other church in England with the blacksmith's saint for patron.

Greta Bridge. It is part of a lovely countryside which lives in our literature, and its old stone bridge of one wide arch, with a balustraded parapet and a background of trees, built by J. A. Morritt in 1774, was painted by John Cotman. It was designed by Sir Thomas Robinson. At one side of the bridge is the old inn with golden walls, on the other are grassy mounds marking the site of a Roman camp, and an entrance to Rokeby Park, where Scott was the guest of John Morritt. The Greta comes to the bridge after a lovely journey through Brignall Banks, and flows on through Rokeby to its meeting with the Tees. A scene painted by Turner, Mortham Tower, on the east side of the park, and Egglestone Abbey, two miles away, are immortalised in Scott.

It was to an old inn half a mile from Greta Bridge that the coach brought Dickens and Hablot Browne one snowy night in 1838. They were in search of what were known as Yorkshire boy-farms, cruel schools where boys were condemned to years of wretchedness; and the inn where Dickens stayed impressed him so much that he put it into *Nicholas Nickleby* as the place at which Squeers and Nicholas alighted with the unhappy boys who had been gathered in London. We read:

"Put the boys and the boxes into the cart," said Squeers, rubbing his hands, "and the young man and me will go on in the chaise. Get in, Nickleby." Nicholas obeyed. Mr Squeers with some difficulty inducing the pony to obey also, they started off, leaving the cartload of infant misery to follow at leisure.

Grinton. The loveliness and grandeur of Swaledale is all about this grey village, where an old three-arched bridge with projecting bays carries the highway across the river. The church and the inn are by the bridge; the hills rise majestically on each side of the valley; and to the west, on the slope of Harkerside Moor, are two barrows and the circular ramparts known as Maiden Castle, thought to have been here when the Romans came this way. South of the village is Grinton Lodge with an embattled tower, above the stream flowing through Cogden Gill to the Swale.

The splendid church is a reminder that although the village is small the parish extends for miles. Everything inside is on a grand scale, but the great width of nave and chancel, aisles and chapels, gives it an almost crouching appearance. The unbuttressed tower of diminishing stages is 400 years old, and has a fine Norman window over the sturdy arch, which comes from the close of the 12th century. Other Norman work is seen in the clustered shafts and battered capitals on the north side of the chancel arch, which for the rest is 13th century, tilting and soaring. By it are the old rood stairs. Finely set in front of the tower arch is the font, its Norman bowl carved with zigzag and crowned with a 15th century pinnacled cover.

The porch has a richly moulded archway of the 13th century. The lofty arcades are mediaeval. Early in the 16th century were built the small vaulted vestry (entered by an old door in the chancel) and the south chapel, which has its original screenwork, one of the tiniest piscinas we have seen, and a peephole to its altar from the churchyard. Mediaeval screenwork divides the north chapel from the chancel. There are splendid old roofs with rough massive timbers, and richly carved panels in the Jacobean pulpit, whose pillars and canopy are modern. Chained to an old reading-desk is a New Testament commentary.

Some of the windows have old glass showing shields, a fine saint, a splendid St George slaying a dragon, and a medley of fragments. In charming glass by A. J. Davies is the Madonna and Child in white and blue, in a setting of flowers; and the Good Shepherd among the moorland heather, with a picture of sheep being led to the fold.

Gristhorpe. It has little more to show than a hall which has become a guest house, and white cottages with pantiled roofs on a pretty little road just off the highway; but it gave Scarborough an old, old man. He was found in a tumulus hereabouts over 100 years ago, his coffin the trunk of an oak 8 feet long and 3 feet wide. For centuries he had been lying with his weapons and ornaments, a wicker basket at his side, a sprig of mistletoe in his hand. Today we may see him in Scarborough Museum, an Ancient Briton who may have been living when Moses was leading the Israelites towards the Promised Land.

Grosmont. It lies on the bright side of a hill dropping steeply from the moors to the River Esk.

The name of the village reminds us of the priory which Johanna Fossard founded here about 1200, as a cell to Grosmont or Grandimont in Normandy. The priory has gone, but in the 19th century church (with a granite boulder at its door) is a font which may have belonged to it. Gone too is the home of the Salvins, where the wife of Sir Ralph Salvin was kidnapped while saying mass. A plan is afoot to reopen the Grosmont–Goathland–Pickering railway line, closed in 1965. The line was planned by George Stevenson and was opened in 1836.

Guisborough. Men of peace and war have had their day and ceased to be in this old market town, lying under the wooded slopes of the Cleveland Hills, in the midst of a rich iron-mining countryside. Attractive as seen from the hilltops, it has on close acquaintance a leisured charm, its medley of red-roofed old buildings lining a long wide street with cobbled verges and rows of trees, the old market cross with a sundial, the church sheltering a unique monument, a magnificent fragment of a vanished priory, and a school in beautiful gardens near the ruins.

Both the school and the priory recall a Tudor Vicar of Bray, who founded one as a grammar school and surrendered the other to the imperious demands of Henry VIII. He was Robert Pursglove, who became a Protestant bishop under Edward VI and a Papist under Mary, and has a splendid brass portrait in Tideswell church, Derbyshire, where he sleeps.

The remains of the priory are in the lovely grounds of Guisborough Hall, a 19th century successor to the house built from the old stones when Sir Thomas Chaloner acquired the priory lands. Sir Thomas was a brilliant ambassador at the Spanish Court, and his son, who travelled much in Europe, was the man who stole the Pope's secret for making alum, and with the help of miners brought secretly from Italy opened here in Yorkshire what may have been the first alum mines in England. Charles I confiscated the mines, and there was a Thomas Chaloner of the third generation who put his name to the king's death-warrant, fleeing to Holland, where he died in melancholy exile. The story of Sir Thomas and the alum mines is that he was allowed to see the Pope's mines at Puteoli, and, realising that the conditions were similar to those on his own estate, he managed to smuggle into this country some of the Pope's workmen; it is said they were hidden in casks. What is certain is that Sir Thomas was excommunicated by the Pope for this offence.

We may walk in the gardens, treading where the monks walked long ago. There are delightful paths, grand old trees, a charming stone dovecot, a rose garden, a fishpond, and the old stocks; and there are steps set between two sea-horses, and an avenue shaded by about 80 old limes, giants every one. Monarch of all is a superb chestnut which was probably a sapling when the monks were turned out. Its trunk is 23 feet round, and its huge limbs have embraced the ground and taken root.

Founded about 1119 by Robert de Bruce, the priory became one of the richest in the North, and one of the most magnificent. Only a few stones here and there are left of the monastic buildings, but the splendid Norman gateway stands by the road, and of the great church the wonderful east end is still towering above the bases of pillars of the nave's north arcade. A tribute to the genius of the early 14th century builders, it is all that is left of the third church on this site.

The tip of its traceried gable is nearly 100 feet from the ground. The mighty window below it, 60 feet high and 24 feet wide, has vine leaves and grapes in its beautiful mouldings, fragments of tracery, and shields. At each side are the fine east windows of the choir aisles. There are gabled buttresses, delicate niches, and leafy pinnacles adding to the richness of this noble end of a church which had a length of 350 feet. Beautiful heraldic tiles and gravestones have been found.

The vine moulding carved on the east window over six centuries ago has inspired the design for a beautiful kneeler for the altar-rail in the parish church of St Nicholas, worked in rich coloured wools by 80 members of the Women's Institute. It is 24 feet long.

Guisborough had a church in Domesday Book, but the church of today has nothing older than about 1500—the time of the tower, the nave arcades, and part of the chancel. The rest was refashioned in the 18th century, but has been finely restored. Its arresting feature is its sense of space, the long nave and the chancel (both of one great width and at one level) measuring from east to west 145 feet. The tower stands within the nave, and its restored west window and doorway are framed in a great arch. The east window is new; in the old one it replaced (now at the west end) are fragments of glass of about 1500, some showing the Madonna and Child, John the Baptist, Our Wounded Lord, the Trinity, and part of a Doom.

One of the memorial windows to the Chaloners is to Richard Hume Chaloner killed in the Great War. There are two crosses from Flanders, and an inscription to a middy of 15 who went down with his ship in 1914. We see a table made from timbers of the old roof, the works of a clock made by a local smith 200 years ago, an ironbound chest, and a reredos of modern needlework showing angels worshipping. A brass inscription of 1641 has curious lines to a virtuous wife, Susanna Pyckering.

One of the priory's great possessions found shelter in St Nicholas Church at the Dissolution of the Monasteries. Known as the Bruce Cenotaph, it is a monument like a tomb, as historically interesting as it is richly carved. It was presented to the priory (probably by Margaret Tudor, daughter of Henry VII) in the time of James Cockerel, the prior whose name is represented in sculpture on the tomb—his Christian name by the scallop-shell of St James, the surname by a cock on a reel. On the east end the prior is with his kneeling canons. On one side are the statues of five Bruces of Annandale, and on the other five Bruces of Skelton-in-Cleveland, all of them knights with helmets, swords, and shields. Between the Scottish Bruces are figures of the Four Evangelists with their symbols; the Four Latin Doctors separate the English Bruces. One of the knights on the Scottish side represents Robert Bruce, who was known as the Competitor from his claim to the crown of Scotland, and was carried from Lochmaben to his resting-place in Guisborough priory when he died in 1295. The figure of his grandson, King Robert the Bruce, is said to have been sculptured on the west end of the tomb, now lost.

It was here that in 1779 the famous linguist John Oxlee was born. As a boy he would walk 50 miles from his father's farm to buy a book, and he became the most renowned linguist of his day, a self-taught grammarian, and author of an amazing book in which our commonest words are given in 100 languages. All this distinction he won for himself before he lost the sight of one of his eyes. He was a master at Tonbridge School when this happened, and at once forgot his misfortune by beginning to learn more languages.

Hackness. Few villages have a lovelier setting than this countryside of little dales, grand hills draped with trees, and breezy moors with fine views, earthworks, and ancient graves. At Hackness the River Derwent turns south on its way to the charming Forge Valley and then to the Vale of Pickering. To the north are Suffield Moor (a lofty ridge), Silpho Moor with miles of heather, and beyond it Harwood Dale. From the little hamlet of Broxa (2 miles up the valley from Hackness) are magnificent views 500 feet above the sea. Extensive afforestation has taken place in this area, and indeed in many others on the moors. The Forestry Commission have planned several forest walks and drives for the public, some of the best of which are hereabouts.

Below a hill, like a vast green pyramid, stands Hackness Hall, with fine gardens and terraces and a lake. Near by is the embattled church, its massive 13th century tower crowned with a sturdy spire two centuries younger. The chancel, made new in the 13th century, has windows as old as the spire, but its simple round arch to the nave is believed to have stood since Saxon days, and has carving of knotwork. The south arcade of two bays, with scalloped capitals, is Norman, and over it are remains of a Saxon window. The three bays leading to the north aisle are from about 1200. But the most arresting thing in this striking interior is the 13th century arch of the tower, massive and beautiful, its rich mouldings resting on a tilting cluster of five shafts at each side. Over 400 years old are the stalls, with carved misericords, and the fine cover of the font has rich carving of tracery, pinnacle-work, and eight saints. From the Jacobean pulpit Charles Johnson preached for 59 years out of last century into this. Chantrey sculptured the monument to Margaret Johnstone, showing a man kneeling by his wife and child; Leopold Johnstone, a boy of 19 who went down with the *Invincible* at Jutland a century later, has an inscription.

A rare possession for this small place are two fragments of an inscribed Anglian cross, believed to commemorate abbesses of the early days of the convent founded here by St Hilda of Whitby in her old age. They are in the south aisle. One fragment is enriched with knotwork and floral scrolls, and the other with simple carving.

Hackness gave London a famous sculptor, for here Matthew Noble was born. We have come upon his work all over the country. It was he who carved London statues of the Earl of Derby in Parliament Square, Sir John Franklin in Waterloo Place, and Sir James Outram on the Embankment, and he exhibited over a hundred works at the Royal Academy. He is represented in Liverpool and Manchester and by the statue of Isaac Barrow in Trinity College, Cambridge. He was always delicate, and never got over the tragedy of his son's death in a railway accident. His grave is at Brompton.

Hardrow. A mile from Hawes, it has a cluster of grey houses, a neat 19th century church with a window to a vicar who preached for 59 years, a fine old bridge, and, more than all, a stream which falls 100 feet near the churchyard on its way to the Ure.

It is the stream that brings hundreds of people to Hardrow every year. Coming to life on the slopes of Great Shunner Fell, Yorkshire's fourth highest mountain, it is at first two streams, the Hearne Beck and the Fossdale Gill, which meet at Fossdale before giving England one of its grandest waterfalls. Known as Hardrow Force, it is in a natural quarry where the walls overhang alarmingly, and the stream falls in a sheer drop of 100 feet from the edge of a projecting scar. The amazing thing is that we can stand behind the shining curtain of water. Turner thought it wonderful enough to paint, and both Wordsworth and Ruskin were captivated by it.

Near the Force runs the Butter Tubs Pass, the wild mountain road linking Muker, in Swaledale, with Hawes in Wensleydale.

Hart Leap Well. A wild moorland ride on the old road from Leyburn to Richmond brings us to this spot, amid a magnificent

Hardrow Force

Hovingham Church

The entrance to
Hovingham Hall

panorama of moors and fells. There is only a trickle of water over stones in the bracken, with a shrivelled and leaning tree, covered with lichen, for company, but it comes into one of Wordsworth's poems, and has a story for all huntsmen. After hunting a hart for 13 hours a knight ran it to earth at this spot, and found that the beast had come down the fell in three leaps, dropping dead by the stream. The knight had stones set up and trees planted to show the path it had taken, but the stones fell, and the trees withered, and neither horse nor sheep would drink from the well. Wordsworth suggests that Nature was stirred with pity for the hunted animal, for he wrote of it:

> *One lesson, Shepherd, let us two divide,*
> *Taught both by what she shows and what conceals:*
> *Never to blend our pleasure or our pride*
> *With sorrow of the meanest thing that feels.*

Hauxwell. It is East and West Hauxwell, with a few people between them. The houses look out on a magnificent view of lovely country and away to the fells. Below them is the fine little church in the park of Hauxwell Hall, an Elizabethan house extended in modern days.

Coming down to the church we pass what was last century the rectory, and remember that this is Sister Dora's village. She was born in this house in 1832 and lived here for 29 years before leaving this lovely spot to become the ministering angel of the Black Country. She was Dorothy Wyndlow Pattison, daughter of the rector and sister of Mark Pattison.

It was Dorothy's ambition go to out to the Crimea with Florence Nightingale, but she was prevented by her father, and took the name of Sister Dora on joining the Sisterhood of the Good Samaritan. She found herself in charge of the Sisters during a smallpox epidemic in Walsall, where she is still remembered for her tremendous courage and endurance.

The church has noble beeches for company, and a stream runs by the wall of the churchyard, in which stands a beautiful Saxon cross with interlacing work. The walls of the nave and chancel have much herringbone masonry of the Conqueror's day, but the old windows still left are 13th and 14th century. The tower is 700 years old, its massive arch wider than itself, but two of the belfry windows are 15th century and the battlements are modern. The Norman south doorway has zigzag carving and a diapered tympanum, and a crudely carved Saxon stone serves as the lintel of the north doorway. The fine Norman chancel arch has rich mouldings, and clusters of shafts with scalloped capitals.

A shield of old glass is 16th century, the mediaeval piscina has a shelf, the cover of the font may be Jacobean, and the dragon and pelican poppyheads of two old bench-ends have been copied in the modern seats. Two tiny coffin-lids have crosses and swords.

On a brass of 1611 are portraits of Henry Thoresby and his wife kneeling at a desk, he in civil dress, she in a Paris hat and turn-back collar. An inscription tells of a grandson of John Dalton who was killed at Burton-on-Trent while conducting Henrietta Maria to Oxford in 1644; the Daltons are still at the hall. Worn stone figures of a cross-legged knight and a lady in a gown of many folds lie in the porch, and may represent Sir Walter de Barden and his wife of the 13th century.

Hawes. It is one of the highest market towns in the land, its claim to beauty being its place in Wensleydale at the end of Butter Tubs Pass, with the wild green fells and magnificent scenery on every hand. From Hawes we can well explore this countryside of moors and dales and waterfalls, the famous Hardrow Force being little more than a mile away. The mountain stream called Duerley Beck comes hurrying through, and is a wonderful sight in time of flood as it tumbles down the rocky ledges with a deafening roar. The old mill by the bridge is silent now, and the old houses at this lower end of the town stand higgledy-piggledy in narrow twisting streets. In the more spacious part is the lofty 19th century church with soaring arcades, a black-and-white roof looking down on the nave, and a richly-carved pulpit growing out of the low chancel screen. It is the centre for the production of Wensleydale Cheese.

Hawnby. A faraway spot among the wooded glens of the Hambleton Hills, it looks down on the lovely valley of the Rye which gathers the waters of the River Seph on its way to the noble ruin of Rievaulx Abbey. Turning from the road which goes north through Bilsdale, we drop steeply down a long lane, crossing the Rye and threading the slopes of the valley, till suddenly Hawnby's red roofs are seen clustering on the side of a curious hill rising 965 feet. The church is not in this picture; it lies in a sleepy hollow where the Rye splashes over its rocky bed.

In the woods beyond the church is Arden Hall at the foot of a delightful glen. The seat of the Earl of Mexborough, it is chiefly 17th century, but it has a Tudor wing, and an old chimney believed to be a fragment of the nunnery founded here in the 12th century. Not far from the hall is the Nuns Well, a round stone basin through which a spring of pure water flows. Mary Queen of Scots is said to have spent a night here.

The church is a simple nave and chancel with a bell-turret, coming chiefly from the 14th and 15th centuries, but there are Norman remains at the west end of the nave. In a corner here is a shaft with a capital showing a man's quaint face, vines growing from his beard. A blocked north doorway, its arch almost round and its imposts carved with small crude heads, comes from the 12th century. A small ancient cross with three bosses stands in the church, to which we come through a modern door on mediaeval hinges.

Ralph Tankard of 1601, who lived at the hall, has a memorial with his medallion portrait in colour, showing him with a white beard and fine eyes, wearing armour and a ruff; above him are an hourglass and a tree. Little Ann Tankard, who died in 1608 before she was two, is seen in a painting asleep in a cradle, by which a rose bush and a lily are growing, and above her is a clock pointing between one and two.

Hawsker. It is High and Low Hawsker, with a 19th century church away from them both, standing where the highway turns west to Stainsacre. There is an old windmill without sails, and a vicarage with the shield of St Hilda's Abbey over the door. The abbey comes into the fine view seen from the church, which is a landmark hereabouts.

Between its simple nave and chancel is a tower with a pyramid roof, opening to them both with two enormous cinquefoiled arches. In the golden-hued glass in some of the windows are unusual scenes.

One is of Adam and Eve in the Garden; another represents Youth and Old Age; a third, illustrating how hard is the way to Heaven, has a maze in which are men, a dog leading a blind man, and an angel on a tower by the sea, guiding a man holding a rope. In yet another we see an old man asleep in a chair as the sun sets and Death tolls a bell.

In a garden at Low Hawsker stands the shaft of a cross about 6 feet high, on the spot where it is believed to have stood for a thousand years. Though much weathered, it still has traces of Saxon ornament with dragons, a bird, and knotwork.

Between Stainsacre and Ruswarp are the lovely Larpool woods and glades, and Cock Mill with its little waterfall. Another beauty spot hereabouts is Rigg Mill with its old wheel and woodland setting.

Haxby. Near the River Foss and within a few miles of York, Haxby has a long narrow green, a big ivied house with a porticoed front, and two chestnuts guarding the church which was rebuilt last century and enlarged in ours. Its Norman story is told by old work remaining in a doorway and three windows of the vestry. Among the saints in modern glass are Cuthbert, Bede, Hilda, and Helen. The massive belfry has a weathercock turning in the wind, and the churchyard has remains of the old cross.

Helmsley. The great castle is a spectacular ruin, but is scheduled to be cared for for all time. The old church is made almost new, and the great house in the park, the ancestral home of the Duncombe family, Earls of Feversham, is now a school. But the trim little market town in a hollow of the hills lives on serenely, delightful with its wide streets and its spacious market square, round which are clustered red-roofed houses and shops, some of the walls draped with creeper, wistaria, and even a vine. Here is the inn which made Dorothy Wordsworth's heart jump for joy when she arrived three years before Trafalgar. A house at one corner is charmingly timbered. The fine old cross in the square, standing on its old steps but having its head restored, is a modest companion for Sir Gilbert Scott's elaborate canopied monument to the Lord Feversham who died in 1867, his statue sculptured by Matthew Noble showing him in his peer's robes.

Just behind the square stands the church, its tower with turret pinnacles rising above gabled roofs and trees. On the north side of the churchyard is an E-shaped house with a timbered storey; it is known as Canon Garth and comes from Tudor days, with a 19th century wing. It was probably the house of the canons of Kirkham.

Rebuilding has left the church a little of its fine old work. The lower part of the tower is 13th century, with a massive arch opening to the nave. The Normans built the lovely south doorway enriched with zigzag, and the splendid chancel arch with zigzag and beak-heads, but both have been restored. The pointed arcade of the nave is only a little later. The aisle has a battered piscina, and the porch shelters a broken hogback of the 11th century, crudely carved at the top. On a stone are the worn brass portraits of a lady in horned headdress and her knight in armour, probably Thomas Lord Ros, who was executed after the Battle of Hexham. There are three lances which were once carried into the market-place by constables, and a wooden yoke which was taken off a slave by an Archbishop of Capetown who was the father of one of Helmsley's vicars, and a friend of David Livingstone. Here we may see one of Livingstone's letters, written from Africa.

In the north aisle we glean something of the story of Helmsley and of the noble ruins of the Abbey of Rievaulx not far away; in modern glass there are pictures of events, and in trees and vines painted on the walls are names and shields, including those of vicars of Helmsley, Abbots of Rievaulx, and Archbishops of York. Better wall-painting in the south transept shows scenes in the lives of St Aidan and St Oswald, and a knight fighting an enormous dragon, driving it over a cliff. This transept is St Columba's chapel, and in glass which is a beautiful study in blue we see pictures of his life, from his boyhood to his death.

The River Rye flows at the south end of the town under an old stone bridge. It has come through Duncombe Park on its way from Rievaulx, and makes a big loop between a curving belt of wood and a famous terrace made in 1758, a half-mile stretch of greensward with a temple at each end and an impressive view of the ruined abbey below. It was Sir Charles Duncombe, a rich London banker, who bought Helmsley in 1689, and the castle fell into disuse when the great house was built in the park by Sir John Vanbrugh. Sir Charles Barry designed the curving wings detached at each side, but there was much rebuilding in the original style after fires last century. It is now a girls' school. The lovely views from the park embrace not only the ruins of Rievaulx, but Helmsley Castle on the edge of the park, its grey stone gleaming in the sun as it rises above the town's red roofs. The main entrance is a triumphal arch dedicated to Lord Nelson.

The fragments remaining of the castle bear witness to its strength and impregnability. Rising from a rocky ridge, it is built round a ward 100 yards long and 70 yards wide, in shape a rough rectangle, with corner towers. Protecting it on all sides is a double ditch—huge earthworks which are now deep green valleys and may have been raised when the castle was built. The outer ditch turns on the north and south sides as if it may have enclosed other courts.

It is thought to have been begun by Walter Espec, a warrior with jet black hair, piercing eyes, and a voice like a trumpet. He was one of the leaders in the Battle of the Standard in 1138, but was really a man of peace, for he founded the abbeys of Rievaulx and Kirkham. From him Helmsley passed to his sister's husband, Peter de Roos, and was held by this family till Edmund Roos died early in the 16th century. Then it passed to the son of Eleanor de Roos, Sir George Manners, whose son Thomas, 13th Lord Ros, was created Earl of Rutland in 1525. Through his marriage with Katherine Manners the notorious George Villiers, 1st Duke of Buckingham, came into possession of the castle, and was followed here after his assassination by his son.

The Civil War was the beginning of the end for the castle. In 1644 Sir Jordan Crossland held it for the king, holding out against Sir Thomas Fairfax in a three-month siege, and then honourably surrendering. In 1657 the second George Villiers returned to England and married Mary Fairfax, daughter of the man who had battered the walls of his castle. The duke made some repairs to the ruins, and here thirty years later he spent his last days, still chattering vainly, and walking in mincing steps, the disgraced favourite of whom Pope wrote:

> *Stiff in opinion, always in the wrong,*
> *Was everything by starts and nothing long;*
> *But in the course of one revolving moon*
> *Was chemist, fiddler, statesman, and buffoon.*

It was from the castle that he set out one day when he was taken ill while hunting near Kirbymoorside, and lay at a house there till his death. With the coming of the Duncombes and the great house in the park the castle was left to its fate.

The plan of the castle was simple, and can easily be followed in the fragments that remain. The piers of the bridges which crossed the ditches can still be seen.

Of Walter Espec's day there is nothing left, except perhaps the earthworks, which were probably defended by timber palisades. The oldest work is that of Robert Fursan, lord of Helmsley from about 1186 to 1227. To his time belongs the little that is left of the outer walls, the corner towers, and the gateways; the fine fragment of the keep (which lost its unusual apse east end in the Civil War, but keeps two turrets of its 14th century embattled top storey), and the lower part of the west tower and the range of buildings adjoining it.

The two barbicans followed about the middle of the 13th century. The main barbican on the south side remains, a fine outwork very impressive with the ribbed gateway between two drum towers, and round towers flanking the courtyard walls. In the 14th and 15th centuries were built the kitchens and buttery, and the great hall on the west side, its foundations showing it to have been 25 yards long and 16 wide. A flight of steps leads down to the dark vaulted basement of the south-west tower, which may have served as a cellar.

Except for their original basements, the west tower and buildings finely grouped beyond the site of the hall were remodelled in Elizabeth I's day by Edward Manners, 3rd Earl of Rutland, who gave them the windows with transoms and the two oriels looking on to the earthworks. His arms are still seen in a room with a plaster ceiling and frieze, some old panelling, and an oak fireplace. Still farther along this side of the ward are traces of more domestic buildings, with an old oven, and within are some of the walls of the 13th century chapel still standing near the keep. Not all is old in Helmsley, for it has one of the few purpose-built Youth Hostels in the county, and is the start of a walk, officially "opened" in 1969, the Cleveland Way, which traverses the North Yorkshire Moors for 100 miles, ending near Filey on the coast.

At Beadlam Grange near by a Roman villa has been excavated

which has yielded coins of A.D. 390. This now becomes the most northerly Roman villa found in England since previously the now-buried villa at Hovingham held this distinction.

Hilton. Halfway between Yarm and Stokesley, it looks over rolling countryside to the long line of the Cleveland Hills. A mile and a half away the River Leven is crossed by a bridge. Standing on a knoll by the roadside, near a neat row of ivied cottages, the lowly little church has in its stout old walls great stones which show the marks where tools or weapons have been sharpened. A double bellcote rises above the pantiled roof covering nave and chancel, and the oak beams of the roof inside still have the marks of the adze. The Normans built the chancel arch, and two doorways are enriched with their zigzag. Carved on a stone near the south door is a dragon biting its tail. The chancel has no east window.

Hinderwell. Between Borrowby Dale and the sea, it has the stump of an old windmill, a well from which the village takes its name, and a church rebuilt in the 18th and 19th centuries.

The water still flows in the well which St Hilda of Whitby is said to have blessed 13 centuries ago. It is under a crude stone shelter in the churchyard, with rough steps in the deep hollow in which it lies. The church is a simple oblong with a low embattled tower, showing in one window St Hilda praying for those in peril on the sea, and in another our Lord Risen, St Michael, and St Gabriel. There is the head of an ancient cross, and part of the shaft of a Norman piscina with a cushion capital is set on what seems to be an old leafy pinnacle.

Port Mulgrave's few houses are on top of the cliffs near by, and deep down below is an unused quay. It was built as an outlet for ironstone, mined far inland, which arrived here through a mile-long tunnel. The coastline is wild and rugged.

Hipswell. The church and cottages are dotted about the green (on which grow two fine trees), and the old hall still has its battlements and mullioned windows. The church is 19th century, but in its walls are some of the stones of the mediaeval church which stood

94

by the hall before it. The top of one of the old windows is in the vestry wall.

But it is for none of these things that we come; we come because, as far as we know, it was the birthplace of John Wycliffe. Somewhere in this Yorkshire countryside he came into the world about 1320, and almost certainly it was at Hipswell, a few miles from the village of Wycliffe where Wycliffes came over with the Normans.

It was a time of confusion and corruption in the Church when John Wycliffe was born, and he was appalled by it. A scholar of Balliol, he obtained a lasting influence over the thought of teachers and students, and the aim of his life was to clear the Church of its abuses, its superstitions, its craze for wealth and power. He translated the Bible, and sent out a band of preachers to spread his ideas far and wide. Nothing could withstand him; though his enemies appealed to the Pope, who issued bulls against him and ordered his arrest, nobody took any notice, and with the help of John of Gaunt, who befriended him, Wycliffe went on. At last, however, he denounced the central Romanist doctrine of transubstantiation, which says that the bread and wine actually change into the body and blood of Christ, and for this he was condemned and expelled from Oxford. He was allowed to withdraw to his rectory at Lutterworth, where he quietly continued his work of leading men back to the Gospel. It was at a service in his church that he was seized with a stroke. They laid him to rest in the little Leicestershire village, and years afterwards, by the decree of a foreign council in a foreign land, this noble Yorkshireman's memory was subjected to bitter indignity, and his bones were dug up and flung into the River Swift. The men who did this thing have perished, but Wycliffe is immortal.

Holwick. It is Yorkshire's Farthest North, with a few houses above the Tees and a fine view of the valley. Holwick Scar frowns above it, and only 6 miles away is Yorkshire's highest mountain, Mickle Fell, climbing to 2591 feet. A mile from the village Yorkshire and Durham are linked by the Wynch Bridge (a 19th century suspension bridge), and here the Tees makes the striking cascade known as Low Force. Two miles up stream is the High Force, one of the noblest waterfalls in England, where the river plunges over 70 feet into a deep pool shut in by the dark rocks.

Hornby. Winding lanes bring us to Hornby's stone cottages and to the ancient church on the edge of the great park which, like the castle within it, has lost its great days, for the estate has been split up into farms. Once a proud pile, but now partly demolished and only a corner of it inhabited, the castle has been since the 14th century the home of the St Quintins, the Conyers, the Darcys, and the Osbornes, and until 1930 of the Duke of Leeds. It grew in the 15th and 16th centuries round a courtyard, and here is still the original St Quintin's Tower. With the old trees round about are a giant beech and a magnificent chestnut whose huge branches sweep the ground like a peacock's tail.

The church was old when the castle was new. The three lower stages of the tower have stood since the second half of the 11th century, and are an example of the combination of the Saxon and Norman styles—the Saxon influence seen in the third stage, where the windows are divided into openings by recessed shafts with crude capitals. The bottom stage has flat buttresses and restored windows, and the top stage with its high battlements was added in the 15th century.

The Normans refashioned the earlier nave and chancel, and of their work there now remain the side walls of the chancel and the fine north arcade of the nave, its clustered shafts supporting three round-headed arches, of which two are enriched with zigzag ornament. The east end of the chancel and the chancel arch have been made new. The north aisle is 14th century, and the clerestory, the south aisle, and the south chapel are 15th. A document exists, dated January 28, 1409, for the building of the south aisle. From the 14th century come two trefoiled piscinas, and the beautiful font standing in front of the tall narrow Norman arch of the tower; the ten sides of the bowl are adorned with leafy gables, and fashioned at the foot into delicate canopies for the waisted stem. Between the south chapel and the aisle is a 15th century screen with painted panels; the chancel screen is partly old. A poor box has two cherubs holding a wreath.

There are some remains of mediaeval glass with saints, leaves and acorns, and memorial windows by Christopher Whall; old gravestones; a battered figure of a woman; and the alabaster figures of Sir John Conyers and his wife of Agincourt days. He founded the south aisle. In a north aisle recess lies a knight in chain armour and surcoat, his wife wearing a wimple and a flowing gown; he is thought to be Sir Thomas Burgh, who rebuilt this aisle where he was laid in 1322. Engraved in brass are the 15th century portraits of Thomas Mountford, his wife, and their 15 children; and a wall monument from which boys are looking down is to Thomas Darcy's wife, who was daughter of Lord Conyers and died in Elizabeth I's day.

Hovingham. On the road from Malton to Helmsley, it is charming in itself and in its setting of woods and hills. On or around the village green, shaded by stately trees, are the old houses, the school with a lovely oriel, a church with a remarkable tower, and the gateway of the imposing hall, standing in a park with a lake, filled by a stream crossed by fords and small bridges.

We come by the lovely road through the park to this delightful spectacle of a village clustering round its old church tower and its stately hall. We stand where Romans, Saxons, and Normans have stood, for the hall is on the site of a Roman villa, the church tower is Saxon, and the mark of the Normans is still to be seen, though the church was almost rebuilt last century. Hovingham Hall was planned and built by Thomas Worsley, a friend of George III who gave him one of its great possessions, Giovanni's great statue of Samson slaying the Philistine. The long front of the 18th century house is charming among the larches and beeches, with the little Saxon tower at one end of it, and the spectacle is enhanced by the great lawn which the village uses as its cricket ground, bounded on one side by a massive yew hedge and on the other by a grove of beeches. A cricket festival has been held here annually for well over a hundred years, and many famous players have appeared here. The hall, church, and village gather round like a happy family, and if we forget the Romans the scene goes back a thousand years. The church tower, with a modern cap, is of three stages. Crude windows (splayed outside) light the middle storey, and the windows of the belfry have pillars between the lights. The west doorway is heavy and massive, its arch of plain and roll mouldings resting on shafts and very impressive is the tower inside, with its quaint patchwork of stones, some herringbone masonry, and its small but massive arch.

The restored doorway opening to the church was built at the end

97

of Norman days; the chancel has a Norman window. On a bracket is a splendid fragment of a Saxon cross, the head and part of the shaft, carved with knotwork; and a Saxon stone, about 5 feet long, is carved with eight figures under round arches, two of the figures being Mary and Gabriel. On the road to Cawton are the Spa House and its three springs of spa water which attracted numbers of people at the opening of the nineteenth century.

Hudswell. The only old things its 19th century church has to show us are a few coffin-lids with crosses and swords, lancet windows in the vestry, a piscina, and a stoup; but the view from the church-yard of the wonderful valley of the Swale, with the cliffs and woods which Turner loved, is well worth coming to see. Another lovely view is of Richmond, its neighbour a mile or so away, from the hill dropping down to the old bridge. The woods are now the property of the National Trust.

Huntington. The River Foss, crossed by a small bridge, flows between the village and the church, which hides by the trees of the great ivied hall. The 19th century made the church almost new, except for the eastern part of the chancel, with 15th century win-dows, a simple sedilia, and a piscina. The pillar of the arcade lead-ing to the north chapel is old, and there are broken fragments of an old font outside. The tower serves as a porch, sheltering a doorway built by the last of the Normans. On the splendid 17th century pulpit are the words: *Where there is no vision the people perish.* The old cross in the churchyard has a new head. It was this church which about 400 years ago received a legacy from a vicar of a number of beehives, the revenue from which was to provide the oil to keep the lamps always burning above the altar.

Hurst. Rich in scenes of beauty and stern grandeur is the road threading the hills to this most desolate and forsaken spot in the silent heart of the moors, touched with the misty hand of the clouds which sometimes veil the handful of houses, scattered and grim, and the scars of old lead mines. The old hall is a farmhouse now, and near by is the shell of an inn. One or two chimneys still stand among the ruins of the mines, which are believed to be among the oldest in the land. It is thought that this place was a settlement for Roman convicts, a Botany Bay of nearly 20 centuries ago.

Husthwaite. Over the hills and far away, Husthwaite is a pretty village with gardens and orchards, 17th century houses, a timbered inn, a tiny green, and a charming little church of amber stone on a high bank by the wayside. The 15th century tower has a bell which is said to have been ringing in Elizabeth I's day. The nave and chancel are chiefly Norman, with several Norman windows in the leaning walls. Battered now but very beautiful is the Norman doorway through which we enter, low and massive, enriched with zigzag ornaments, the grooves in its capitals and sides said to have been made by villagers sharpening their knives and shuttles. The old door has its original hinges. The low chancel arch (with a peephole close by) and the blocked north doorway are Norman.

The box-pews, the altar-rails, the font cover, and the fine pulpit are all 17th century. Under the canopy of the pulpit is a rare treasure of the 13th century, a small leaden cross with the Crucifixion, found in the churchyard and said to be a coffin cross. The fine oak roof is of our century, and six of Mr Thompson's Kilburn mice tell of his rich woodwork in the finely traceried altar, the reredos extending across the east wall, and the litany desk. An inscription to John Winter who died in 1873 at 91 tells us that he was curate here and vicar of Birdforth near by for 65 years.

There is rich reward for all who climb Beacon Banks high above the village, for at the top, where there are entrenchments made centuries before our history was written, we look far over the Hambleton Hills, the Plain of York, and the Pennines. Four miles north is the White Horse of Kilburn.

Hutton Buscel. Beauty and peace go hand in hand in this village on a green hill, lying just off the highway six miles from Scarborough. Its stone houses are old and new, and its church, tucked away among trees, has for company in the churchyard an old cross with a new head on the tall shaft. By it are two fine Chile pines.

It was the home of the Buscels as far back as the 12th century, and the earliest of them would see the building of the church. The massive tower of that time still stands, though it has been restored in our century after damage by lightning. Its lower walls are Norman; the belfry stage was added when the Norman style was passing, and the parapet is 15th century. The tower arch to the nave is curious for being on one side high and pointed, and on the other side low and almost round. The arcades, too, are odd. The three sturdy bays on the north side, with bell capitals, are 13th century; the two bays of the south arcade, the clerestory, the chancel arch, and much of the chancel itself, are 15th. The pulpit is Jacobean, and a window is in memory of Elizabeth Monkman whom the village blessed for her kindness to all sick folk. The old sanctus bellcote is still on the nave gable, and a sundial tells us not to waste time.

Hutton-le-Hole. A charming little place to find in a green hollow of the moors, it is all up and down, with a hurrying stream winding among houses scattered here and there, standing at all angles. There are bridges for us to walk over, and water-splashes for a car. There is a neat little church for which the villagers saved up 40 years, sheltering an oak reredos richly carved, and traceried altar-rails on which we find the mouse of Mr Thompson of Kilburn.

On a house which has been an inn is a stone with the words *By Hammer and Hand all Arts do Stand*, and the initials of Emmanuel and Betty Strickland, who built the inn in 1784. At a cottage with the initials J. R. and the date 1695 lived John Richard, who died here in 1753. A devout Quaker and a friend of William Penn, he began preaching when he was 18, rode 4000 miles on a white horse in America, and took part in a council between white men and Redskins. After such adventures he came back to England to end his days in this quiet spot, and sleeps at Kirbymoorside. In their early days the Friends had a Meeting House in Hutton, and a Quaker burial-ground is still to be seen 2 miles away, in a wood not far from Lowna Bridge crossing the River Dove. Here we found a place worth coming many miles to see—the Ryedale Folk Museum. Originally housed in a small cottage in the village, it has expanded to include a fully-equipped blacksmith's shop and a reconstructed mediaeval cruck-framed house (Stang End, from Danby)—and the ultimate idea of having a Folk Park is well on its way to realisation. A great deal of the work has been done by Mr Bertram Frank, now curator of the museum, and a friend of the late R. W. Crosland whose personal collection of antiquities forms a major part of the exhibits. We talked with Mr Frank when we visited the place and found him immensely knowledgeable about the whole area hereabouts—indeed he has published a history of iron-working in Rosedale, and when we called was working on a history of turf-cutting and its implements. The museum covers many country crafts, including the recently discovered glass workings at Rosedale; an odd feature of the house is its collection of the curious witch-posts so common a feature of the old houses of the area.

Hutton Lowcross. A delightful lane from Guisborough brings us to the remains of an old cross by the park, which is famed for its rhododendrons, and to the woods with magnificent chestnuts, copper beeches, silver birches, and dark pines by the stream—all sheltering under Highcliff Nab, a splendid view-point 1000 feet above the sea. The gabled hall in the park replaced an older house last century, and has a fine sight of the Cleveland Hills. In the walls of the farm are one or two stones from St Leonard's Hospital which was founded hereabouts and given to Guisborough Priory, and here also was founded a Cistercian nunnery.

Hutton Rudby. Between the River Tees and the Cleveland Hills (and sometimes known as Rudby-in-Cleveland), it has a fine church by the old bridge, looking down on the wooded glen where the River Leven tumbles over the weir, and looking up to the houses clustered round the spacious hilltop green.

Reached by a beautiful oak lychgate, the church is chiefly 14th century, though the chancel has remains of lancets a century older and the tower is a century younger. The base of the tower, serving as the porch, has a stout ribbed roof and a doorway with fine gates. The nave has arches on clustered shafts, and a lofty roof with arched beams. The aisle has many old bobbin-ended pews, two fine old brass candelabras hang in the sanctuary, and the handsome Elizabethan pulpit is adorned with panels of marquetry. It was the gift of Thomas Milner, who has a memorial in the nave. There is a shield in 15th century glass, and some fragments are probably older. The beautiful modern glass showing St Nicholas, St Michael, and St Francis in the west window, and Faith, Hope, and Charity in another, is in memory of the Ropners of Skutterskelfe Hall, the great house in a park east of the village. A lovely blue window has St Catherine, the Madonna, and John the Baptist.

A niche in the sanctuary was perhaps meant for an Easter Sepulchre. In a splendid trefoiled niche in the aisle lies the figure of a mediaeval priest in vestments finely draped. He holds a chalice, and round his head is a rich leafy cross. The silent tongues of three old bells are near the door. There are fragments of carved Saxon stones and the head of an ancient cross, and (in a case) a fine bassoon used here a hundred years ago and a silver penny minted at Durham in the 16th century.

Huttons Ambo. It is really High and Low Hutton, two villages in pleasant setting between the road and the River Derwent which meet 3 miles away at Malton. Here the countryside is beautifully wooded, and the river, dividing the North and East Ridings, is delightful. High Hutton has a 19th century church by a yew-bordered drive leading to the hall among noble trees, and Low Hutton nearer the river has traces of a Roman camp, the ancient ramparts still plain for us to see.

Ingleby Arncliffe. Its cottages in long gardens, and the stone water tower set up by Sir Hugh Bell, are on a little hill. On the highway below is Ingleby Cross, as spick and span a hamlet as we could wish to find, where the stone cottages bordered with flowers, the village hall, and the inn with a swinging sign of fine ironwork, are gathered round a small green trimmed like a lawn.

A pretty lane brings us to the church and the hall, snugly embosomed in trees at the foot of the hanging woods which mantle the steep cliff climbing to about 1000 feet above the sea. The story of the Colvilles is linked with both church and hall. Only the moat of their old home is left. The big stone house we see, with fine woodwork and beautiful ceilings, was built by Thomas Mauleverer in the 18th century, and enlarged in 1900 by Sir Lowthian Bell. It is said that when Thomas built it he left four rooms unfinished, wishing four generations after him to finish one room each.

Dwarfed by its great neighbour, the plain little church is a re-building of 1821, but its older story is told by the Norman capitals of

A doorway at Jervaulx Abbey

Norman capitals on the chancel arch in Liverton Church

Thirteenth-century coffin lid in Middleton Tyas Church

the west doorway of the tower (in which we heard the pigeons coo-
ing), old benches, box-pews, and a three-decker pulpit. The altar
plate includes an Elizabethan cup. In the remains of 14th century
glass in the east window are the arms of the St Quintin and Fauconberg families, to which belonged the two wives of a 14th century
Colville.

Lying in the sanctuary are two stone knights, wearing chain
armour, surcoats, ornamented belts, swords, and shields. Interesting
to antiquarians as two of the few examples in England showing the
ailettes on the shoulders, they represent two Colvilles of the 14th
century, probably Sir Robert who fought the Scots and helped to
get Piers Gaveston executed, and another Robert who may have
been his son.

Ingleby Greenhow. Tucked away in a lovely glen which cuts
into the Cleveland Hills, here rising steeply and grandly from the
plain, it has a stream flowing from Greenhow Moor on its way to
the River Leven, and is sheltered from the east winds by Ingleby
Moor with a tumulus 1300 feet up. Only a few miles away we see
Easby Moor crowned with Captain Cook's obelisk, and the sugar-
loaf mass of Roseberry Topping, both rising more than 1000 feet
above sea-level. Half a mile from the village is Ingleby Manor, a
beautiful house for 300 years, approached by one of the noblest lime
avenues in Yorkshire.

The lowly church with ivied walls bears the mark of 18th century
rebuilding, but the lower part of the tiny tower is as the Normans left
it, preparing us for the surprise awaiting us within. Here the rugged
simplicity of the Norman church is much in evidence. The nave
opens to the tower with a narrow and lofty Norman arch, and to the
chancel with a low massive Norman arch with a big peephole at
each side. The Norman arcade leading to the aisle has five arches
on massive pillars whose capitals have extraordinary carvings of
grotesques, faces, and foliage; there are twisted dragons, animals
with bodies like balloons, a wild animal like a panther which seems
to be stalking a pig with a curly tail, a laughing dog, and a panting
animal.

There are old coffin-lids and fragments here and there, and two
stone figures (probably 14th century) under two arches of the

arcade; one wearing a loose robe with a sword from his belt may belong to the Eure family, and the other is a priest with a chalice and a missal by him. The font is about 600 years old. The church is of surprising length, and the floor mounts in six steps to the altar. The impressive modern East window is a memorial to Sir David Foulis, a descendant of the Foulis and Sidney families who worshipped here from 1609 to 1951. It was dedicated on May 27, 1966.

Jervaulx Abbey. The River Ure flows through a peace profound by the broken walls of this mediaeval splendour, founded by a few monks 800 years ago and growing rich for 400 years till its long peace came to an end with the execution of its abbot, Adam Sedbergh, for taking part in the Pilgrimage of Grace.

It was in the autumn of 1536 that a great company calling themselves Pilgrims of Grace invaded these quiet meadows and hammered at the abbey door. Declaring themselves friends, they stated their intention of marching on London to compel Henry VIII to spare the monasteries, and they desired the abbot to join them. But Abbot Sedbergh, not wishing to be implicated in an insurrection, slipped away and took refuge on Whitton Fell. Meanwhile the rebels roved the dale but constantly returned to Jervaulx, angrily demanding to see the abbot, and in the end threatening to burn the monastery. In desperation the monks sent messengers in search of Adam Sedbergh, and from his hiding-place they pointed to clouds of smoke already rising from the Abbey. His heart sank, but down the hill he went, to find himself faced with the choice of execution or of joining the angry mob. So against his will the unlucky abbot rode off with them, knowing in his heart that dire misfortune must follow. So it proved. The king tricked the pilgrims by offering them pardon, but afterwards took revenge on them. Jervaulx, like all other monasteries, was ransacked and destroyed, and Adam Sedbergh was imprisoned in the Tower; his name can be seen scratched on a wall there. He was executed at Tyburn in 1537.

The ruins, slight though they are, are fascinating for showing us the ground plan of a great Cistercian abbey. The church has almost disappeared, but we can trace its size in outline, and there are portions of low walling, piled-up fragments of stones, and bases of pillars. Chiefly 12th and 13th century, the abbey had the shape of a cross 264 feet from east to west, and 115 feet along the transept, each arm of which had eastern chapels.

There is a little of the platform on which the high altar stood, and here are still the two long steps which led to five altars at the east end, where stone coffins are now, in the shade of trees standing like a sheltering screen. In a north transept chapel is an altar on three steps, with a broken stone keeping its five crosses. There is the battered figure of a knight thought to be a Fitzhugh, and one of half a dozen gravestones in the nave has on it a cross and a chalice.

On the south side of the cloister (now a lawn shaded by two weeping willows) we see the plan of the kitchen, the warming house, and the refectory, which extended from north to south between them. On the east are remains of the 13th century chapter house, separated from the transept of the church by a narrow passage with a recess in which the monks kept their books. The chapter house has lost its 12th century doorway, but it has the Norman windows which kept it company, the flight of six steps, the raised seats round the walls, and four of the fine octagonal pillars of the aisles, their capitals carved with overhanging foliage. A gravestone of a 15th century abbot has a cross, a chalice, a mitre, and a staff; two others are of 13th century abbots, and one is of a monk whose joy it was to adorn the altars with jewels and gold.

In this eastern range was the dormitory of the monks, and where it extended above a vaulted chamber is the most spectacular part of the ruins, a high wall with a fine row of lancet windows and a pointed doorway. We see the springers of the vaulting, bases, and fragments of pillars, and a small fire place. In the imposing block east of this extension was the 15th century kitchen, still with traces of cupboards, serving hatches, ovens, and fireplaces reddened with the fires of long ago. Outside the abbot's chapel is a fine hand-mill for grinding flour, its outlet like a spout.

Keld. In a deep hollow of the Pennines, 1100 feet above the sea, it is one of England's most isolated villages.

The noble grandeur of Upper Swaledale is all about it—wild moors and crags, mountain slopes with little hollows, beautiful waterfalls, and the river making its lovely way between the rugged cliffs.

There are thrilling rides whichever way we choose to come, the low road giving us the glory of the valley looking up to mountain tops, the rougher roads over the moors awe-inspiring in their loneliness and desolation. The long road from Reeth brings us round the moor to Tan Hill, where the white walls of the highest inn in England are 1732 feet above the sea. From here the road runs above the wild ravine where the Stonesdale Beck gathers many little streams, then drops precipitously down to an old bridge to find the Beck falling with a lovely cascade into the Swale. Half a mile below the bridge the grey houses look over the Swale to sheer walls of rock crowned with overhanging trees. From here it is only a few hundred yards to Kisdon Force, a waterfall tumbling 30 feet into a rocky glen. Two miles away as the crow flies Rogan's Seat climbs to 2204 feet, the highest point between Swaledale and Arkengarthdale.

Kettleness. High above the crumbling headland and the rocky shoals, its few farms and cottages look across Runswick Bay to Runswick's houses clinging to the cliffside, red roofs crowning their white walls. In 1829 a landslide at Kettleness carried thousands of tons of the cliff into the sea, and the people were rescued by a vessel carrying the alum which used to be mined here. While men were digging up a Roman lookout station which once stood hereabouts they found the bones of a man with a dog at his side, its paws on his shoulders. It is a fine place for fossil-hunters.

Kilburn. As we ride from Thirsk there bursts upon us a wonderful view of the Vale of York, with a striking sight of Kilburn's White Horse across the deep valley. The great horse cut in the turf on the face of the plateau stretches east from Roulston Scar, a sheer rampart in the long line of the Hambleton Hills. With an eye big enough for twenty people to sit on, the Kilburn Horse is about 314 feet long and 228 feet high. It was made in 1857 by the village schoolmaster Thomas Taylor with 30 men to help him, and is said to have been paid for by a villager who made a fortune in London. The giant is wearing a coat of lime weighing six tons, and is a landmark for miles around.

Six hundred feet below the Scar, Kilburn is an attractive place.

It has a stream running by wayside gardens and crossed by little bridges, a hall begun in Tudor days, a green with a shapely sycamore and a mounting stone, an inn with a seat commemorating the coronation of George VI and Elizabeth and a charming old timbered house. There is a link between the house and the seat, on which we see the mouse which tells of something well done; it is the mark of a Yorkshire artist, Robert Thompson, who lived in the old house, a fine setting for much beautiful woodwork within. By the house are his workshops, where the chairs and tables, the pulpits, lecterns, and screens which we come across on our journey through this countryside are made. As if inspired by the carvers of old, Robert Thompson used an adze instead of a plane, and gave to our churches and schools woodwork which is a veritable tribute to the craftsmanship of our century. His mouse, which we have come across so often, is in Kilburn's church, on the traceried pulpit, on a desk in the sanctuary, and again with a crocodile on the lectern. Robert Thompson died in 1955.

Side by side with Robert Thompson's fine carving, beautiful work of eight centuries ago survives in the church. The imposing Norman doorway through which we enter has three orders of rich zigzag and original capitals, though the shafts are new. The 15th century tower has a plain Norman arch to the nave, and another is between the aisle and the north chapel. The Norman chancel arch has zigzag and roll moulding under a carved hood, but some of the shafts are new and most of the capitals are copies of an original one which is carved with a lion. The nave arcade has pointed arches resting on beautiful capitals of stiff leaves. The chancel has a 13th century lancet and an old low window in its south wall. An old gravestone showing a pastoral staff is perhaps of an Abbot of Byland; another, carved with a cross, a round target, and a hammer, may be 13th century. From the 17th century come the aisle pews and a bell now silent on the floor.

Two miles from Kilburn as the crow flies, Hode Grange has memories of a band of monks who, with the faithful Abbot Gerald, broke away from Furness Abbey and after long wandering founded Byland Abbey in 1177. At Hode they are said to have stayed four years, and here Roger de Mowbray established a priory and a church. The walls of the church still exist in a barn, and built into one wall is a coffin in which Abbot Gerald is believed to have lain.

Kildale. The wild moors are above, but Kildale's farms and cottages lie snugly sheltered by trees in the narrow valley of the River Leven, and on the hillside. Here lived Vikings whose bones were dug up when the old church was rebuilt last century, and here the Percys had a house, though only traces of its moat remain, by the churchyard. Two of four enormous gravestones now in the porch have the Percy shield on them. A Norman font stands under the tower, which has a pyramid cap, and in the rich glass of three windows we see the Crucifixion, the Wise Men at Bethlehem, and St George.

Kiplin. Its handful of farms and cottages are clustered by the 120-acre park of Kiplin Hall, a gabled house with domed towers which has been enlarged since Sir George Calvert, 1st Lord Baltimore, built it in the time of James I, from designs by Inigo Jones. But its great days are gone, though the park and gardens are often open to all. There is a fine beech hedge about 50 yards long, and the big lake is filled by a stream which joins the River Swale not far away. It was from the park here that a piece of turf was sent to Baltimore for the 300th anniversary of the founding of Maryland by the son of the first Lord Baltimore. The father, an Elizabethan statesman, became interested in the colonising of America after the sailing of the *Mayflower*, and himself went out to settle a colony. Returning home to obtain a charter, he died before the colony could be formally established, and his son Cecilius carried on his work and thus became the nominal founder of the capital city of Baltimore and the State of Maryland.

Kirby Hill. It lies between the old and the new Great North Roads, a mile from Boroughbridge, and has a windmill from which a magnificent view embraces 18 churches and two castles. Its own little church is one of the most interesting in the county, coming from Saxon, Norman, and mediaeval days, though its north side has been made new.

Crowned with a pyramid spire, the tower was built about 1090 and refashioned last century, but its original round arch still opens to the Saxon nave, and in its south wall is a carved Roman stone which may have been brought from Aldborough, the site of the Roman Isurium, across the River Ure. The round arches of the Norman arcade have their inner order resting on separate shafts and showing traces of old painting; on the pillars are fine mason's marks —a star, a bow with an arrow, and many letter As. A mediaeval arch made new leads to the chancel, which is 13th century and has an arch opening to the north chapel, which has a peephole.

About the church and in the modern porch is a collection of over a dozen stones from Saxon England. Two carved with horses and one with two human figures come from about the year 1000, and the shaft of a cross in two pieces is 200 years younger. There are fragments with knotwork, an early coffin-lid with a cross, and a mediaeval door with quaint old hinges like a great fork hangs in the nave's 11th century doorway. Recessed in the wall by the doorway is a long stone in the place the Saxons gave it about 11 centuries ago; it is carved with circles of worn interlacing, and some of the stones of its original arch may still be above the later doorway. The Norman font has an 18th century cover, and some bench-ends 500 years old.

Kirby Hill. It is the Kirby near Richmond, looking out from a lovely hilltop to a vast green countryside, with the old castle and red roofs of Ravensworth in the valley below. The road just glances at the homely little gathering of stone houses, the old grammar school, and the fine old church round a green like a small court, the stalwart church tower like a guardian for the rest and a landmark from afar. The school, with tiny windows, was founded by John Dakyn, a rector who died in 1558 and sleeps in the church, where hang the rules he made for the boys, written neatly in his own hand in a book with wooden covers. Matthew Hutton, who became Archbishop of York and the friend of George II, learned to read and write at this school.

The tower seems to have been built for defence in the 14th century; its vaulted roof springs from two crouching men, and its curious arch is acutely pointed and lob-sided. The fine nave arcades and the chancel arch (with tilting sides) are mediaeval. The Norman chancel has an original window with a tiny slit below it, a piscina with a projecting bowl like a shell, and two little old chairs. There is some 300-year-old woodwork with poppyheads and a roof is 15th century, but the fine chancel screen and the pulpit are modern.

Among the interesting sculpture on the walls outside is a cross-legged little man with a fiddle, sitting on the old porch with leafy pinnacles. A man blowing a horn and a face with its tongue out are on the tower, and under the Norman corbel table of the chancel a quaint little man shelters. Near him is a laughing face.

Kirby Knowle. Slumbering in a sheltered fold of the moors, it is a delightful place to find. From the small sandstone church is a peep of the fells beyond the great Plain, but from the little road over Primrose Hill the magnificent view surpasses even that from Upsall. From the moors which rise behind the village like the rim of a bowl the panorama is superb.

Upsall people come to this church, which was made new last century. It stands in a churchyard where the old font bowl, used as a flower vase, has for company the shafts of two old crosses, one having a round head which probably does not belong to it. The embattled tower serves as the porch. Of the earlier building there are two fragments of Saxon carving, a mediaeval gravestone carved with a cross, and a row of 18th century inscriptions adorned with shields and cherubs on a long step in the sanctuary. The west window has Kempe's rich glass of the Annunciation.

Finely carved with tracery and flowers by Mr Thompson of Kilburn (whose mouse is at the foot), the lectern is a memorial to Brigadier-General Hotham, who died in 1932. He lived at the great house which peeps above the treetops to the west of the village and has the misleading name of New Building, it being an old house which James Danby enlarged after buying it from the Constables in the 17th century. It has some curious hiding-places.

Kirby Misperton. Its other name, Kirby-over-Carr, reminds us that it lies in the heart of the Vale, with Pickering 4 miles away. Facing the pond on a lovely tree-shaded road is the 15th century church with a chancel made partly new, and the hall near by shelters among the stately trees of its 50-acre park with lawns and lakes. It is now made into the very popular Flamingo Park Zoo, with a wide variety of animals including the flamingoes after which it is named. Beyond it the Costa Beck goes on its way to the Rye. Attractive outside, the church has a light nave and a dim chancel which still has some of its old walling. The nave arcade is without capitals, and the old font has a stem bigger than its bowl. With the old stones built into the walls are heads of crosses, fragments of Saxon knotwork, and stones with inscriptions.

Kirbymoorside. It comes into history, for here one of the most dazzling courtiers of all time is said to have breathed his last. Once fabulously rich and immensely powerful, he died all but penniless and alone in this small market town.

There have been few changes here since then, the days of the notorious George Villiers. Here are the headquarters of the Sinnington Hunt, claimed to be the oldest in the country and connected with Villiers. Kirbymoorside is an attractive place, still in its lovely setting where the northern moors and glens come down to the Vale of Pickering. The highway from Helmsley to Pickering runs through it, broadening out in a dignified square near where the church stands in company with charming old houses on cobbled ways.

It is a grey-walled and red-roofed town. An inn with yellow walls has a quaint wooden porch 300 years old, and the Tolbooth, said to have been built of stones from castles, was made new after fire in 1871. Behind it, in a little square, is an old cross on many steps.

Above a ravine to the north of the town are scant remains of the castle of the Nevilles, who forfeited their estate here by rebelling against Elizabeth I. James I gave it to the Duke of Buckingham. Tall trees and a ditch on Vivers Hill (east of the market-place) mark the site where the castle of the Norman Stutevilles stood.

The tower of the church was being rebuilt when Wordsworth came by on his wedding day. Sir Gilbert Scott made the chancel new in 1874, but mediaeval and Norman masonry remain and there is also an old mass dial. The massive porch, rather like a tunnel with its stone roof, has an upper room reached by a flight of steps which give a pretty touch to the south aisle. The nave arcades are from about 1200, with the mediaeval clerestory above. The chancel arch is chiefly 13th century. A fragment of mediaeval glass is supposed to represent the face of God the Father, and a brass portrait is of Lady Brooke, an Elizabethan lady, kneeling with her 11 children.

The reredos in the north chapel has four mediaeval panels carved with two scenes of the Annunciation, a Garden of Eden, and Abraham about to sacrifice Isaac. The central panel by a modern craftsman has Our Lord with the children, one in His arms, and another playing with a dog. Five of six lions dividing the panels are old.

On a windowsill is a fragment of a Saxon cross, and four other fragments are in the vicarage porch. The reredos and rails in the chancel, and the oak screens, were designed by Mr Temple Moore who also designed the cross in the churchyard in memory of those who fell in the Great War.

A quaint entry in the church register reads: 1687, George Vilaus, lord dooke of bookingham. Thus is recorded the death of that brilliant wit and king's favourite George Villiers, 2nd Duke of Buckingham. The house where he died is facing the Tolbooth, its gabled walls covered with creeper. It has changed much since his day, but the original door is here with its old hinges, its lock, and its barn-door fastening, and here too is the small staircase bringing us to the room where the fallen favourite came to his end. The oak panelling has gone, but an oak cupboard remains, and two little windows look out on the market-place.

Hated, ridiculed, defamed, he had long been supreme at Court, the favourite of Charles II. He had ruled England as if he were king, and had pleased or offended everyone. Stripped of wealth and influence, he scraped up enough money to restore part of Helmsley Castle, where he lived an aimless life, frittering away his days with dancing, drinking, and quarrelling. One April day he went hunting, was taken ill suddenly in the saddle, and was carried into Kirby-moorside.

The Slingsby glider works, the only factory devoted solely to the production of gliders, is to the south of the town—which is hardly surprising since there are two large gliding centres on the moors near by.

Kirby Sigston. The farms are scattered. The attractive old church stands finely at an end of a ridge of the moors, looking down on a tiny stream to its one companion, the old rectory, which was being refashioned when we called and has in its garden a copper beech and a cedar.

It is a restored Norman church, though the tower, with battlements only just topping the nave, is much later. The long chancel has a plain parapet and ugly gargoyles, and the low porch shelters an old door with strap hinges and latch. We go down three steps to the nave, up three to the chancel, and down three more to the aisle.

Except for the narrow pointed western bay, the tall arcade of the nave is Norman, with capitals of stiff leaves and carved hoods. A plain Norman arch leads to the chancel, which has a 14th century arcade of two bays built into its north wall. The capitals have battered carving of dragons, and between the arches are crouching animals. Built into the south wall is the head of a Norman window with zigzag and criss-cross carving. There are traces of windows a little later, and the east window is 15th century. The Jacobean font is on a Norman stem, and the simple pulpit is also 17th century. In the few remains of mediaeval glass are shields and a two-headed eagle, the shield of the Sigstons, whose castle stood on the moated site half a mile from the church. There are fragments of old coffin-lids and carved Saxon stones, the small stone coffin of a child, a mediaeval stone bench in the aisle, and a beautiful wimpled lady sculptured in stone. She has two angels at her head, and her graceful gown is caught up in her arm. In an inscription to Thomas Lascelles of 1705 we read that with gentle hands he restored sight to the blind.

Kirby Wiske. It is Roger Ascham's village; here was born the scholar who taught Elizabeth and was Latin secretary to Mary Tudor. His book on *The Schoolmaster* is still read, and we have nearly 300 of his letters. We may imagine him as a boy walking by the River Wiske, which flows between the village and the road to Northallerton, nearing the end of its slow 24-mile journey to the Swale. At the bridge over the stream is a raised causeway for use in floodtime, but if we come in summer we see the meadows golden with flowers.

On the two banks of the river to the south of the village stand the house called Sion Hill and the site of Breckenbrough Castle, where the Lascelles lived for centuries. The road to Sand Hutton runs by the park of Breckenbrough Hall, with an avenue of trees leading from the brick and timber lodge. We have a peep of the lovely house with its curved gables and clustered chimneys—the home in the last years of last century of one whose beautiful marble monument, showing a woman nursing two children, is in Kirby Wiske church, standing on the bank by the bridge.

The sturdy embattled tower is 15th century; during the 14th were built the chancel, the north chapel, and the nave arcades. The oldest fragment is the splendid south doorway, built by the Normans and much restored, with zigzag and beak-heads in the arch and crude heads on the hood. Over a head with a hanging tongue is a holy lamb in a circle. Built into the outside wall by the vestry are several stones with Norman carving of grotesques and an animal's head, and a Norman panel showing a figure with arms akimbo.

The most beautiful part of a surprisingly fine interior is the chancel, 600 years old. The east window shines with Capronnier's colours in a picture of Christ preaching to a little crowd, and at each side is a restored niche with old brackets of a grotesque and the head of a king. There are three charming stone seats with rich trefoiled arches and leafy hoods ending in heads, and heads at each side of the piscina. A plain coffin-lid lies in the founder's recess, and high over all is a modern barrel roof of open timbering. The church has a battered 600-year-old font no longer used, and on a windowsill in the vestry is part of a coffin-lid with shears.

There are portraits in the porch and the vestry of three famous sons of the village, Roger Ascham and the two village boys who became bishops. They were George Hickes, who suffered persecution because he refused to acknowledge William and Mary, though he afterwards became Bishop of Thetford; and William Palliser, a scholar born here in 1646, who became Bishop of Cashel and built up a fine library, which he gave to Trinity College, Dublin. As for Roger Ascham, the portrait of him in the vestry shows his meeting with Lady Jane Grey at Bradgate Park in Leicestershire.

Kirkby Fleetham. Old houses look on to the cricket green, dotted with trees. On one side of the village are green mounds and traces of a dry moat; from the other side a lovely road runs for a mile to the church, which is charmingly grouped with the hall, sheltering in a wooded hollow of the park where a stream is flowing to the River Swale.

A majestic chestnut is growing near the church, which was re-fashioned last century. There is new work in the fine doorway carved with zigzag and cable moulding, but the fine mediaeval tower still stands and a mediaeval arcade leads to the south aisle. Parts of old coffin-lids are in the porch walls, and the round bowl of the font is 700 years old.

The treasure here is the exceptionally fine figure of a knight lying on a tomb enriched with quatrefoils. Wonderfully preserved, perfect in every detail but for the missing tip of his nose, he is in chain armour and helmet and a finely draped surcoat, and carries a great sword and a shield. His hands are at prayer, his legs are crossed, and a lion leans its head curiously against one of his feet. He is believed to be Sir Nicholas Stapleton, who fought at Bannockburn.

A beautiful Flaxman monument has the bust of William Laurence of 1785 on a pedestal by which a woman sits weeping. William's books and little heaps of money are carved on the foot of the pedestal, and below it is an inscription to his father.

Kirkby-in-Cleveland. The moors rise above it like great ramparts, their heads often wrapped in the clouds. Facing a charming row of stone cottages, some with ivied walls and gardens glowing with colour, the church stands on a bank among fine sycamores. The plain nave was made new in Waterloo year; its windows frame lovely views of the switchback lines of the hills.

In startling contrast to the nave, from which it is divided by three graceful arches, is the beautiful chancel, refashioned in our own century. Fine arcades without capitals are between it and the chapels, and the small windows of the clerestory above them continue in the sanctuary. The east window reaches the roof, from which hang two fine brass candelabra. An eight-sided font looks mediaeval, but built into the wall of the south chapel are carved stones which make the story of the church centuries older still. Three are fragments of a Saxon cross. Two believed to be Norman show a knight on horseback holding up his sword, and a woman with long hanging sleeves, seeming to hold a fan and a bunch of flowers. Of our own day is a cross from Flanders. Broken and battered with long exposure in the churchyard are figures of a man and a woman who may belong to the Eure family, who had land here.

Kirkdale. Its name is that of a parish with half a dozen small places, and of a romantic glen where the Hodge Beck winds under thickly wooded banks. It has come from the lonely moorland valley of Bransdale, and is on its way to meet the River Dove in the Vale of Pickering. Kirkdale's fame is in a cave where the light of day has never penetrated, and in a church with what we may regard as the rarest sundial in the land. Farther down the dale is Welburn Hall, now a school, which dates in part from Jacobean times.

The church has one of those delightful situations so easily missed, though within a mile of the busy road. Trees shelter it like a green wall. The roof of the nave is topped by the roofs of the chancel and the slender tower, and from the south wall projects a big porch with a timber gable and oak gates with wooden grilles. There is a sundial on the gable, but the sundial which makes this place renowned is away from the sun and safe from wind and rain inside the porch.

Set in the wall over the simple Norman doorway, the dial is a stone about 7 feet long, with an inscription in perfect lettering and a dial marked with the eight hours of the Saxon day. On the dial are the words, "This is day's sun-marker at each tide"; and at the sides is the longest message which has come down to us engraved in stone from Saxon England. Most of us can make out much of the inscription, and it thrills us to read something written in the English of a few years before the Norman Conquest, and to find here the names of people who are in our history books. This is what we read in this ancient epitaph:

Orm the son of Gamal bought St Gregory's Church when it was all utterly broke and fallen, and caused it to be made anew from the ground, to Christ and St Gregory, in the days of King Edward and in the days of Earl Tosti. Hawarth wrought me, and Brand the Prior.

Tosti was Tostig, brother of Harold of England; and one of the crimes for which he was banished a year before Hastings was the murder of the Gamal whose son rebuilt Kirkdale church. Harold and Tostig met at Stamford Bridge in Yorkshire, where Tostig earned 7 feet of English soil.

The tower is 19th century, and the 13th century chancel has been made partly new, but we can still see Orm's church in the walling of the nave, in the lofty and narrow tower arch with great stones in its sides, and in the sides of the chancel arch, the later head of which is almost like a pointed gable. The sides of the arch leading to the north chapel look old enough to be Saxon, the arch itself being perhaps 13th century.

The lofty pointed arcade leading to the aisle has stood since the end of Norman days, two of its capitals carved with early leaf ornament. The font is as old as the arcade and has a Jacobean cover. In the fine group of three restored lancets in the east wall of the chancel are the Crucifixion and two saints in glass. The reredos, with its carvings of two saints and the Adoration of the Wise Men, is a part of much beautiful woodwork adding to the simple charm of the interior. There are stone seats along the walls of the nave and aisle, and old carved stones within and without. Sheltered in the church are fragments of coffin-lids and Saxon crosses, part of a battered figure found in the churchyard, and two remarkable gravestones. One of these is carved with strapwork and circles, and has on the edges a pattern like knotted fringe; the other has a fine cross with scrollwork and a hole as if for a gem. Antiquaries think they may be from the 10th century.

There are two coffin-lids in the porch, and built into the west wall of the nave outside is a fragment of a Saxon cross. Under the 15th century window in the south wall is a Saxon stone with a worn Crucifixion. The chancel has a mass dial by the priest's doorway, and a stone with fine plaitwork.

In a dip of the lane below the church the stream runs over a rocky bed, flooding the road in stormy weather. In the deep quarry on the other side is the entrance to the cave which a quarryman discovered in 1821. Dr Buckland explored it and found it to be about 100 yards long; and here he discovered the bones of 22 kinds of animals, including wolves, elephants, ox, bears, and deer, all lying with the tools and weapons of Stone Age Men.

Kirkleatham. It is a place of noble trees. The great house is now demolished, its stables forming the greater part of Kirkleatham Hall ESN school for the North Riding Education Authority. The first church was old enough to come into Domesday Book, but this one was rebuilt in 1763, from designs by a village architect. It is in classical style, with six columns supporting the roof, and has an unusual appearance outside owing to the huge mausoleum dwarfing the chancel. The roof is like a stumpy spire crowned with a vase.

Chomley Turner built the mausoleum in 1740 as a resting-place for his son Marwood William Turner, who had died the year before at Lyons when on his way to Italy; we see him standing with his books about him. Chomley's own monument, by Scheemakers, shows him standing at an urn. Westmacott's monument to Charles Turner of 1810 has the figure of a woman by a sarcophagus. In the middle of the mausoleum is a marble sarcophagus to one whom Kirkleatham has good cause to remember, Sir William Turner, woollen draper and Lord Mayor of London; he founded the beautiful almshouses here, and died in 1692. In a rich recess in the sanctuary is the marble statue of his brother John, wearing the robes of a serjeant-at-law, and carrying his gloves.

The small brass portrait of a child, looking like a little Queen Elizabeth in her quaint dress, is of Dorothy Turner, who was only four when she died in 1628, a few years after William Turner acquired the estate. There is a fine brass portrait of Robert Coulthirst in rich robes; he was 90 when they buried him here in 1631, having lived in six reigns. To the 14th century belong a gravestone carved with a cross and a dagger, and the worn figure of a wimpled lady who was probably Eva de Bulmer. The stone coffin of a child in the mausoleum is said to be Danish.

An ironbound chest with carving of tracery and birds above leafy gables is mediaeval. To the 18th century belong the oak seats, the inlaid pulpit and reading-desk, and the graceful font with a fine oak cover adorned with foliage, cherubs, and pinnacles like acorns. There is rich modern carving in the poppyheads of the stalls, and the altar is enriched with cherub-heads. On the altar is beautiful plate given by Sir William when he was Lord Mayor, and a silver dish said to have been washed ashore at Coatham in 1740. The church register goes back to 1559. The east window has A. K. Nicholson's lovely glass showing Our Lord with a rainbow, St Hilda with a goose beside her and a picture of Whitby Abbey, and St Cuthbert with a spade and an otter, on a rocky shore. On a rich mosaic ground in another window are Ruth and Naomi, and Moses with the Children of Israel.

Built round three sides of a square, with splendid gates and railings on the fourth side, the Lord Mayor's Hospital for poor folk and young folk is most imposing. By the gates is the stump of an elm planted in 1705 and now grown into a great tree, and in the court-yard is a statue of Justice by Christopher Wren. In the central range of the brick buildings is the stone chapel of 1742, crowned with a domed tower, and here and there on the walls are two sundials, statues of a boy and a girl, an old man leaning on his stick, and an old woman drawing her shawl about her shoulders. The chapel is delightful, with a small gallery, a marble floor, a fine roof, mahogany stalls, ornate candelabra, and two gilded chairs given to Sir William by Charles II. In the beautiful glass of the east window (glowing with orange and scarlet) are the Wise Men bringing gifts to a smiling Jesus in the arms of a blue Madonna, and beside them are Sir William in his mayoral robes and his brother John in scarlet.

Among hundreds of books in the library are many priceless first editions, an old service book from Salisbury, a rare set of Van Dyck etchings, and a manuscript translation of Boethius, every page illuminated with gold and colour. Here also are Sir William Turner's account books, kept in his own neat hand; at the top of every page written during the Plague are the words "Praise God", and on another page a balance of £50,000 is followed by the words, "Blessed be Almighty God who has blessed me with this estate".

There are many treasures in the museum of the hospital, but the most amazing of all is a piece of boxwood believed to have been carved by an English sailor imprisoned in France. About 20 inches high, it is crowded with a host of tiny people, rearing horses, and lizards. St George is slaying the dragon, the princess turning away; and below the castle is a cave in which queer creatures are hiding. No Chinese ivory is more astonishing than this small carving, for which the British Museum is said to have offered £6000. We were told that the captive sailor spent 12 years on it, and that every detail is carved out of a single piece of wood.

The delightful village near by, of some 16 houses, has some of the few Georgian lamp-posts still in use.

Kirk Leavington. The Saxons and the Normans knew this place, and the great Yorkshire Bruces had a fortress where the steep mound known as Castle Hill stands in a loop of the River Leven two miles away. The deep surrounding ditch, the hollow entrenchment at the summit, and a narrow earthwork shaped like a crescent can still be seen.

There are big houses among trees. The church on a bank has a nave refashioned in 1882, and a beautiful 13th century chancel with fine lancets in its side walls and a modern group at the east end. Three steps climb to it from the nave, and the beautiful Norman chancel arch is carved with zigzag, which also enriches the low massive Norman doorway within the porch.

Some of the rich store of Saxon fragments and old coffin-lids are built into the walls, others are loose. One of two fine coffin stones in the porch has a cross with a leafy stem, and a splendid one in the chancel wall has a rich cross with a book and chalice by the stem. Two others have shears. Some of the Saxon fragments are carved with Crucifixions and knotwork; one panel has figures of two men side by side, and another has a man with two birds on his arms. With these are four stone heads of mediaeval people. There is an old six-sided font not used now, and in the churchyard is a stone coffin and part of a mediaeval cross.

Mr Thompson's mouse is running along the base of his traceried screen to the vestry. Other rich woodwork is seen in the panelling of the sanctuary, in the reredos with a bishop and a knight under canopies, and on the pulpit with a cornice of vine and grape.

Kirklington. Near the A1, riding as straight as a foot-rule between Boroughbridge and Catterick, this delightful village has old houses round the green, shaded by trees and criss-crossed by roads. Away from the rest is the gabled old hall, looking out to the tower of the church among the trees.

A fine church, it stands finely at a corner by the green. Much of it is 14th century, but the tower and the clerestory come from the 15th, and the older chancel (about 1200) has windows of all three mediaeval centuries. In the north porch is a neat little 13th century doorway with the fine head of a man on each side.

The 600-year-old arcades have an odd array of arches of varying heights and out of shape, and between them is an extraordinary collection of carved corbels showing two faces joined by a branch from their mouths, a quaint man with a body like a seal, three grotesques entwined, and three grinning faces with the ears of two in the mouth of the middle one. The splendid Jacobean pulpit has arcaded panels and a grape border, an old reading-desk has a chained book, and the south door is still barred with a huge beam which slides into a hole in the wall. The roofs of the nave and chancel rest on 26 angels, and mediaeval relics are a double piscina and a coffin-lid with a cross, chalice, and book.

The east windows of the aisles have lovely glass, one showing Our Lord with children and leading a flock of sheep, another with a knight at prayer, a young man playing a harp, and pictures of soldiers and choir boys; it is a tribute to one of the Wandesfords. In what is left of old glass are saints, a dragon, an eagle, and a roundel with the crest of the Wandesfords (a church). The motto of this family was "All for the Church", and the crest is seen again on a helmet hanging with their flags and gauntlets; and also above the tomb of Sir Christopher Wandesford, who lies surrounded by the shields of his house, wearing armour as Elizabeth I saw him when she knighted him at Greenwich. A brass tablet to one of them has been here since 1463. Their descendants are still at the hall after all these centuries.

Within two recesses lie the fine figures of a 14th century knight and lady, perfect in detail. He wears armour and has a fine lion on his shield, and another at his feet; she has a simple gown and mantle square headdress, and a dog at her feet, which are in pointed shoes. They may be Alexander Mowbray (son of a judge) and his wife.

Laithkirk. The houses are dotted on the steep hillside, and the ivy-walled church is tucked into the hilltop. Trim and lowly, it has a bellcote, modern windows in stout old walls, an old stoup in the porch, a sundial, and a massive screen dividing the nave and chancel, its cross touching the roof.

Below the church the River Lune roars over its stony bed in a deep glen. Looking north we see the broad valley of the Tees, with white farms on the moorsides, and fields giving way to the heather.

Mickleton is on the other side of the Lune, not far from its meeting with the Tees, and beyond it are the wild moors of Durham.

In its journey through the deep valley (known as Lunedale and skirted by the highway) the Lune flows 12 miles, coming to life in countless little streams from the slopes of the fells—some from Little Fell in Westmorland (rising 2446 feet), some from Mickle Fell, Yorkshire's highest mountain, with a cairn on the top 2591 feet above the sea. It is a crescent-shaped hill, with a curious hollow known as the Boot of Mickle Fell, and the long climb to the summit has for reward a magnificent panorama into which come the Lake-land Fells, Wild Boar Fell in Westmorland, and most of Yorkshire's famous heights.

The river's spectacular feat on its way through Lunedale is the filling of the Grassholme Reservoir, a lake nearly 2 miles long, cover-ing 160 acres and holding 140 million gallons.

Lartington. A mile from Deepdale, a glen loved by Sir Walter Scott, Lartington has much to delight us. Cottages in charming gardens line one side of the wooded road leading to the hall in its beautiful park, bounded by the little Scur Beck on its way to the Tees. Coming from Stuart times, the house has lovely gardens and terraces with statues. Even the railway station has its interest. The unassuming clock in the waiting-room is said to have been made by Master Humphrey. Immortalised by Dickens, Master Humphrey carried on business in Barnard Castle till he went to spend his last days at Hartlepool, his clock ticking away there before keeping rail-way time here.

Lastingham. Aloof from the world in a green moorland hollow is this small place of great distinction and with an ancient tale to tell. Through it runs a prattling stream from Spaunton Moor, on its way to the River Seven flowing through heather-decked Rosedale. The village is linked with Appleton-le-Moors by the road up Lidsty Hill; from a massive cross there are fine views, with a picture of Lasting-ham's jumble of stone walls and red roofs clustering below the noble church. The Saxons gave the village its name, but the Romans had been before them, finding here the powerful Brigantes whose graves, known as howes, are on the moors.

We learn of the earliest days of the church from Bede, who tells us that St Cedd, Bishop of East Anglia, came here with a band of monks to found a church where King Ethelwald might worship and find a last resting-place. This first church, probably of wattle and clay, was built in 660, and when St Cedd died of plague he was buried outside its walls. He was succeeded as abbot by his brother Chad, who became Archbishop of York and Bishop of Lichfield.

When Bede visited the monastery a stone church had risen on the site, and the bones of St Cedd had been buried by the altar. In the next century the monastery and the church were probably destroyed by the Danes, and it was not until 1078, when the Conqueror gave leave to Abbot Stephen and his monks to leave Whitby and settle at Lastingham, that order began to grow out of devastation.

Abbot Stephen built a crypt over St Cedd's grave (probably as a shrine for pilgrims). Above the crypt he began a great church which was to be part of an abbey; but his plans were never completed, and when he retired to York, where he founded St Mary's Abbey, only the crypt and the eastern end of his church had materialised.

There is still much of Abbot Stephen's work to be seen. His crypt stands much as when he left it. When his church was adapted for the use of the parish in 1228 the present west wall was built at the end of the crossing, leaving two massive columns partly outside and two in the nave. At the same time the aisles and the arcades were built, but their windows were renewed when the south aisle was widened in the 14th century. The tower is about 1400.

Early in last century the interior of the apse was made to look like a Greek temple, and John Jackson, a painter of great distinction born in the village, gave it, for an altarpiece, his copy of Correggio's *Agony in the Garden,* now in the north chapel. Later in the century John Pearson, the architect of Truro Cathedral, designed the beautiful stone vault, inspired by the Norman roof of the crypt. The font may be of Abbot Stephen's time; the gravestone forming the lintel of the south doorway may be older still, and a stoup in the west wall is 14th century. From Jacobean days come a table, a chair, and the Litany desk. Beautiful glass in an aisle window shows the two brothers of long ago whose memory is fragrant here, St Cedd with a book, and St Chad with a model of Lichfield Cathedral.

We come down a flight of steps of the Abbot's crypt, rare for its apse, and unique as a complete church in itself, with chancel, nave, and two aisles. The arches are simple and massive. The pillars are short, and their bases and capitals heavy. Some of the carved capitals have the ram's horn.

Still older than the Norman crypt are some of the treasures within it. St Chad may have known the altar. A block of carved stone, hollowed at the top, is thought to have been a Roman incense altar used at Cawthorn Camps. A fragment of a great cross (the middle of the head and one limb) was found a century ago and may be as old as the first stone church here. There are some beautiful fragments of an 8th century cross, a 10th century cross shaft, the shaft of a Viking cross, and two daintily carved stones which may have been in the doorposts of the Saxon church. There is a Danish hogback, the old Ainhowe cross from the moors (where a modern cross now marks its site); old wooden beams are carved with dragons; and the church has a bier older than the Reformation.

John Jackson, born here in 1778, was a tailor's son who commanded attention by clever drawings of his schoolfellows and was given an opportunity of art studies by two generous patrons. His first colours were such as he found in the village glazier's workshop. Being enabled to travel abroad, he astonished Rome by his portrait of Canova. He made a good income, but his generosity kept him poor. A Methodist and perhaps over-serious, he was liberal enough in his opinions to give the altarpiece to the church of his village.

Leake. From the highway between Thirsk and Yarm an avenue of limes leads to an old church standing in a field by the 17th century hall, now a farmhouse. Behind rises the long smooth lines of the Hambleton Hills.

Built by the Normans about 1100, the church's imposing tower rises through the west gable of the nave, which is flanked by the aisles. The belfry storey is enriched with arcading and a corbel table; over the 15th century west window is set the head of a Saxon cross, and a round-headed arch opens to the nave. By a sundial on the south aisle wall is a Norman stone carved with a dragon.

The north arcade of the nave comes from Norman days, and the capitals on which the round arches rest are a striking example of stiff-leaf carving. The south aisle was added about 1300, and on one of the capitals are oak leaves and acorns. Most of the windows are 14th century, and very charming are those in the side walls of the chancel, glowing with a rich gallery of saints in memory of an Admiral. The east window is 15th century.

The door with a wicket through which we enter the church is an introduction to much old woodwork within. There are 16th and 17th century benches, a beautiful altar-table of about 1600, handsome old rails, a Jacobean font cover and two Jacobean chairs, a lectern with a Jacobean desk and a three-legged stem, and an ancient ladder to the belfry.

Exquisite are two 16th century bench-ends in the chancel, said to be from Bridlington Priory. Each has a poppyhead with lovely undercut carving, and a detached pillar richly carved and canopied. One has a dragon, tracery, and the rebus of a prior, Peter Hardy. The other has a lion, and wonderfully fine carving in the canopy which shelters a figure of John the Baptist standing on a barrel.

John Watson and his wife, who died over 400 years ago, are here in brass, he a civilian, she in kennel headdress.

Lealholm. A much-loved village of Eskdale, it is famous for what are said to be the biggest rock gardens in England. They follow the winding river which flows through Crunkly Gill over great boulders and between rocky walls shaded by trees and overgrown with countless plants, flowers, and ferns, many of them rare specimens. For naturalists, for all who love charming scenes, this is a paradise indeed. The 20th century church has a red roof and a tower so small that it is only about 6 feet wide at the base. Standing here on the hillside, we look down on the houses nestling in the valley with its green fields by the silver Esk, and a one-arched bridge near the spot where the river comes through a narrow gorge.

Levisham. There are beautiful views from this remote place, perched on the edge of a moorland plateau, which has many interesting tumuli and earthworks.

A tremendous hill, one of the steepest in Yorkshire, drops down to the valley, green and narrow and charming, through which flows the musical Levisham Beck. By the bridge is a delightful water-mill, and near a little waterfall down the stream hides the small church of St Mary, hemmed in by the hills which rise like ramparts and are draped with trees and heather. Its story goes back to the 11th century, and of that time the chancel still has its simple round arch on imposts, part of a stone on which a dragon is crudely carved, and a fragment of a cross in the wall outside. The sturdy tower and the windows are part of 19th century rebuilding. The Norman font, with cable moulding, is in the modern church.

Leyburn. A small town high above the River Ure (and nearly 700 feet above the sea), Leyburn has grey houses, wide streets, and a spacious market-place with the 19th century town hall. A cross from the grave of a soldier who fell on the Marne is in the church, built last century in the style of six centuries ago, and crowned with an embattled tower. The old chapel which it replaced stood near the hall, whose gates are at a corner of the market-place.

A great surprise is in store for the stranger who takes the path to Leyburn Shawl, a natural limestone terrace continuing for a mile along a rocky ridge. Dark yews and firs, old oaks and sycamores, shade the walks along this great platform, from which we see a vast panorama of moors and half the glory of Wensleydale, hearing at times the roar of Aysgarth Force. Penhill over the river, and the ruined castles of Bolton and Middleham on each hand, come into the view.

Tradition says that Mary Queen of Scots was captured on Leyburn Shawl after escaping from Bolton Castle, and the town has another claim to fame. Here is said to have been born the Lass of Richmond, Frances I'Anson, who afterwards went to live at Richmond. She was so neat and sweet that Leonard MacNally fell in love with her, and the song he wrote about her is still a favourite:

> On Richmond Hill there lives a lass,
> More bright than Mayday morn,
> Whose charms all other maids surpass,
> A rose without a thorn.
> > This lass so neat,
> > With smile so sweet,
> Has won my right goodwill.
> > I'd crowns resign
> > To call her mine,
> Sweet lass of Richmond Hill.

Liverton. On a breezy upland between the moors and the sea, it has a few cottages and farms, and a small cared-for church aloof. It is only a nave and chancel, and is much rebuilt, but keeps some of its Norman walling and a massive Norman chancel arch which reaches nearly to the roof. It is an astonishing possession for this little place. The arch is of three orders—two adorned with rich zigzag, one with pairs of grotesque heads which have leaves coming from their mouths. The imposts are carved with honeysuckle, and the capitals are a very fascinating study. On one side we see the huntsman blowing his horn and three dogs attacking a boar, a quaint face from which leaves are growing, and a solemn Adam and faintly-smiling Eve, with the tree between them and the Angel standing by. On the other side are two dragons snarling at a grotesque in foliage, fine beaded plaitwork, a wild animal snarling at a bird with crossed wings (perched on the edge of a capital), and a dragon biting its tail. One of two old bells standing by the arch has a Latin inscription. A mediaeval coffin-lid has a cross and a shield, and in two pleasing windows are Abraham and Isaac, and the Madonna with her mother St Anne. The Waterwheel Inn has an old wheel outside. Liverton Mines soon scar the landscape.

Lockton. A village of the moors, it is set on a hill above a deep glen which is like a vast furrow ploughed by a giant. Above the headlong descent to the valley are the old cottages and farms, and the quaint grey church with a 15th century tower not much higher than the nave, wearing a gabled cap within the battlements.

The nave and chancel are mediaeval, with some later windows, and between them is a 14th century arch. There are old altar-rails, a Jacobean pulpit with crude carving, a font shaped like an egg-cup perhaps in Norman days, and a scratch dial (on the chancel wall) which may be older still.

Loftus. A busy town built on a steep hillside, it has the great iron and steel works of Skinningrove in a deep valley near the sea. There is little that is beautiful here except the splendid sunsets behind the smoke. The church has an arcade without capitals, a waggon roof running from east to west, and a chancel with rich woodwork. The sanctuary is panelled. The reredos has a rich canopy of tracery and a border of vine and grape. The fine traceried screen has a figure of

St Leonard (the patron saint) over the entrance, and angels holding Passion symbols in a cornice from which springs the graceful vaulting, like bell-shaped flowers, on the east and west sides. One of two Jacobean chairs has a carved back, and a beautiful little blue window has two saints—Hilda and the Madonna. Near the church is a fountain in memory of the men who fell in the Great War.

Lythe. All Yorkshire motorists know Lythe Bank, the long steep hill climbing from Sandsend to this village looking far over the North Sea from a height of 450 feet. Aloof from the houses, the church stands magnificently, with nothing to hinder its view of cornfields sloping to the high cliffs, ships passing for ever along the coast, and Whitby with its quays. Many mariners sleep in the ancient churchyard, and on a stone cross with the names of 17 men of the village who died for peace is a record of seven unknown sailors washed ashore in the war years from 1914.

Begun by the Saxons and refashioned by the Normans, the church was made new 700 years ago, and has been beautifully restored in our century. The north aisle is on the old foundations. The south aisle, the strong tower with a stone spire like a nightcap, the fine porch with a floral boss in its vaulted roof, and the striking vaulted chapel with rose bosses, are all made with the old stones.

Many massive buttresses are a feature of the handsome exterior of this place, built to stand against every wind that blows. Beautiful wood lends its aid to the attractive interior, in the benches, the pulpit and choir seats, and the lovely traceried screens. The chancel screen has a vaulted loft supporting a carved and painted organ case. Two lancet windows in the east wall, a fine double piscina, and a trefoiled niche are all part of the 13th century church. In a spacious crypt under the tower are treasured many fragments found during restoration—mediaeval, Norman, and some with fine Saxon carving of two men wrestling and a figure thought to be Adam under the Tree of Knowledge. Among these are also fragments of hogbacks.

There are many memorials to the Phipps, Earls and Lords of Mulgrave, in this fine church. Their great house, Mulgrave Castle, is on the slopes of a wooded ravine to the south of the village, where a stream winds to the sea. Parallel with this ravine is another glen through which the East Row Beck flows, and on the narrow ridge between them stand the picturesque remains of the Old Castle which was garrisoned for Charles I and became derelict soon after. Supposed to have been founded in the 8th century by Duke Wada, founder of the Waddington family, the castle was made a stronghold towards the end of the 12th century, and was probably given its now fragmentary towers a century later. Facing the ruined pile is the Hermitage, said to stand where stood the Hermitage of Mulgrif, which was given to the Abbey of Whitby in the 12th century.

The woods with their many paths are a fair background for the 18th century Mulgrave Castle, imposing with its tower and battlements. From the windows are charming views of land and sea, and of the terrace known as the quarterdeck, which delighted Dickens so much that he wanted to dance on it.

The home of the Marquis of Normanby, Mulgrave Castle was dear to Henry Phipps, 1st Earl of Mulgrave, who spoke against the abolition of slavery on the ground that in 12 years in Jamaica he had never seen a slave ill-treated. Curiously enough it fell to the lot of Sir Charles Phipps, Governor of Jamaica in 1832, to go from plantation to plantation telling the slaves they were free, and to still another Phipps to pay compensation to the owners of slaves when Wilberforce's dream had become a glorious reality. Constantine John Phipps, second Baron Mulgrave, was a bold captain who sailed as near the North Pole as he could, and had Nelson as a middy on his ship.

Another great man remembered here was Bishop John Fisher, who was vicar of Lythe for five years out of the 15th into the 16th century.

Malton. Many roads come to this busy little town above the Derwent, here flowing in a green valley where a stone bridge crosses to Norton and the East Riding. There are old yellow houses, narrow streets, a spacious market-place where the old church of St Michael keeps watch, and an inn (the Cross Keys in Wheelgate) with a Norman crypt which is said to have had some association with the priory at Old Malton.

New Malton, as the town is sometimes called, is said to have been given this name on its rebuilding 800 years ago, after it had been burned to drive out the Scots. But it was old even then, for it was important in Roman times, and is one of the places which claim to be the Roman station Derventio. Be that as it may, the Romans certainly had here a rectangular camp of about 8 acres, its site marked today by a cross among the grassy mounds in Orchard Field. During excavation the plan of the camp was made plain, and many treasures which came to light are in the Roman Museum. Here we may see flints and stone weapons used by men before the Romans came, part of a Roman spade which may have been used to throw up these ramparts, fragments of plaster from the walls, and the sandals a Roman wore as he walked about the camp when all was bustle and stir. There are bone woolcombers and buttons, pins, knife-handles, skeletons of children who once romped within the fort, fragments of Roman window glass, and bits of pottery. These, with remains from a Roman house at Langton, and other possessions, are housed in one of the best little museums of its kind in Yorkshire.

Of the Norman castle built on the site of the camp nothing is left, but of the great house which followed it about 1600 an imposing fragment stands, a high wall of weathered stone in which are three fine archways. Behind it is Malton Lodge, charming with battlements and mullioned windows. Some of it is modern, but the rest was built with the stone of Lord Eure's house, which is said to have been pulled down in Stuart days because two heiresses quarrelled over it. The sheriff, declaring that they had equal right to it, ordered them, Solomon-like, to break down the walls and share the stones. Close by is a neat row of old houses with stepped-gabled windows in the roofs.

At each end of a cluster of buildings on an island site in the market-place are the town hall and St Michael's church (without a church-yard). The town hall has a balconied entrance, battlements, and a small lantern with a spire. The church has a sturdy 15th century tower and modern transepts, but the fine clerestoried nave, the narrow aisles, and the chancel stand almost as they were built by the Normans in the middle of the 12th century. Round arches are everywhere, in windows and arcades. Flat buttresses and corbels adorn the walls outside, and the old stringcourse, carved with zigzag, forms hoods for the clerestory windows.

Hiding among old houses on a little hill, St Leonard's church, with a quaint tower and spire, still has Norman arcades between nave and aisle, chancel and chapel, and a Norman font with a Jacobean cover. Over the lofty arches of the nave are many grotesque corbels. The east window, showing Gideon, David, Jonathan, an officer in khaki with York Minster in the background, and a sailor with a battleship behind him, is in memory of officers and men of the Yorkshire Regiment who fell in the Great War.

A quaint possession is the portrait brass of Arthur Gibson, who died in 1837. He is said to have engraved it himself, and it is the only one of its kind we have seen, for it shows his vices as well as his virtues, giving us a portrait in which we see him drinking from a tankard and another where he is kneeling in prayer.

In the cemetery lies a hero of our own day, Dr G. C. Parkin, who laid down his life for others in the darkest hour Malton has ever known. He was only 31 when a typhoid epidemic raged here in 1933. Day after day Dr Parkin devoted all his energies to fighting the plague, never sparing himself, never afraid of taking risks.

Manfield. Near a straight stretch of Roman road, Manfield looks over Tees meadows and cornfields to Durham less than a mile away. Fine trees shelter the church the Normans began and modern days have made partly new. The sturdy tower is 16th century, the south arcade is 13th, the north arcade and the chancel are 600 years old; but most of the windows (including the round ones of the clerestory) are modern. The south aisle has an old lancet; the chancel has a priest's doorway with a Norman arch enriched by zigzag and a Norman pillar piscina under a 14th century niche. A fine coffin-lid has a sword, and roses and leaves by the stem of a rich cross; and on one of five fragments of other lids is a pair of shears. A richly carved chest and two chairs are 17th century, and in the sanctuary are two tall candlesticks like bedposts.

In the churchyard sleeps a woman who, we are told, was harvesting in the fields when she was 106, and lived two years to boast of it.

Marrick. From the lonely village high on the hillside an old stone causeway leads down to all that is left of Marrick Priory, standing by the river in an entrancing wooded stretch of Swaledale, where the stream rushes over its rocky bed, and the bare moorland rises like a rampart above it. With the grey cluster of farm and church, the slender tower rising in the midst, and all enclosed by low stone walls, it is an exquisite picture seen from the highway through the dale. The priory was founded in the 12th century as a house for Benedictine nuns, perhaps by Roger de Aske, who endowed it and gave to it the parish church. The nuns used the chancel, now in ruins, and the people used the nave, which was rebuilt in 1811. The tower is 13th century. On a coffin-lid is a chalice and a book. There are quaint box-pews, a Jacobean pulpit, and old glass fragments. We found the place about to come to life again, for it was being restored and extended to make an Adventure Centre for the use of young people—an admirable enterprise on the part of the Diocese of Ripon.

There is no quieter spot in all the dale, and we think here of the story they tell of the prioress who did a beautiful thing before she closed the door for the last time in 1539. To this little place had come a lovely girl seeking sanctuary with the nuns, for Henry VIII had sought to marry her. She was Isabella Beaufort, a rich and beautiful maid-of-honour. Here for nearly four years she lived in hiding; and the story tells us that the prioress was very human, for she wrote secretly to Edward Herbert, who was in love with Isabella, telling him they might write to each other. Then came the sad day when the King closed this and all the other priories and monasteries throughout the land, and sadly the nuns left their old home. But it was a happy day for Isabella, for Edward Herbert carried her away to Somerset where, as in the old stories, they were married and lived happily ever after.

Marske. The winding road by the Swale gives us vista after vista of magnificent foliage in one of the loveliest valleys of Yorkshire, and the old road over the hills has fine views before dropping down to the deep glen in which the village lies. We should come when the woods are russet and golden.

A charming bow bridge, perhaps seven centuries old, crosses a turbulent stream on its way to the Swale, making cascades, flowing under trees, and running through the beautiful lawns and gardens of the hall. One of the trees is an Austrian pine about 20 feet round and 70 feet high. The hall has been made new, but it is still the home of the Huttons, descendants of the family which gave us two archbishops. An obelisk rising 60 feet in the park is a memorial to Captain Matthew Hutton, who died just before Waterloo.

Looking down on the bridge from the other bank is the church, to which we climb 22 steps. Its 17th century restoration has left it an old-fashioned air, with box-pews, a two-decker pulpit, and a squire's pew. The walls are stout, the bellcote is mediaeval, and the simple doorway is Norman. Only a little later is the unusual nave arcade, with round arches on capitals striking for their boldness and simplicity, eight stiff sycamore leaves growing from the eight sides of the pillars. A wide round arch leads to the chancel, which has a north arcade of two massive round arches on square pillars. Two chairs are Jacobean. The top of a 14th century window is set in a recess in which lies a grinning head. The porch has parts of a 15th century inscription with beautiful lettering and borders of flowers, and there is a sundial of 1700.

Marske-by-the-Sea. The old village between the hills and the sea has become a trim little town for holiday-makers. A few old houses, a thatched cottage, and an old barn are still to be seen, and Marske Hall, now a Cheshire Home, has lost nothing of its old charm. Seen beyond a palisaded wall and lawns, it is a many-windowed stone house of 1625, its façade having three domed towers, with projecting bays between them.

By the hall is the 19th century church of St Mark, a spacious place in 13th century style guarding two old treasures. One is the square Norman font, with corner shafts and sides richly carved with scroll-work, wheel pattern, and zigzag; the other is a wayside cross believed to be 13th century, with a lovely head of pierced carving.

The font belonged to the old church of St Germain which was blown up with gunpowder in 1820. The church built on its foundations is on the brink of the cliff. It has little more for us to see than its quaint benches and a two-decker pulpit, but in its old church-yard lies the father of England's greatest navigator, Captain Cook. It is said of him that he lived 70 years without knowing his alphabet, and that in his old age he learned to read so that he could spell his way through his son's account of his voyages.

Marton-in-Cleveland. It is Captain Cook's village, for ever linked with Yorkshire's great seaman, who first saw the light in a cottage which unhappily has been lost. It stood in the fine 110-acre park of Marton Hall, now known as Stewart Park after the man who gave it to Middlesbrough. A granite vase marks the spot where Cook's cottage stood. The hall, rebuilt last century after a fire, now houses a museum with a collection of birds, objects illustrating the races of mankind, and relics of local interest. Among the weapons and implements from the South Seas are clubs used by the people Captain Cook made friends with, and relics of his voyages.

Travellers for miles round know his monument on Easby Moor a few miles away, pointing to the sky from a thousand feet above the sea. Marton built the village school to his memory. In the church-yard, shaded by many old trees dwarfing the church, sleeps Mary Walker, who gave Cook a good meal in the days when he was often hungry. Cook worked for her husband when he was only eight; she lived to be nearly 90, and to know that her pupil had won undying fame.

Shaped like a cross, the church in which Cook was baptised was rebuilt in its old style a century ago, but the north arcade stands much as it stood towards the close of the 12th century. Some of its capitals are carved with stiff leaves, and two are notable for their extraordinary sculpture, one with a curious company of odd little men and animals among leaves; the other with wriggling dragons eating leaves, and a shepherd attending sheep which are nibbling leaves. The modern chancel has two lovely mediaeval piscinas, and an oak chair said to have come from Byland Abbey. An old grave-stone, partly hidden by a pew, has an engraving of a carpenter's square. In rich glass is a Crucifixion Scene and three saints, Hilda, Christopher, and Elfleda; in another window is St Nicholas.

Marton-in-the-Forest. Near the River Foss in what was once the Forest of Galtres, it has a very odd little church coming chiefly from the 15th century, though its stout chancel arch (with a slit in the gable above it) tells of its Norman origin, and the tower (only 6 feet square inside) is 16th century.

Stepped gables at the east and west ends, and between the nave and chancel, give the exterior an unusual appearance, helped by the tower, which mounts steplike to the parapet and is supported by stepped buttresses looking like wings to the south doorway. The

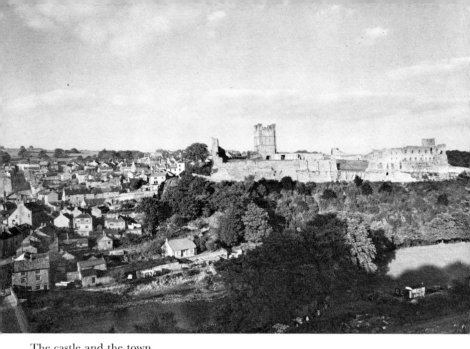

The castle and the town

Richmond

The square, with the obelisk and the church

The Greyfriars Tower, Richmond

hanging tracery of this doorway may have come from Marton Priory, and over it is a worn canopied figure. A 15th century door opens to the interior, which is simplicity itself. There are crude old bench-ends, a Jacobean chest, and a 13th century font. A low window in the chancel has its original oak lintel, the roofs rest on old wall-plates, and a little old glass is like rays of golden light.

The site of Marton Priory is over a mile away, by the road to Helmsley, but nothing is left of the old place except fragments in the farmhouse, Marton Abbey. Of Moxby Nunnery, a mile south of Marton, there are traces of a moat.

Masham. There is an air of repose about Masham, a fine picture of Old England with its dignified houses, quaint almshouses, the lovely old church with a spire, and the spacious market-place with a maypole and a slender old cross.

A fine tree-lined road goes down to the River Ure, which has come from Wensleydale and is crossed by a beautiful 18th century bridge. Near the town it is joined by the Burn, and across this little river is the lovely Swinton Park of 300 acres, now used as a Conservative College. It was the last home of Lord Masham, the great Yorkshire inventor and philanthropist, known as the Plush King. Two stately beeches guard the imposing entrance to the park, and deer browse by its lakes.

Masham has nothing older than the astonishing round pillar in the churchyard. Higher than a man, with worn figures representing Our Lord and the Twelve Disciples, it is believed to be part of an enormous cross carved over a thousand years ago. The church may have some Saxon masonry in its west wall, and in its collection of ancient stones are parts of two Saxon crosses.

The Norman tower was given its octagonal lantern and its lovely spire in the middle of the 15th century, when the clerestory was added to the nave. About 1330 the rest of the church had been made new, perhaps by one of the Scropes, whose name will always be associated with this place. The vaulted porch with leafy pinnacles is 1520, and the little bay of the north aisle is 100 years younger. The modern font is a copy of the Norman one lying in the tower. There are old coffin-lids and a *Breeches Bible*. A painting above the chancel arch, showing an angel on a cloud, is said to be part of a

Nativity by Sir Joshua Reynolds which was damaged by fire at Belvoir Castle.

Among the memorials to the Harcourts of Swinton Park is a tablet to Octavius, an archbishop's son who went to sea a middy and came home an admiral. He built a church at Healey, restored this one, and built some of the almshouses here, dying in 1863.

A classical wall monument of 1727 has the bust of Sir Abstrupus Danby, one of the family who followed the Scropes at Masham. Magdalen Danby and her husband, Sir Marmaduke Wyvell, are reclining, with their faces resting on their hands, in a 17th century monument with figures of Father Time and a winged boy blowing bubbles. Below them are six sons in armour and two daughters in ruffs and farthingales.

It is the pride of Masham that here sleep three men who were notable in their day, one of them a Julius Caesar. He was Julius Caesar Ibbetson, famous in the 18th century as a painter of country scenes, especially of the Lake Country. The second was an artist of last century, George Cuitt, remembered for his exquisite etchings of castles and abbeys; he died in 1854. The third notable man of the village, who lies in the churchyard, was the miller musician William Jackson, born in Waterloo year. Even as a boy he could play 15 instruments, and walked to York to hear an Oratorio in the Minster. He made an organ before he left school, and at 17 became organist here. He made a name as a composer of anthems and beautiful settings for the Psalms; and wrote a singing manual long used in our schools.

Melsonby. Lanes from two Roman roads bring us to this village, where a stream trickles through a deep hollow, the old stone rectory and the church standing on opposite banks. There is a fragment of a 12th century nunnery near the rectory. Though the church was made partly new last century, much of it is about 1200, and fragments are older still. Sturdy and bold enough to have been described as a Norman keep in miniature, the tower has walls with massive stones, but the astonishing thing is the enormous pointed arch to the nave, resting on clustered shafts. In the great space of the tower stands the simple font on two round steps.

The nave impresses us with its tilting arcades, which may have been part of the Norman church. Over the arcades is a fine Norman clerestory, and a wide arch leads to the chancel.

Three notable possessions are a coffin-lid with a face in the middle of a cross; a coped Saxon stone carved with knotwork and foliage, a quaint animal, and two dogs biting two birds; and a 14th century recess reaching the roof of the south aisle, its carved foliage lying gracefully on the gabled canopy, which has elaborate cusping tipped with faces. The battered figure under the tower may be Sir John Stapleton of 1332.

Middleham. To this little grey town clings the memory of the proud Nevilles whose fierce hates brought generations of warfare, whose wealth and power made them masters of kings and princes. Their splendour faded half a thousand years ago, their castle is a ruin, but their memory lives in this small place which was old when the Nevilles came. The story of the castle goes back to Norman times, and Roman remains have been found.

Coming from East Witton, the road crosses the River Cover near its meeting with the Ure, flowing through Wensleydale. If we come from Leyburn we cross the Ure on a picturesque suspension bridge hung between embattled towers, and climb the hillside where Middleham (crowned by the castle) looks over the green beauty of the dale.

There are steep streets, old inns and houses, and two market-places, one with a restored old cross. The other (the Swine Market) is by the massive north curtain of the castle, and has the old bull-ring near what is known as the Swine Cross, a curious erection of two stone blocks on a two-sided flight of steps. The battered animal on one block may represent the boar of Richard III or the bear of the Warwicks. Looking on to this square is the tower of the 19th century school. The place often sounds with the beat of horses' hooves, for it is renowned as a training centre for racehorses.

A cobbled path by cottages and flower-beds ends at the church, reached through a lychgate or by a flight of steps. By the footpath beyond the other side of the churchyard is the Well of St Alkelda, the Saxon princess who shares with St Mary the dedication of the church, in which tradition says she was buried. On a pillar in Middleham church is an inscription saying that what are believed to have been her bones were found here in the nave. She is supposed to have been strangled by two Danish women, and in the jumble of mediaeval glass in a north aisle window we see the women pulling at a handkerchief tied round her neck. Two brilliant medallions of glass in one of the vestry windows, showing her martyrdom and angels bearing her up to heaven, have come from a yacht known as *The Alkelda*. A stone in the vestry wall, carved with crude interlacing, is believed to be part of her tombstone.

The church is chiefly 14th century, but the top of the tower, the clerestory, and most of the windows of the aisles, are 15th century. The south doorway has a modern arch on 13th century sides, and above it is a 14th century sculpture of the Crucifixion believed to have come from the castle. High in the north aisle wall is a Norman fragment carved with zigzag.

A mediaeval font has come back to church from a garden, and the modern font which took its place has a restored 15th century canopy, like an open tower and spire richly carved and brightly painted. This was found in the rectory loft, and the old altar-rails have been recovered from a stable. A Jacobean cupboard has ornate panels, and the north aisle has a rich modern screen and a curious old gallery seeming to hang behind two massive arches of the arcade. There are gravestones serving as lintels of windows, and others built into a fireplace in a room of the tower. Very unusual is the great 16th century tombstone against a wall of the tower, deeply carved (on a fine background like brocade) with a mitre and staff, of which the point pierces a barrel as if it were a thorn. It represents in sculpture the name of Robert Thornton, Abbot of Jervaulx, whose tomb and remains were probably brought here for safety at the Dissolution of the Monasteries.

The south aisle has an east window with Capronnier's glass showing Christ preaching, and a west window in memory of Richard III, one of the actors in Middleham's brilliant pageantry, having received it as a gift from his brother Edward IV after the death of Warwick the Kingmaker at Barnet. The window was set here in 1934 by those who believe that this king was not so foul as history has painted him. His window is of two lights, and the glass is in the fashion of his day. There are big figures of St Richard of Chichester (in his robes and mitre), and St Anne teaching her daughter to read, Mary wearing a crown and a blue mantle dotted with fleur-de-lys. In the foot of the window are small kneeling figures of Richard (in purple mantle) and his queen Anne Neville, daughter of the Kingmaker. Her mantle is richly emblazoned with the alliances of her house. Behind his father kneels their only son, Edward Prince of Wales, who was born at Middleham Castle and died there in 1484 when he was eight. Under the window are replicas of Richard III's seals. Richard gave Middleham church a college, which was dissolved in 1856, Charles Kingsley being one of the last of the canons. The rectory is still known as The Deanery, and has three mediaeval doorways.

For about 200 years the castle, one of the grandest in the north, was a chief stronghold of the Nevilles, their wealth and love of ostentation bringing to it armies of soldiers and brilliant companies of courtiers. Middleham first knew them about 1270, when Ralph Fitzranulph's heiress married Robert Neville of Raby. The Nevilles refashioned the curtain wall and the domestic buildings set against it, but the great keep is for the most part the Norman stronghold erected between 1170 and 1190, probably by Robert FitzRalph. His grandfather, Ribald, is said to have built Middleham's first fortress where now a grassy mound rises above the town, a few hundred yards away. Known as St William's Hill, it looks down on its battered successor, which has seen a splendour scarcely surpassed in the Courts of our Tudor kings, and is now a fearful and sinister place with gaunt masses of masonry, gaping holes, and dark cellars, its silence broken only by jackdaws and pigeons.

The keep, 105 feet long and 78 wide, is one of the biggest in England, with walls about 10 feet thick and 55 feet high, though the battlements and turrets which adorned it are gone. It was residence as well as fortress, divided by a central wall into two divisions which once had gabled roofs. A flight of steps outside the east wall led to the entrance on the first floor. The vaulted rooms of the ground floor were cellars and kitchen, and here are still two wells and a great fireplace. The eastern room of the first floor was the great hall, with a tiny vaulted chapel at one end, and the pantry and buttery at the other. There are traces of another floor built above the great hall in the 15th century, reached by a fine newel stairway, up which we can climb to see an impressive picture of the keep within its moated enclosure, and a marvellous panorama of the countryside. The river winds far down the dale, the wolds are away in the east, and the fells rising one after another towards the west horizon.

There are turrets on the south and west walls of the keep, and projecting from the east side are remains from the 13th century.

Making a rectangle 240 feet long and 190 feet wide, the walls and domestic buildings made new by the Nevilles are linked by three towers and the 14th century gatehouse. The round tower is known as the Prince's Tower, from a story that Prince Edward was born in it. Over the bakehouse joining it was a long room called the nursery. The 14th century north-west tower was made higher a century later. In the south range are remains of the horse-mill and a great oven.

We come to the vaulted gatehouse by a wooden bridge where once a drawbridge crossed the moat. Its battlements are gone, but here are the corbels which supported them, the turrets climbing at the angles, the little door leading to the guard chamber, and the fine archways, one with the grooves in which the portcullis went up and down. On the ground lie stone figures of armed men which may have stood on the battlements. One and a half miles to the south-west is Braithwaite Hall, a fine 17th century farmhouse now in the care of the National Trust.

Middlesbrough. A small place of 40 people long after Waterloo, it has become the capital of Cleveland and the only county borough in the Riding; it is now part of the administrative area, comprising towns in Yorkshire and County Durham, known collectively as Teesside, and has expanded vastly since the 1939–45 war. It has regiments of streets, its churches include a Roman Catholic cathedral, and there are fine public buildings, its boundaries having grown till they enclose 7000 acres, with fine parks. It is its place on the map that has made possible this growth. Seven miles from the sea but only one from the mouth of the Tees, it lies in a bend of the river and has a water frontage of about 5 miles.

Its industries are legion, but we know it chiefly for its iron and steel works, its docks and shipyards, its chemical, salt, and engineering works, and its export of coal. ICI have installations at Wilton, claimed to be the largest chemical complex in Europe; Shell and BP have the biggest oil-storage depot in Britain here, and Tarmac's roadstone plant is the biggest in Europe. The story of the modern town is chiefly a romance of iron and steel; it was really born about 1830, when a few far-seeing men decided that it would be a better port for the shipment of coal than Stockton-on-Tees. Joseph Pease and his partners bought 500 acres of land and formed as a company The Owners of the Middlesbrough Estate, building the first roads and laying the foundation of many industries. The extension of the Stockton and Darlington railway to Middlesbrough was due to Edward Pease. It was the Owners who opened the first dock.

When the dock was opened Middlesbrough had about 6000 people, and after 1850 the number began to go up in leaps and bounds. It reached 90,000 by the end of the century, for in that year iron ore was discovered in the Cleveland Hills, and Henry Bolckow and John Vaughan established here the first works for smelting.

Henry Bolckow, one of the town's benefactors, was a remarkable German who became a naturalised English citizen a century ago and with John Vaughan acquired collieries, quarries, gasworks, factories, and brickfields. Theirs was one of the first colossal firms in the North, and the rapid growth of the town, consequent on this enterprise, led Mr Gladstone to describe Middlesbrough as the youngest child of England's enterprise. It is claimed that half the steel buildings in the world have Middlesbrough girders. Its engines are throbbing in ships on every sea. Its tools and machines are in the workshops of every continent. Its wires and cables cross almost every land. Its fame as a builder of bridges is unrivalled. It is interesting to remember that the ironworks founded by Henry Bolckow and John Vaughan were refounded by a firm which has given the world some of its greatest bridges, the famous firm of Dorman Long, whose works cover many hundreds of acres here, including the first universal beam mill in Europe.

One of the supreme triumphs of modern engineering is the marvellous Sydney Harbour Bridge, the giant child of Middlesbrough. The town also built Lambeth Bridge (which gives the Londoner one of the most glorious views of the capital), the wonderful iron bridge over the White Nile, and the Storstroem Bridge in Denmark (the biggest in Europe), the Volta River Bridge in Ghana; and it has given itself two remarkable bridges across the Tees. One is the famous Transporter, crossing the Tees from the end of Ferry

Road to Port Clarence on the Durham side; it is 850 feet long and 225 above the water, graceful in spite of its size. It rises above miles of docks and quays where huge cranes work and coaling machines handle 550 tons an hour. There is room for about nine vehicles and 600 people in this huge transporter car. The other remarkable bridge here is the Newport Bridge on the west side of the town, the first vertical lift-bridge in England, and the biggest of its kind in existence. It has over 6000 tons of steel, and cost over half a million pounds. One of its two high towers is on the Yorkshire side and the other on the Durham side of the Tees. The lifting span is 270 feet long and 66 wide, weighing about 2500 tons, yet at the touch of a hand it rises 100 feet in 45 seconds.

At one end of Victoria Square (a small park in front of the municipal buildings) is a statue of John Vaughan, the panels on his pedestal showing iron manufacture. At the other end stands Sir Samuel Sadler, MP and three times mayor. Their portraits are in the impressive panelled council chamber of the town hall, which dates from 1889, the year Middlesbrough became a county borough. Among famous men of Middlesbrough with portraits here are Henry Bolckow, Sir Joseph Pease, and Sir Lowthian Bell. The Hugh Bell Schools are on the south side of the square; on another side is the public library, with eight columns supporting a cornice on its front, and inside, among its treasures, an almost complete collection of Greek Bibles since the Reformation, and a valuable collection of books relating to iron and steel. By the gates of the square are big boulders with fossil forms. Not far off is the Constantine College with a splendid Hydraulics Laboratory and Experimental Foundry.

The figure of Henry Bolckow stands just inside the gates of Albert Park, 72 very pleasant acres he gave to this matter-of-fact town. He looks out from his pedestal across fine lawns and gay flower-beds. Here, too, we see the trunk of a huge tree found in the Tees, a boulder dredged up from the Tees at Newport, and a sundial telling the time here, in New York, and in Melbourne. By the beautiful iron gates of the park are 22 bronze panels with the names of 3000 men who fell in the Great War, a fitting background for the great cenotaph standing proudly here.

A companion for the Great War cenotaph is the Dorman Memorial Museum at the park entrance, crowned with a green

MIDDLETON

copper dome. It was the gift of Sir Arthur Dorman in memory of
his son and the men of a Yorkshire Regiment who died in the Boer
War. Here are prehistoric flints, tools, and burial urns; Roman
remains including a stone coffin and a 2nd century sarcophagus; and
a collection of shells, flowers, birds, and animals. The head of an
ichthyosaurus, a monster which died in the early morning of the
Earth's long day, was found in the Carlin Howe iron mines. Here
we see Sir Lowthian Bell's collection of ores, an iron rail of the
world's first railway, a case of pottery from prehistoric times to the
19th century, and lovely models of all kinds of ships, fascinating to
old and young. There are English ships of olden and modern days,
a Venetian galley, Spanish galleons, and little sailing ships in bottles.
Near by is the attractive small Art Gallery which has a good
permanent collection and frequently mounts exhibitions of the work
of modern artists.

The Roman Catholic Cathedral is an impressive building with a
fine canopied pulpit and a beautiful little Chapel of the Blessed
Sacrament. Middlesbrough has also a notable group of 19th and
20th century churches, some of them attractive architecturally. St
Hilda's, at a corner of the market-place, shelters a Norman font with
a crude St Andrew's Cross, and has ancient stones said to belong to
an older church on this site, where a cell was consecrated to St
Cuthbert. The modern St Cuthbert's Church has an austere beauty
with lofty arches soaring on square piers, striking aisles, and a fine
round crucifixion window. The richly decorated All Saints has a
lovely rose window above the altar. St John's has an elaborate
carved reredos, the Seamen's Chapel has an altar painting showing
Christ walking on the water, and St Barnabas's has a wide chancel
screen with canopied saints. On the outskirts of the town is an
attractive Little Theatre, which can claim the distinction of being
the first new theatre built in England after the Second World War.

Middleton. A mile from Pickering lies this trim village with grass
verges, creepered cottages, and a church with its roots in Saxon
England.

Nine centuries have gone since the Saxons began this splendid
tower, with its huge corner stones in the crude long-and-short style,
and a Saxon doorway (with a projecting hood) now blocked in the

143

west wall, an oval window breaking into its arch. The head of a cross above this window is one of half-a-dozen Saxon fragments treasured here, one carved with knotwork, one with a quaint little man. In the north aisle is a fine small cross, probably 11th century, adorned with crude plait and knotwork, and quite complete.

The tower was completed about the year 1200, when its arch to the nave was altered. The Norman arcade leading to the north aisle has massive pillars and arches, in striking contrast to the south arcade, which comes from the end of the 12th century and has the simplest of natural foliage carved on its cross-shaped capitals. The clerestory and the restored roof of the nave are Tudor. The 13th century chancel was made almost new half a century ago. Worn but still beautiful is the 700-year-old south doorway with a trefoiled arch and rich mouldings, its light stone framing a grand 15th century door gnarled and black with age. Probably as old as this door are two bench-ends making a seat in the chancel, and four stalls of which one has a misericord seat carved with the figure of a man. The pulpit (from which John Wesley preached) has a sounding board beautifully inlaid with a star. The north aisle has a stone bench, and the south aisle has a piscina and a peephole. Peering into the nave is the ugly head of an animal, and near the tower is an old coffin with its lid, probably a relic of the nunnery which stood in the field known as Nun's Garth.

Middleton Tyas. Magnificent trees shade its maze of twisting ways, and the mighty beeches of the park round Middleton Lodge shade the lane which brings us from the Roman highway. On the other side of the village a fine avenue leads to the church hiding in the fields, guarded by oaks, elms, and beeches, and roofed with lead. Much of it is 13th and 14th century, the 700-year-old tower crowned with a modern spire; but the splendid north arcade, with six round arches, is Norman. The chancel arch (with a modern screen) is about 1300, the time of the south arcade, whose only carved capital has beautiful sprays of oak, sycamore, ivy, and hawthorn. One window, notable for its curious shape, is like the quarter of a circle with two upright mullions; another has lovely modern glass showing John the Baptist in purple and St Francis in brown. But it is in a recess of the south aisle that we find the great treasure of this attractive church, an exquisite coffin-lid whose beauty is perhaps un-surpassed; its edges are wreathed with leaves, eight lilies form the head of the cross, and by the stem are trailing stalks and leaves. An old tombstone with a shield is by the north door.

A pompous inscription to John Mawer, a vicar who died in 1763, tells us that he knew 22 languages and was descended *from the royal family of Mawer*, whatever that may be.

Moulton. A village of the byways, with a Roman road over a mile away, it has two beautiful old houses, and a carpenter's shop which was a chapel in mediaeval days. It still has the old piscina and some of the old roof beams. Stately and tall, with projecting wings, the fine manor house stands in friendly fashion, looking down on the cottages gathered round the meeting of the ways. It is older than the Elizabethan Hall, now in the care of the National Trust, which has many curved gables, and rises from a lawn among the trees. The story is that James I rested at the hall on his way from Scotland to take the English throne, and if so he would know the carved oak staircase.

Mount Grace Priory. Sheltering under the glorious woods of Ingleby Arncliffe, with buttercup fields below, this lovely spot was for 140 years the home of monks who sought seclusion from the world, and even from each other, giving themselves to hard work, meditation, and great privation, wearing shirts of hair cloth and finding recreation in their gardens.

The only Carthusian priory in Yorkshire, and one of only nine in England, Mount Grace was founded by a nephew of Richard II, Thomas Holland, who became Duke of Surrey and was executed at Cirencester for conspiring against Henry IV. Twelve years after-wards he was brought to rest in his priory.

Fragmentary as the ruins are, they serve as a fine example of the Carthusian plan; the austerity which governed the lives of the monks seems to be proclaimed by the ragged walls, but that is only on close acquaintance. The first picture to greet us as we come from the highway is of the charming house Thomas Lascelles fashioned in 1654 from part of the west range of the buildings; the date and his initials are over the entrance of the two-storeyed porch, in front of which are two fine bronze boys. Set on a terrace above the beautiful garden, the house has an array of mullioned windows, walls with battlements and gables, and a pantiled roof with dormers.

The priory had two big courts of irregular shape, each having only two of its four sides parallel. At one end of the house is the old three-arched gateway (roofless now) leading into the south or outer court. On the north side of the court is the priory church, its slender tower rising above lofty fragments of the nave walls (with a triangular-headed window over the west doorway), the north transept with a high arch, and the south transept with a great window. The tower and transepts were added about 1420. Of the great choir to the east only traces are left.

Immediately north of the church are remains of the range which divided the south court from the inner or cloister court. In the 15 cells round three sides of the cloister lived 15 monks, each in his own small dwelling of two storeys, with a ladder to the upper floor. Here each monk lived, prayed, and slept. Each cell had its own doorway to the court, and a curious hatch in the wall through which food was served to the monk without his being able to see who served it. The monk's little garden joined his cell. One of the cells has been restored as it was in days gone by, and on the opposite side of the court is the old lavabo at which the monks would wash their hands. When the church was enlarged in 1420, more accommodation for monks was made in a corner of the south court, bringing the total number of cells and gardens to over twenty.

There are old fishponds below the ruins, and in the woods near by is a Wishing Well which was long famous. On the hilltop are traces of a chapel where the monks are said to have been buried, and from it there is a glorious view reaching to the Pennines beyond the Plain of York.

Muker. The wild grandeur of Upper Swaledale, where the narrow green valley is like a yawning abyss shut in by the steep sides of the desolate fells, is all about this charming grey village of a hundred folk, their houses perched one above another. The small church looks over the roofs to the prattling beck which makes a pretty waterfall on its way from Thwaite, and runs under Muker's one-arched bridge before joining the Swale.

146

On their way from Keld to Muker, the Swale and the Beck make almost an island of Kisdon, a lofty height 1636 feet above the sea— the river flowing on its north and east sides, the stream having the company of the road for the rest. As the river goes on through the hamlets of Ivelet and Gunnerside, it gathers the stream which makes the triple cascade of 100 feet known as Yew Scar Falls, and the Gunnerside Gill which has carved its way through a deep gorge after rising between Rogan's Seat (2203 feet) and Water Crag (source of many streams) only 20 feet less.

Of the great fells to the south there is a magnificent view from Butter Tubs Pass, the mountain road which runs between Great Shunner Fell and Lovely Seat, and links Muker with Hawes in Wensleydale. The road reaches 1726 feet, its highest point, near the Butter Tubs which give it its name, a series of strange shafts in the limestone with a depth of from 50 to 100 feet. In them the Cliff Beck comes to life, then runs below the road to the Muker Beck. From the top of the road the views could hardly be surpassed; turning from the beauty of Swaledale we see the fells in all their glory, with the long ridge of Widdale crowned at 2203 feet by Knoutberry Hill, and Ingleborough, 16 miles from where we stand, rising to 2373 feet.

It is all a magnificent setting for this small village, which boasts of one of the churches built in Elizabeth I's day, though most of its windows are modern, and its thatched roof went in 18th century alterations. The nave and chancel are an oblong (only 22 feet wide and three times as long), and the tiny tower is less than 8 feet square. The two bells are older than the church, and were probably brought here from Ellerton Priory. The font was found in 1900 buried under the floor. High in the east wall are two stones which may have come from Coverham Abbey.

Muker is proud to remember that two brothers, Richard and Cherry Kearton, came here to the little school, walking every day from Thwaite, where they were born, and receiving here the beginnings of that scholarship which was to make them famous as naturalists and lecturers.

Myton-on-Swale. The Hall with golden walls stands in a beautiful park where the Stapletons have lived since Charles I's day. The river flowing by is near the end of its journey as the Swale, for, after skirting the village, it joins with the Ure to become the Ouse.

Standing by the wayside, with poplars for company, the neat church comes chiefly from the 13th and 15th centuries. The tower is built within the church, almost hiding the western arch of the arcade, which leads to a very narrow aisle. Between the arches are old carved stones, and under the tower is a coffin-lid with a cross. Rich glass shows the Annunciation, and figures of Peter and Paul; and in a lovely window to one of the Stapletons we see St George with banner and sword, and St Nicholas with three boys looking at the apples he is holding. Another striking window has a king with sceptre and sphere, and St Martin on a black horse, sharing his cloak with the beggar. The oak screen of the Stapleton chapel has Moses and Aaron in coloured glass, and within the chapel is a brass to one of the family who was a sea captain. It has a scene in enamel of the sea opening to let crosses ascend to the sun.

Nawton. This neat village of grey houses, halfway between Kirbymoorside and Helmsley, has an unusual memorial on its tiny green, where the trunk of a shapely sycamore serves as the central pillar of a canopied shelter, shaded by the branches. With its round roof of wooden posts, the shelter reminds us of a market cross, and has within it a seat, round the tree trunk, in memory of a boy of 17. The small church in lancet style has an oak panel with a finely carved border of roses in memory of one of the Duncombes, and a marble panel with a beautiful woman in a wealth of drapery. She is Lilian Duncombe who was 34 when she died in 1904.

She belonged to the family of the Earls of Feversham, whose great house, known as Nawton Tower, is nearly 3 miles away.

Nether Silton. It has a fine hall in a frame of trees, a green from where we get a wonderful view of the Hambleton Hills, on which the tiny village stands, and a small modern church which shelters a massive Norman font adorned with a bold band of cable, a carved Jacobean chair, and altar-rails with twisted balusters, made from the wood of H.M.S. *Dreadnought* of Lord Nelson's day.

A magnificent view of the hills and the plain is seen from a great monolith standing in a field by the church. On the stone is cut a puzzling inscription of which only the first letters of the words are given. Three lines are said to mean:

Here the grand old manor house stood,
The black beams were oak, the great walls were good,
The walls of the east wing are hidden here.

But it is difficult to find a meaning for the other lines, which are:

ATCLABWHEY
AD 1765
AWPSAYAA

Part of the old house stands, a farm with mullioned windows in gabled walls.

Newby Wiske. The road from South Otterington is carried over the River Wiske by a graceful old bridge of five arches, and the delightful old cottages, with ivied walls and in gay little gardens, are facing the fine yew hedge and luxuriant trees of the park. The stone hall in the park is said to have been begun when Charles II was king and can be seen from the road.

Newton-in-Cleveland. It has only a handful of houses, an inn, and a small church, but its place under Cleveland's famous hill gives it distinction. Perched on the western edge of the moorland plateau above the green plain near the Tees, Roseberry Topping rises 1057 feet above the sea, shaped like a cone of which the top is blunted through having been quarried for stone. Climbed from Newton (or more easily from Great Ayton), it has from the top a magnificent panorama of the countryside, reaching to Yorkshire's western fells, over Middlesbrough and the Tees to Durham, and beyond the harbour far out to sea.

Restoration has been kind to the little church of nave and chancel with massive walls, a tiny porch which seems to be old except for its roof, and a sturdy tower of 1901 which has a stone screen within it. The Norman chancel arch has at each side a tiny peephole, one of them only about four inches wide. The beautiful Norman font is enriched with arcading and cable moulding. St Oswald and a youthful St Christopher are in two of the windows.

Several interesting old stones are in the walls outside. One of two in the tower shows a dragon preening its wings; the other has two animals fighting, one like a wolf, the other a dragon with a head at the end of its tail. Engraved on a coffin-lid over the entrance to the porch is a cross, the shaft resting on a dog which is on the top of the steps forming the base. By the porch are a stone coffin and a lid with a cross.

Newton-upon-Ouse. We should come in the spring when the glory of the cherry trees is a sight to be remembered, or in autumn to see the splendour of Beningbrough Park in red and gold. The park is now in the care of the National Trust and is open to the public.

The park is bounded on two sides by the Ouse and the Nidd, which meet at its southern corner. To the north lies Newton, whose old-time quiet has been enlivened by the coming of an aerodrome at Linton a mile away. Between the two villages the Ouse is joined by the little River Kyle, which has gathered the streams flowing through Linton Woods.

The churchyard has a fine lychgate and a wide view over the great Plain. In the middle of last century the church was rebuilt except for its Norman tower, from which a graceful spire with flying buttresses rises to 150 feet. The lofty arch of the tower is the most impressive feature within, its massive half-pillars crowned with great capitals. A bell is 500 years old, and a lovely silver chalice is Elizabethan. There are magnificent brass portraits of Viscount Downe of 1846 and his wife, he wearing clerical robes with two lions at his feet, she a bonnet, with her feet on a cushion and a dog to guard her.

Normanby. It is the Normanby in the green Vale of Pickering, sheltering under a hillock by the road winding from Kirbymoorside to Malton. The small bellcote church facing the smithy looks rather new outside with rebuilding and restoration, but its old age is apparent within. The doorway through which we enter has a few of its Norman stones. The nave arcade is Norman but much restored; the font has a Norman bowl, and in the porch and the nave are frag-

The abbey from the south-east

Rievaulx

Inside the refectory

The Esplanade

Scarborough

The town, the beach and the castle

ments of Norman carving, Saxon crosses, and mediaeval gravestones. The fine 14th century chancel arch has capitals sadly hacked
away, but showing dragons and leaves and a face. The altar-rails
are Jacobean, and a quaint old almsbox is shaped like a baluster.

Northallerton. The home of a few thousand folk, it has a medley
of old houses and shops and inns along the broad street, one of the
finest churches in the Riding (of which it is the capital), and
memories of far-off days.

The Romans had a settlement here, and a small Roman altar was
found when the railway was made. The Conqueror is believed to
have encamped here, and to have built a fortress on Castle Hills.
The castle was destroyed but in the 12th century a palace was built
nearer the church. Five centuries after this also was in ruins, and all
that is left of it are traces of the moat and earthworks. We see them
in the cemetery.

Near the 19th century cross in the market-place is the town's oldest
house, which has long been an inn, the Old Fleece; its stone walls,
two timber gables, and great oak beams charmed Charles Dickens.
There are many interesting old buildings about the church, which
stands finely at the spacious north end of the town, with small greens
and trees about it. One is the grammar school, with memories going
back 600 years. The scholars attend a new school now, but the old
one has a roll of notable scholars. Here were taught John Kettlewell,
a 17th century writer of great charm; John Radcliffe, the doctor who
dared to tell Queen Anne that there was nothing wrong with her;
Thomas Burnet, Latin scholar; Thomas Rymer, historian; George
Hickes, master of many languages, who came here with the brother
who was executed for joining Monmouth's rebellion; and William
Palliser, who left his desk for the pulpit and became an archbishop.

Facing the school is a house with wide bay windows, its name
(The Friarage) reminding us that there were once several religious
houses in the town. The small brick almshouse known as Maison
Dieu has a 15th century foundation, and the Rutson hospital was
founded in 1876 in the lovely old house with a vine growing over its
walls; the trunk of the vine is 4 feet round and some of the branches
are 100 feet long.

Opposite the church is the Porch House, attractive with its ivied brick walls and pantiled roofs, and a stone porch so small that we must bend our heads as we enter. Charles I must have stooped to enter, for he was twice a guest and once a prisoner here.

The church, dignified and impressive without and within, has the shape of a cross, and its central tower, built in the 15th century and rising grandly to its pinnacled crown, is a landmark dominating the town. The chancel has been made new, but the rest is Norman and mediaeval.

The Normans built the sturdy north arcade of the nave, and the doorway in the west wall. From the 13th century come the tilting south arcade, the beautiful south doorway, and the two transepts. In the gable of the north transept is an oval window. The south transept has an old sundial, and there is a stone coffin by the gabled porch. There are fragments of Norman stones and Saxon crosses, an old gravestone built into the west wall, a stout ironbound chest, a wonderful table with an inlaid star, a chair on which two cherubs are holding a crown, part of an old screen with pinnacled buttresses, and on a pillar a curious engraving of a man's head in a wig, probably 18th century. The font, its pinnacled cover, and a carved chair are Jacobean. There are fine modern roofs, red stones telling of fire when the Scots burned and plundered the town 600 years ago, and two saints under lovely canopies by the east window. Very fine soaring arches support the tower.

Two miles away on the road to Darlington is a stone obelisk in memory of the Battle of the Standard fought here in 1138, taking its name from the curious standard raised by the English; it was the mast of a ship, fastened to a carriage on four wheels, having at the top of the mast a pyx containing the Host. A bronze shield showing the singular standard is on the monument. It was here that the barons of the north met the Scots whom they had determined to drive out of England. The English are said to have left their horses a mile behind so that retreat was impossible, and the Scots, under King David, came riding into battle on their famous Galloway ponies. The Scots gave a great shout when the battle began, but the English archers shot high into the air so that a rain of arrows destroyed 12,000 of the enemy. It was a complete defeat.

North Otterington. Nearer to Northallerton than its twin village, it has a small squat church with one or two old houses for company, looking west over the Wiske meadows, and east to the Hambleton Hills. Built in the 12th century and made partly new, it has a few carved Saxon stones, a Norman doorway and traces of a Norman window in the chancel, and a doorway built when the Norman style was passing, sheltered by an old porch which has on its walls marks like those caused by the sharpening of tools or weapons. Near it is a scratch dial. The stout 14th century arcade leads to a narrow aisle with 15th century windows and a piscina, and a low mediaeval arch leads to the long chancel which has two low side windows, and a curious wall about three feet high projecting at the east end.

Norton-le-Clay. A small place with a few farms and cottages and a brick church of 1840. On the wall of a house with a pantiled roof is a stone inscription to a Belgian refugee, who is described as a noble woman.

Nunnington. Grey houses above the lovely River Rye, and a beautiful avenue of sycamores climbing almost to the top of the green hill known as Caukleys Bank, belong to old Nunnington which has charming views of hills and dales. There are quaint buildings founded by Ranald Graham as almshouses and a school in the 17th century, and a hall stands on the site of a nunnery. Made new in the 17th century, the hall is a charming picture with its gabled walls, mullioned windows, and clustered chimneys, standing amid smooth lawns and noble trees by the old bridge over the river. It has memories of the Grahams whose memorials are in the church which guards the village from its high place on the hill. It is now occasionally open to the public.

With stately firs for company, it is a fine little restored church of the 13th century, with a tower of 1672 resting on a modern arch. The mediaeval door still swings on its original fleur-de-lys hinges, and the old font, like a pillar, has a lid as old as the Jacobean pulpit. Within a recess in the nave lies the stone figure of a knight with crossed legs, Sir Walter Teye, whose fighting days were done in 1325.

Wearing chain mail, he holds a heart, and the lion at his feet has a paw resting on his sword.

A marble memorial in the chancel reminds us of Sir Richard Graham, Viscount Preston, who finished an adventurous career in 1695. A friend of Charles II, and ambassador at the brilliant court of Louis XV, he plotted to restore the Stuarts to power after William and Mary came to the throne. In 1690 he was on a secret mission to France when he was captured and brought back to England where, after being condemned to death, he was imprisoned till he gave the names of other conspirators. He spent the last five years of his life at Nunnington Hall and sleeps in the church.

Another Royalist sleeping here is William Widdrington, a friend of the Old Pretender, who has a memorial in the nave. Like Richard Graham, whose sister he married, he narrowly missed execution, his plea being that he was the last to take up arms in the rebellion of 1715, and the first to put them down.

Nunthorpe. A little neighbour of Great Ayton, it has a few old houses shaded by trees, the great house (Grey Towers) in its park, and a 20th century church in solitary setting on the hill. Conspicuous in its view of the ragged line of the Cleveland Hills are Roseberry Topping rising over 1000 feet, and the obelisk to Captain Cook crowning Easby Moor.

As simple and beautiful as any within 50 miles, the church, built of lovely golden stone, is shaped like a cross, with a central tower and a west porch. It is a picture of solidarity and strength, well fitting its place near the rugged moors. There are fine arches supporting the tower, and others at each side of the chancel. Graceful lancet windows filling it with light, and the rich-hued oak of the massive benches, the pulpit, and the lectern, all contribute to a harmonious whole.

Old Byland. At the head of a ravine in the Hambleton Hills, running to the River Rye, it has grey cottages by the wide sloping green. Hiding behind the cottages is the tiny church, old enough to have been given in 1143 to the monks who had left the brotherhood at Furness Abbey nine years before to found a colony at Calder in

Cumberland. After several years there and a few more at Hode near Thirsk, they came to Old Byland and built here a cell, but finding the nearness of Rievaulx Abbey a disturbing factor (for each monastery could hear the sound of the other's bells over the river), they moved on again in 1147 to Stocking near Kilburn, finally ending their long wanderings when they built Byland Abbey 30 years later. Their cell at Old Byland became a grange, and is said to survive in the old farmhouse known by this name on the other side of the ravine.

The church is very quaint with its low chancel and higher nave, the eaves of which are only just topped by the tower, which is barely nine feet square outside. Most of the tower is modern (as is the east end of the chancel), but its doorway has a Norman arch, and a band at each side of it with Norman carving of two winged dragons, their tails knotted, and two capitals with star pattern, knotwork, and a face. The belfry has an original window with twisted pillars and a sill patterned with diaper. On the east wall of the tower is a Saxon sundial with an inscription upside down, meaning probably Huscarl made me for Sumerlethi.

Most of the windows are 15th century; one in the chancel, like the Norman doorway beside it, has an oak lintel. The fine Norman chancel arch is narrow and massive, and carved at the top of the capitals of its simple shafts are little men with scrolls on their heads, reminding us of the horns of a ram. The low round font is Norman; another old font has a cover like a dunce's hat. On the old oak roof is a boss carved with a man's head.

Old Malton. A charming little spot a mile from Malton itself, it has long been a place of pilgrimage for all who love old stones. The yellow houses and the thatched cottages are prettily strung along the road, and between the road and the River Derwent winding through the meadows are two delightful companions—the church of St Mary in a trim churchyard and the gabled Abbey House standing in a bright garden with trimmed yews.

St Mary's is a striking fragment of the Gilbertine priory founded by Eustace FitzJohn in the middle of the 12th century. It is only a part of the original church, and is almost all that remains of the priory, though there still survives in the Abbey House a vaulted chamber which was under the refectory, and several of the houses here are said to have been built with the old materials.

The church we see consists of six bays of the old nave, with its west front and the tower. The aisles and the clerestory have gone, but the arcades and the triforium are still in the walls, and the beauty of what is left helps us to imagine how splendid the ancient church must have been with its west and central towers, its transepts with their eastern chapels, and an aisled choir. In the scant remains outside the church are the foundations of the north-west tower, fragments of the nave aisles, and the western piers of the central tower destroyed 300 years ago. By these piers are four stone coffins, one of enormous length, and one (with a cross inside) for a child. On the south side is the doorway to the cloisters, and on the north is a Norman doorway, carved with zigzag and beak-heads.

Except for the big 15th century window in the west front, and the fine restoration of half a century ago, the church comes chiefly from Norman days and the 13th century. The late 12th century work is seen in the south arcade (with later clustered shafts in the western bays), and the three eastern arches of the north arcade. Of the same time is the lovely triforium over all these arches—a series of round arches, each enclosing two small pointed ones and separated by lancet openings. The rest of the north arcade was refashioned in the 15th century, when the wall above it was enriched with blind arcading. The original pillar still stands at the meeting of the two periods, but is encased in 15th century panelling. On this pier, and on the angel corbels at the west end, is the rebus of Prior Bolton, a bolt and a tun.

The only remaining tower is a beautiful feature of the west front, where the 13th century style is seen in the pointed arches of arcading and windows, resting on banded shafts. A charming touch are the quatrefoils in circles over the belfry windows. Under the 15th century west window is a beautiful 12th century doorway, looking curiously grimy and black compared with the rest of the building, though its detail is wonderfully preserved. The round arch is adorned with zigzag, flowers, and other ornament, and the capitals of the six banded shafts at each side are carved with stiff leaves. The stout oak door for which it is a frame has traceried panels, and the little mouse proclaiming it to be the work of Mr Thompson of

156

Kilburn. We see the mouse again on the beautiful pulpit and lectern.

In the quaint carving of the rich modern stalls are angels, animals, grotesques, a man hewing down a tree, a miser putting a bag of money into a chest, men fighting a lion, and the spies with the grapes. Carved on the misericords of the few massive old stalls are a rabbit, an eagle, a griffin, an owl, and a dromedary. There are fragments of old gravestones, a battered 14th century niche on a nave pillar, and two fine brass candelabra hanging in the chancel.

In the churchyard sleeps Charles Smithson, who was only 39 when he died. One of the best friends Charles Dickens ever had, he lived in the lovely old house known as Easthorpe Hall, three miles west of Malton. There was no spot in England Dickens loved more, and he has left us a record of happy days spent in this green corner of the world where he heard the sound of birds all day long. Charles Smithson was the lawyer who helped Dickens to concoct what they called a pious fraud, a plot in which they brought into the world an imaginary boy whom Dickens was to send to a Yorkshire school, all an excuse for his visits to some of the schools he afterwards wrote about in Nicholas Nickleby. A sad day it was for Dickens when he stood by the open grave of his friend in the shadow of this old church.

Old Richmond. A few green mounds where a village stood long centuries ago, separated from Durham by the River Tees, Old Richmond is silent and deserted now, but a sentinel keeps watch over the site of the vanished hamlet, a pathetic ruin to which few pilgrims come. An old bridge and a lonely track bring us to all that is left of St Laurence's chapel, built in the 13th century. Perched above the river, some of its walls are about ten feet high. There is a kitchen with two fireplaces and a great chimney rising forlorn above the tiniest of churches. The stone aumbry is still here, and there are little lancet windows, three of them in the east wall from which the altar has been torn away. Close by is a small round dovecote of ancient stones.

Ormesby. Magnificent trees, especially beeches, are the glory of this village of yellow cottages, near the fine park of Ormesby Hall, and an inn by the highway where we look across the plain to the Tees and the Durham hills. Built by the daughter of an 18th century Archbishop of Canterbury, the hall has long been the home of the Pennymans, and still is. It is recorded that a Pennyman of Charles I's day wept in Parliament when asked to give evidence against Strafford, but he was a fine soldier, and fought for the king at Edgehill. Another Pennyman was a mystic who declared that he heard voices, as did Joan of Arc. It is occasionally open to the public.

A lychgate opens to a pretty causeway which carries us over the tiny stream, flowing between steep banks, to the church with a tower of golden stone crowned by a shingled spire. Most of it is new, but there is old masonry on the south, and built into the walls outside are fragments of old coffin-lids, crosses, and Saxon carving. There is also an ancient stone figure of an unknown woman. A stone coffin, old capitals, and the broken bowl of a font are in the churchyard. There are windows, a screen, and a reredos in memory of the Pennymans, and the font cover is like a tower and spire with its pinnacles.

Osbaldwick. The red-roofed houses gather by the green, and a green mound tells of the days when a Saxon chief had a fortress here, protected by a moat. A stream which ran by it is still flowing through the village, crossed by small bridges. Restoration has not robbed the plain church of its ancient walling outside, a doorway with two round arches (one seen inside the church), and a bull's-eye window in the west gable. The pulpit is said to have been in York Minster 300 years ago.

At Murton, a mile away, the ruined shell of an old chapel has been restored, and has a small Norman window.

Osmotherley. It is a surprisingly big village to find high up in a cleft of the Hambleton Ridge, with the Cleveland Hills rising grandly in the east, and the Cod Beck, fresh from Osmotherley Moor, flowing in the valley.

Along the green-bordered road are many stone houses, and by the old village cross is a stone table on five pillars which was probably used as a market stall, and served John Wesley for a pulpit. There is a story that a Roman Catholic priest invited him to this out-of-the-way spot, and we know that soon afterwards one of the first Methodist chapels in the land was built here. A simple place with 1754 over the doorway, we come to it through a cobbled alley.

The church has a 15th century tower and porch, and a long nave and chancel with mediaeval walls, probably on Norman foundations. The south aisle and its arcade were added in the restoration of 1892, during which the foundations of a Saxon apse were discovered. There are fragments of Saxon crosses and part of a hogback in the porch, which has marks as of sharpening tools on its entrance. The Norman doorway has an arch with zigzag and beak-heads, but two of its shafts have been renewed. The old strap hinges are on the door. The font is Norman. The fine chancel arch, made new at the close of the 14th century, is unusual for its clustered shafts, rising from above the floor level. The south chapel, opening from the chancel by two arches, was built 400 years ago as a resting-place for Sir James Strangeways and his wife. An earlier Sir James, in the reign of Edward IV, was Speaker of the House of Commons.

A mile or two north of the village starts the Lyke Wake Walk, a 40-mile trek across the North Yorkshire Moors. The idea originally came from Bill Cowley, who farms near Potto, who planned a walk to traverse the highest parts of the North Yorkshire Moors from Osmotherley to Ravenscar at the coast, without touching civilisation. The walk, one of the finest in the North of England, goes through magnificent country, full of all manner of interest; it touches the highest point of the moors at Botton Head, uses part of the old Rosedale railway, passes several of the old crosses in which the moors abound, follows the old jet miners' track for part of the way to the coast, includes a nature reserve, Fen House Bogs, and, near the end, goes very close to the mysterious radomes on Fylingdales Moor. To qualify for the highly successful Lyke Wake Club one is supposed to do the walk in under 24 hours.

Oswaldkirk. It has an ancient church, and memories of two famous men. The antiquarian Roger Dodsworth was born in 1585 at West Newton Grange close by. He lived through the troublous years of the Civil War, but paid little heed to Royalist or Roundhead, preferring to go on with his patient studies in the cloisters of England. He was the chief compiler of the *Monasticon Anglicanum*. The 160 volumes comprising his own work and the original manuscripts he collected, now treasured in the Bodleian Library, are a monumental achievement of great value.

In the fine little church, where Roger Dodsworth was baptised, Archbishop Tillotson is said to have preached his first sermon while visiting the rector in 1661. It was the beginning of a remarkable career which was to make him the most fearless and outspoken preacher of Restoration times.

He may have preached in this pulpit, for it is Jacobean, and the church itself is much as it was in his day. The nave has Norman and 13th century walling on Saxon foundations, with a Norman slit, dainty mediaeval windows, a blocked Norman north doorway with the head of a stoup beside it, and a south doorway of about 1500 which has two capitals 300 years older. Under a crude round-headed recess in the nave is a coffin-lid engraved with a cross and a sword. Part of another gravestone is built into the old priest's doorway, and one with a crozier (in the sanctuary) may have rested over the bones of an abbot of Byland. With the old stones in the porch are two Saxon fragments, one carved with plaitwork, the other with the Madonna and Child. There are a few old glass fragments, a picture of Queen Victoria with orb and sceptre in the 14th century west window, a good oak screen between the nave and chancel, and seven candelabra in the nave, round which runs the old stringcourse. An attractive feature are the three graceful arches at the west end, supporting the bell-turret.

Sheltered by trees and rocks at the end of the Hambleton Hills, the village has many old houses and gay gardens including the Malt Shovel Inn, which probably dates from the 18th century.

Over Silton. An adventurous little road climbs from the valley to this small place of far horizons, set on the Hambleton Hills. It has a few houses and cottages, a tiny school of 1844 now housing motor cars, and a small church with a bellcote and stone-tiled roof standing solitary in the fields. There is a mounting stone in the churchyard, and a mass dial on a buttress. The nave keeps its fine Norman doorway enriched with roll and zigzag mouldings, and the chancel, rebuilt in the 14th century, has a modern arch. The arms of the Scropes and the Nevilles are on the beams of the 15th century roof. The Norman font, like a square with the corners cut off, is one of the smallest we have seen, and has traces of crude carving. A trefoiled piscina niche has a projecting bowl, and an old bench-end, said to have been brought here from Bridlington Priory, has fine carving of delicate tabernacle work.

Patrick Brompton. The trees of the park shade this bit of the highway from Bedale, cottages nestle here and there, and on a bank stands the fine church, with the cream-walled inn at its gate. The tower was rebuilt last century, but the rest of the exceedingly lofty church is chiefly 12th, 13th, and 14th centuries.

Built in the last quarter of the 12th century, the beautiful north arcade shows the passing of the Norman style to the English—the pointed arches enriched with roll and zigzag moulding, the lovely eight-clustered pillars crowned with stiff leaf capitals. The first arches to be built were the eastern arcades; the three western bays on the south are 14th century. The chancel arch has a group of three arches above it; the chancel is an exquisite example of 14th century building and has a high place among the best work of its time. It is the crowning glory of the church, and the finest of three notable chancels hereabouts. A stringcourse runs under the splendid windows, over the charming sedilia and piscina, and over the recess in the north wall which may have been a founder's tomb and an Easter Sepulchre. A bishop and a priest are carved on the sedilia, and a splendid gallery of heads adorns the hoods of the windows. A king and a grotesque man support the brackets of canopied niches on each side of the great east window. A medley of 14th century glass fills a lancet in the north aisle, and an old shield is in a vestry window. The rood stairs are still here, and the top of an old pillar with a capital once served as a font. The doorway through which we come and go is from the 12th century.

Pickering. Above it are the rolling moors; below it is the wide Vale whose name it bears, the fertile plain about 30 miles long and 7 miles wide, which was in prehistoric times a huge lake formed by the water of ice-blocked streams from the enclosing hills. Near the remarkable Keld Head spring, in which the Costa Beck has its source half a mile west of the town, wooden piles and other traces of lake dwellings were found towards the end of last century.

There are narrow winding streets with an old-fashioned air, and a high road and a low road crossing the Pickering Beck, near which is the small Beck Isle Museum. But Pickering's fame is in its fine church and its castle. The church is a venerable pile on rising ground in the middle of the town, dominating the buildings about it, and crowned with a tower and spire which is a landmark over the plain. A stately and beautiful ruin on a commanding site to the north of the town, the castle crowns a steep escarpment above the Pickering Beck.

Rising from a churchyard reached by long flights of steps, and bordered by red-roofed cottages, the weathered old walls are adorned with 15th century battlements, and the great mediaeval porch, set at the top of a five-sided flight of steps, is as lovely an entrance as we could wish to find. Over its doorway is a sundial, and within it is a Jacobean almsbox.

The Saxon church which stood on this site was probably destroyed in the Conqueror's day, and its only remains are a carved fragment of a cross-shaft on a bracket in the south aisle, and probably the font, which was damaged in the Civil War and has had its base repaired.

The church we see has grown from the one the Normans built in the middle of the 12th century, giving it a nave and a north aisle, a chancel with an apse, and probably transepts and a central tower. Something of this early work still survives in the north arcade, showing a fine simplicity of style in the plain round arches and massive round pillars with scalloped capitals. About 1190 the south aisle and its arcade were built. Some of the pillars are eight-sided, and others have half-round shafts. At the same time the base of the tower was built, the rest of the tower and its spire belonging to the 14th century. So does the chancel with its rather odd arch, a piscina, and three fine sedilia with leafy gables, the capitals carved with fighting men and fighting dragons. From the 15th century come the clerestory of the nave and the Roucliffe Chapel on the south side of the chancel. The north transept was rebuilt and the south transept lengthened last century, but each has a 14th century arch. There are mediaeval coffin-lids, a battered stoup, a tower screen with 16th century panelling found in an inn, and beautiful modern woodwork in the chancel screen and the reredos. The chest may be Elizabethan. There are Georgian candelabra, and a Hepplewhite pulpit.

Restoration has made the chapel a fine setting for the worn and battered alabaster figures of Sir David Roucliffe and his wife, from the beginning of the 15th century. Angels are watching over them; a lion is at Sir David's feet, and two small dogs are tugging at Dame Margery's dress. Built in their memory, the chapel had an upper room for a priest, but the floor was removed in 1857, and it was used for a time as a school. In it is what is known as an Act of Parliament clock, made when Parliament taxed the small clocks in 1797.

Near the north transept lies the handsome figure of a knight, wearing an ornate sword-belt; his legs are crossed, a lion is at his feet, and angels are at his head. He was Sir William Bruce, who fought at Boroughbridge in 1322, and left an endowment for a chantry chapel which is thought to have stood on the north side of the chancel. The fragment of a stone figure near the pulpit recalls a famous name, for tradition says it represents John o' Gaunt.

Among many wall-monuments is an inscription to John and William Marshall, both notable agriculturists. William was building a College of Agriculture at Pickering when he died in 1818. There is a massive bronze with the names of men killed in the Great War.

Pickering folk are proud of an old tablet in the sanctuary paying tribute to Robert King and his son, who went from this place to help to plan the city of Washington. By the monument hang the British flag and the Stars and Stripes, the American flag having been given by a New York rector who had met Robert King's descendants during a visit to Pickering, and had preached in this church, where father and son prayed in the 18th century. One of two brass tablets commemorates the brotherhood in arms between Britain and America in 1917; the other is a memorial to Ambassador Page, unveiled in 1924 by Ambassador Kellogg. A fragment of old panelling near these memorials was given in memory of Henry Ware Clarke, an American of Yorkshire descent who fell in the Great War.

It was between 1450 and 1460 that the church was given what is today its crowning glory—a gallery of magnificent wall paintings unequalled by any other church in Yorkshire, and by few anywhere.

Hidden for centuries under whitewash, and covered up again after accidentally coming to light in 1851, they were discovered about 1880 and have been restored to their old splendour of vivid colour, wonderful detail, and dramatic force. They completely fill the north and south walls of the nave, creeping between the arches and between the windows of the clerestory.

At the west end of the north wall is a fine St George in armour, riding a white horse and slaying the dragon. Next to him is Christopher, the traveller's saint, stepping ashore as he leans on his sprouting staff and bears the Child on his shoulder. There is a serpent round his leg, and the head of a sea monster behind him; then come three scenes in one, telling the story of Herod's feast and the martyrdom of St John the Baptist. We see the king with Herodias and courtiers at the table, while Salome dances for their delight, and the saint stands by in disapproval. At the execution of St John Salome waits with the charger; and Salome brings the bearded head to the king. After this are two pictures one above another. One is a striking scene of four archers riddling St Edmund with arrows; the other shows the martyrdom of Thomas Becket, who kneels at the altar while the faithful Edward Grim holds up his hand as if to keep back the four knights, who are drawing their swords.

A fine group of paintings on the south wall are scenes from the life of Catherine of Alexandria. They show her rebuking the Emperor Maximinus for worshipping idols; an angel protecting her when she is put in prison; the conversion of the Emperor's wise men as they hear her defence of Christianity; St Catherine's second imprisonment, her scourging, and whipping, and the visit to her of the converted empress; the torture of the saint on the wheel with sharp spikes; and the executioner with sword upraised to strike off her bowed head. There are fascinating strips of pictures showing the Seven Acts of Mercy, and seven scenes from the Passion of Our Lord. Another scene is of Our Lord's Descent into Hades, with Adam and Eve coming to meet Him from the mouth of a dragon. Angels are with Him as He rises from the tomb in a Resurrection scene, and the soldiers are falling back in amaze.

Like the church, Pickering Castle takes us back to Norman days, though much of what remains is 14th century. The battered grey walls are indeed a romantic sight, crowning a deep moat (now a green dell), rising from lovely carpets of lawn and crowning a noble mound lightly draped with ash and sycamore trees and nearly 700 feet round at the base.

Protected on one side by the steep rocky banks above the Pickering Beck, the whole area has the shape of a rough triangle about 500 feet long and 350 feet wide, enclosed by massive broken walls and towers, and divided into two wards by a stout curtain wall which ascends to the mound in the middle of the site.

The Conqueror is believed to have founded the inner ward, and Henry II replaced the original timber defences with stone. The stone walls of this outer ward, with the entrance gateway and three towers, belong to the 14th century. So do the fragmentary walls of the stone keep on top of the mound. Mill Tower, at the south-west corner of the triangle, rises above the stream. Rosamund's Tower has a prison in the basement. Devil's Tower, at the north-east end of the curtain wall, has doorways in the basement leading to the inner and outer moats.

Much of the Norman wall still stands, and a thrilling climb up the rough flight of steps on the top of it is rewarded by a fine panorama from the keep. Near a blocked Norman doorway stands the 13th century chapel of St Nicholas, new-roofed but a chapel no more.

The castle belongs to the Duchy of Lancaster, and it was long the custom of the Steward of the Duchy to ride down to the market-place to proclaim the Fair. King John was often here, and within these walls Richard II was a prisoner before being done to death at Pontefract—while he was longing for a little grave, or to be buried in the king's highway. In the Civil War the castle was besieged and suffered much damage. On the other side of the Beck is a lofty circular hill crowned with an earthwork.

One of the men Pickering remembers was Francis Nicholson, who won fame as an artist and is known as the Father of English Water Colour Painting. He was born here in 1753, and died in 1844. Other notable men of the town were Ralph Dodwer, who left to make a fortune in London and became Lord Mayor in 1521; James Calvert, who went out to take the Gospel to Fiji; and John Costillo, whose stone is in the Methodist graveyard. A poet who loved this corner of Yorkshire, he wrote dialect poems of much charm, and a verse of one of them is on his stone:

> *Bud noo his een's geean i' deeath,*
> *Nera mare a pilgrim here on eearth.*
> *His sowl flits fra her shell beneeath,*
> > *To reealms o' day,*
> *Whoor carpin care an pain an deeath*
> > *Are deean away.*

Pickhill. It lies serenely in Swale meadows, the church set finely on a knoll above a green hollow where a bridge crosses the brook.

A sturdy 15th century tower crowns the church, which has splendid old work to show. An imposing oak porch with an open gable and traceried sides shelters a lovely Norman doorway with rich zigzag ornament; and a door with charming hinges opens to the trim interior of cream walls and rich mottled stone. Like the doorway, the tall Norman chancel arch has zigzag and scalloped capitals, and from each side of it runs a carved stringcourse; the arch is a fine frame for the modern screen. Other fine carving is in the reredos, with a scene of the Road to Calvary. On an old oak beam are faces, foliage, and a hare, and preserved beneath the altar is the stone altar of mediaeval days.

The nave arcade, with big arches on delicate clustered shafts, is 13th century. The chancel is about 1280. The chapel has a piscina in a peephole, and the base of a font of 1662 may be mediaeval. In a collection of ancient stones are fragments of small Norman pillars and Saxon crosses, and parts of two hogbacks, one carved with knotwork, one with a dragon. A battered stone knight in chain mail, with his sword and shield, may be Sir Andrew Neville of 1295. The railway goes over the foundations of his old home, which was the castle built by the Constables.

Raskelf. The moorland near by is well known to botanists for rare gentians and orchids, and the famous White Horse, seven miles away on a slope of the Hambleton Hills, is seen from the village. There are cottages in gardens with trim hedges in the long street ending at the church. Quaint and oddly-shaped, it is much rebuilt

A painting on the screen
in Hornby Church

The sermon glass in Croft Church

A carving on the reredos
of the chapel in Snape Castle

Pickering Castle

Thwaite

but some of it goes back to the 12th century, and its surprising possession, the only tower in Yorkshire built of wood from ground to summit, is about half as old. It is a plain square tower with a fine weathercock on its pyramid cap.

The wide nave has a north arcade of two bays with great capitals, built when the Norman style was passing. The unusual chancel, as wide as the nave, has a modern roof with massive beams, and is entered by an oak arch with carved spandrels and a black-and-white gable. Its rare feature is an old wooden arcade of two bays leading to the north chapel. There is old heraldic glass in the chancel.

The altar-rails and the cover of the Norman font are 17th century, and there are about a dozen simple old bench-ends in the modern seats. Three old bells hang in the tower, and remains of the old cross are in the churchyard.

In the church is a tribute to Augustus Cavendish Webb who found his immortality at the Charge of the Light Brigade, cheering his men as they rode into the terrible Valley of Death.

Ravensworth. Its houses and inns are gathered in pleasant fashion round a fine green. It is like a meadow on a sunny slope with farmyard animals keeping it trim, and has the base of an old cross under the strangest of sycamore trees. On the edge of the village are the broken walls and roofless tower of a castle, with part of a gateway, green mounds, and a dry moat. It is in Scott's *Rokeby*. The Normans are said to have rebuilt a Saxon stronghold here, but the ruins are of the mediaeval seat of the Fitzhughs who fought the Scots, made pilgrimages to Palestine, and are said to have been friendly with Henry V.

Here was born in 1739 a cobbler's son who became in turn schoolmaster, actor, poet, and journalist, Cuthbert Shaw. Although he wrote some verse of merit, dissipation barred his way to success and he died in squalor in London at 32.

Redcar. Like Coatham, with which it joins hands, Redcar is an old fishing village turned holiday-town for the workers by the Tees. The magnificent beach is a promenade of firm sands, extending on one hand towards Marske, and beyond Coatham to the huge South

Gare Breakwater at the mouth of the river. There are reefs of rocks forming natural breakwaters, a spacious esplanade, and an iron pier.

Redcar's broad main street has a few old houses. The attractive part of the 19th century church is the chancel, with an arcade at each side opening to a chapel. The altar is richly draped, and the great reredos, dazzling with colour and gold, has fine traceried panels with the Madonna and Child and six saints—Cuthbert, Hilda, Aidan, Wilfrid, Oswald, and Columba. On the rich panelling in the sanctuary is the little mouse of Robert Thompson of Kilburn. We read of a soldier of 20 who died in the Libyan Desert, and of Robert Carter who gave his life for a friend.

At Red Barnes House there lived for many years Gertrude Bell, one of the most astonishing women of our time. In an inscription to her memory unveiled in 1935 by her brother she is described as scholar, traveller, administrator, peacemaker, and friend of the Arabs.

In a small museum on the sea front are many curios, models of sailing ships, and a lifeboat, the *Zetland*, said to be the oldest in the world.

Redmire. One of the lovely villages in a richly wooded patch of Wensleydale, it shelters under Redmire Scar and looks to Penhill across the Ure, here a broad river tumbling over ledges of rock in the charming waterfall known as Redmire Force. The road along the hills from Wensley, running by Bolton Park and under Preston Scar, gives us entrancing views of the dale.

The houses are in gay gardens, and on one of several little greens are the steps and base of the old cross with a new pillar. Near it is a fine sycamore walled round, and the great trunk of a curious oak growing in a cottage garden leans on its wall and shades the road with half of its branches.

Down a lane we come to the simple little church, built within sound of the river eight centuries ago. The walls are stout, and the oddly-shaped bellcote is crowned with a cross. The Norman doorway has a hood enriched with zigzag, scalloped capitals, and one of the original carved shafts. There are old oak roofs, and one of the red and gold bosses is carved with flowers and tracery. The crude Norman font is on a worn step, there is a curious Norman mass dial, and high up across a corner of the nave is a big stone with carving of scroll, flowers, and a cross.

Reeth. Clustering round the spacious green on a sunny slope are the grey old houses and inns of this little Swaledale town, reached from Richmond by two lovely roads—the low road through the valley, the older road over the hills. From the war memorial on the green we see all the grandeur of its setting, with wooded hills and bare moorland heights on every hand, their heads often lost in clouds. At the foot of the hill the Arkle Beck flows on its way to the Swale. Old lead mines tell of vanished prosperity in this country-side whose scenes Turner loved.

Richmond. It is the capital of Swaledale. An ancient place where old ways are cherished and old legends remembered, and with the spirit of days gone by imprisoned in a peerless castle, it has river and cliff, rocky crags and beautiful woods, and it is famous in history and song.

Set amid some of the most enchanting scenery in the north of England, this old town has been immortalised by Turner. Coming down from the lonely moors, the Swale sweeps grandly along its superb valley and by the crag where the castle stands. We should see the fortress from the path near the grand old bridge, the vast pile of masonry crowning sheer walls of rock. One of the many fine views of the little town climbing the hill is seen from the enchanting river-side walk to Easby Abbey, which was a house of prayer when Rich-mond Castle was the home of fighting men. Another fine view is from the south bank of the river facing the castle, where the slight remains of St Martin's Priory have farm buildings for company. The monastery was founded about 1100 by the steward of Alan, Earl of Richmond, for a few Benedictine monks from St Mary's Abbey, York; there is still a Norman doorway in fragments of old walling by a cowshed, and a small embattled tower of the 15th century.

A romantic town indeed. Its fortress was so strong that no army dare besiege it. Here are memories of knights and priests, and of a captive King of Scotland. Here Frances I'Anson lived at a house where Leonard MacNally saw her, fell in love with her, and wrote his famous song *The Lass of Richmond Hill*.

There is (of course) the tale of a drummer boy who was lowered down the castle well and went drumming along a passage till his drumming ceased and he was never seen again; and there is the tale they tell of simple Potter Thompson, who found a cave under the castle and came to a chamber where King Arthur lay sleeping with his knights.

We shall hardly find in England a town reminding us more vividly of the Middle Ages. Here are passages between houses crowded on ledges of rock, buildings as surprising as anything at Staithes or Robin Hood's Bay. The streets are cobbled, and many of them have peeps of the castle. The market-place, the heart of Richmond, is steep and roughly cobbled, and round it are houses which have stood for centuries, making a sort of wall in which the market-place is like the courtyard of the castle. The obelisk in the market replaced an ancient cross in the 18th century.

The town of old had walls and gates, and there is still a narrow postern leading into Bargate and down to the bridge, and another in the alley called Friar's Wynd. Tucked away in Friar's Wynd is a quaint building which was long a warehouse, but has been restored to its original function as a theatre. Built in 1788, it was used as a theatre until the 1840s, Kean, Kemble, and Macready appearing there. It is thus one of the two surviving Georgian theatres in England. Very tastefully restored, it has several plays performed each year in addition to solo performances by well-known artists.

Friar's Wynd brings us to one of the loveliest things in Richmond, an exquisite 15th century tower with a graceful archway through, and buttresses climbing to a pinnacled crown of open battlements. With the fragment of walling beside it, it is all that is left of the house of Grey Friars founded in 1258 by Ralph FitzRanulph, whose heart was buried here. The grounds have been made into a garden, and in it Richmond has set up one of its tributes to those who fell in the Great War, a cross on a base with a relief of a sailing ship, the Great Harry warship of Henry VIII. On the stone are the names of 99 men. The Celtic cross in Frenchgate was set up by the Green Howards in memory of 7500 of the regiment who gave their lives in the same war.

There are old stones everywhere. On Anchorage Hill is a small grey building like a church without a tower; it is the Bowes Alms-

house of James I's day, and in it are remains of the ancient chapel of
St Edmund. Of the ancient Hospital of St Nicholas there are slight
fragments in a house on the road to Easby.

In the spacious cobbled street called Newbiggin is the 19th
century Roman Catholic church dedicated to St Joseph and Francis
Xavier. It has richly carved and coloured Stations of the Cross,
with figures in mediaeval dress; a great stone reredos with figures of
Our Lord on the Cross, St Mary, and St John; a stone altar under
which lies a striking figure of Our Lord as in a tomb; a beautiful oak
altar in the lady chapel, made in Belgium; a font with quaint
carvings of the Crucifixion, the Baptism, a man with a fish, and a
dove bringing the olive leaf to Noah, who is at his window in the
Ark.

Richmond's strangest church is Holy Trinity in the market-place,
oddly mixed up with other buildings—its north aisle over shops,
houses on the site of the south aisle, and the tower separated from
the rest of the church by a building used as offices. The tower has a
Norman base and a 15th century top, and belongs to the Corporation, its bell ringing out the curfew morning and night. The chancel
was made new two centuries ago. There is a fine old almsbox of
black oak. The church is a public church no more, but has long
been used as the grammar school chapel.

There is more to see in the church of St Mary in Frenchgate,
rising from the hillside in a setting of great natural beauty. Behind it
are houses on the steep slope, and below is the river flowing under a
handsome stone bridge. The church seems to rise from a mass of
living green (chestnuts, hawthorns, and firs), and here in summer is
a loveliness enchanting even in Richmond, where beauty is a common
thing.

Ancient and modern craftsmen have made St Mary's a rare place,
where the new things are beautiful and the old things interesting.
The slender tower and the north porch are 15th century. The porch
has a vaulted roof with a boss showing a face with leaves coming
from its mouth, and shelters a doorway of the 12th century. The
western bay of each arcade is part of the 12th century church, the
stout pointed arches dwarfed by the other lofty bays. Carved on one
of the capitals are what seem to be a lamb and a donkey feeding, and
a big animal attacking a smaller one. There are fragments of 15th

171

century glass, a curious poorbox of 1547, and a picture of Christ before Pilate by a 16th century artist.

Between the south chapel and the aisle is one of the screens carved by Robert Thompson of Kilburn, whose little mouse is in one corner. In the chapel are sedilia, a piscina, and a fragment of wall painting from mediaeval days, and here too is a book with the names of the 7500 men of the Green Howards who gave their lives in the Great War. Hanging in the chapel are regimental colours greatly prized, a flag found in Richmond Castle in the 18th century, the colours of a Yorkshire battalion which fought in South Africa, and a flag of a battalion of Kitchener's Army. But nothing in Richmond, we imagine, stirs the mind or quickens the pulse more than the Mons banner hanging here, for it was carried at the London Albert Hall service in 1919 in memory of the first seven divisions which faced the German lines in 1914.

The chancel has beautiful modern stalls, and a splendid series of early 16th century stalls from Easby Abbey. Their tracery is tipped with roses, and in an elaborately carved band of vine and grape is a warning in Latin about the sins we should beware of—talking scandal, costly living, gossiping in the cloister, quarrelling in the chapter, and disorder in the choir. On the misericords are flowers and foliage, animals and birds, the most amusing of all showing an old pig playing bagpipes while the little pigs dance to the merry tune. There are many carved chairs from Jacobean days.

One of the most remarkable monuments in Yorkshire is in the chancel; it is dated 1629. Richly carved and gaily painted, it shows Sir Timothy Hutton and his wife kneeling on cushions under a canopy adorned with figures of the Madonna and Child and angels. Sir Timothy has his sword at his side, and his wife wears a black flowing gown. Very quaint is the row of 12 children, four in swaddling clothes and eight kneeling. Each child has a shield, and for each one there is a curious little rhyme.

There are parts of two old coffin-lids in the wall by the north porch, and a fine complete one with a cross and a chalice on the churchyard lawn.

We found here the gravestones of two Richmond men who fought at Waterloo, and here is the Plague Stone, a memorial to over a thousand people who died of plague 300 years ago. Another stone is to William Willance, who had a miraculous escape from death in 1606 at Whitcliffe, where a rugged scar stands out boldly against the sky. William and his horse are said to have gone over it one foggy night, the horse being killed, the rider living to tell the tale. Among the corporation plate is a chalice he gave in gratitude for his escape.

The fame of the town in ancient days, the Castle of Richmond, is still its pride and glory, the noblest ruin of its kind in Yorkshire, a mighty fortress on a mighty hill. Rising high above the market-place, crowning a crag above the river, more beautiful than Helmsley and more imposing than Scarborough, this stupendous pile of walls and towers has a grandeur unsurpassed by any fortress in the North.

The rock on which it stands is a natural stronghold, a triangle impregnable on two sides, and on the third defended against all invaders by a moat and wall. Begun by Earl Alan ten years after the Conquest, the castle was enlarged about 1146 by Earl Conan, who strengthened the walls and built what is the loftiest Norman keep in England.

We come first to the barbican, passing the site of vanished gate-ways. Much of the outer wall is as strong as when the Norman builders finished it. Robin Hood's Tower has three storeys, two with stone vaulted roofs of the Conqueror's century. On the ground floor is a little chapel with traces of arcading, and a small east window between two bull's-eyes. Beyond the fallen tower is a group of ruined 14th century buildings known as the Great Chamber and the Chapel, both with two storeys and roofless. There was a porch and a flight of steps leading to the chapel, and from the Great Chamber two doors opened into Scolland's Hall.

Scolland was an earl, and his hall, built before Domesday Book was finished, is one of the notable parts of the castle. In the base are narrow windows from which we look down on the beautiful castle walk with the river far below. The banqueting hall on the second floor was lighted by windows which are seen as a single arch within and as two lights divided by central shafts outside. Above the windows are the stone corbels on which the roof beams rested, some of them carved with faces.

The gateway to the Cockpit is here still, an ancient frame for the fair lawns and trees which now adorn this old courtyard, once an outer court of the castle, and still protected by a gateway and great walls. Over the inner gate are traces of the balcony from which the ladies of 800 years ago would watch the sport below. A Norman wall and part of a tower rise west of the great court. The south side was never strongly fortified, for the natural rock made it impossible for invaders to enter that way. Standing by the low Norman parapet we look down to the river or across the Great Court (now one of the most perfect lawns outside Oxford) to one more remarkable sight, the supreme wonder of Richmond.

It is the vast keep above the gateway, looking as if it had been built by giants rather than by men. With the exception of the White Tower in London and the Great Tower of Colchester Castle, we believe there has not survived from Norman England another pile of masonry so great as this.

Built above the Norman gateway, the keep rises 114 feet from the bottom of the moat. The simple archway in the south wall, the inner gateway of the Norman entrance to the castle, brings us to a ground floor with a stone roof built about 1330, but the immense central pillar is a century older and is built over a well. There is no Norman structure more nobly preserved, the stones inside and out almost as perfect as if eight years rather than eight centuries had passed over them. A modern flight of steps brings us to the only entrance to the keep, a south doorway opening to a great hall lit by three windows in walls 11 feet thick, the splays and windowsills so deep that the windows themselves are like small rooms. One of the remarkable things about the hall is the central pillar which comes up from the ground, and once carried the weight of the floor above.

What looks like a slanting tunnel in the solid wall brings us by many steps to the second floor, which has a fine room open to the roof and lit by east and west windows. Two rooms on this floor have windows giving peeps of the valley. Another flight of steps in the thickness of the wall goes up to a stair-head lit by two windows, and beyond this more steps bring us to the battlements, the most astonishing viewpoint in Swaledale. We look down on the narrow streets, the spacious market-place, and the river roaring like a cataract over its stony bed. All Richmond is at our feet.

Rievaulx. It has been said that Bolton Abbey is for the artist, Fountains for the historian, and Rievaulx for the poet. Except for

Tintern, there is no abbey in England that has been more beautifully touched by time or set in a more heavenly place. Lying in the valley of the Rye, as its name tells, it is set like a jewel in this romantic glen enfolded by heights of noble trees rising to the moors. Clustering by the ruins are pretty cottages with thatched and pantiled roofs, and on a bank above is the trim little church, its nave partly mediaeval, the chancel and the tower of our own century.

We have a thrilling sight of the upstanding fragments of the great abbey as we stand near the three-arched bridge across the shining river on its way to Duncombe Park, or as we stand on the marvellous green plateau above the ruin. Turner painted the abbey. Cowper was so enchanted by it that he wished he could live in sight of it for ever. Dorothy Wordsworth was spellbound by the spectacle.

What they saw and loved is for us a still nobler heritage, for the care of the Ministry of Works has been bestowed on the ruins for more than fifty years. Dorothy Wordsworth noted the singing of the birds and the wild flowers on the hillocks.

The first Cistercian abbey in Yorkshire, Rievaulx was founded in 1131 by Walter Espec, Lord of Helmsley. It flourished from the beginning, and sent out monks to found daughter houses; in a few years it had 140 monks and 600 lay brothers.

The ruins are of the church and the domestic buildings, all of which were more or less completed before the end of the 12th century, though the buildings on the south of the cloister were reconstructed about 1200, and in the next generation the presbytery, the tower, and the transepts were transformed. It is in this 13th century work that the glory of Rievaulx lies, its superb beauty being in striking contrast to the earlier work, which shows the absolute simplicity enjoined by Cistercian rule.

Owing to the slope of the land the church was set almost due north and south, with the presbytery facing south, but for simplicity of description we assume here that the usual points of the compass have been followed. The aisled nave of nine bays, 170 feet long and 800 years old, is said to have been the earliest Cistercian nave of great size in England; its plan is outlined in the smooth lawn, and there are fragments of its massive pillars, some are still as high as a man. There are traces of the Galilee, with several old gravestones, one having an inscription to 13th century Isabel de Roos. The five or six western bays of the nave were used by the lay brothers till their decline in the 14th century, when the screen walls between the nave piers were removed, and chapels were built in the aisles—four in the north aisle and two in the south. These chapels still have their altars and parts of the old tiled floors, and one has the gravestone of Abbot Burton, who died 500 years ago.

Rising almost to their full height, the two transepts are a patchwork of dark and light masonry, the darker and rougher stonework being as old as the nave. This Norman work is easily seen in the lower parts of their north, south, and west walls; and the 13th century rebuilding is plain in the light stone of the triforium and clerestory stages of the north transept, the clerestory of the south transept, and the whole of the two east ends, each with an aisle divided into two chapels. One of the chapels in the north transept has a fine vaulted roof. Below the group of three lancets in the north wall of this transept is a 13th century doorway which replaced a Norman doorway (now blocked) leading to the cemetery.

The perfection of the 13th century style is seen in the superb presbytery, with three tiers of lovely arcading in the north and south walls, and a double tier of three lancets in the east. Here the idea of plain severity was thrown to the winds, and the original short presbytery allowed by the rule was scrapped for this wonderful structure of seven bays, 145 feet long, a glory in stone with a profusion of exquisite mouldings and chaste ornament. At the foot of the triforium are corbels supporting the shafts of the vanished roof, those on the south rich with foliage. Part of the original stone marks the high altar, and beyond it are the bases of the altars of the five eastern chapels. At the west end is the eastern arch of the central tower, like a light stone bridge high above our heads. The two aisles have gone, but on the north are still fragments of the wall which supported the flying buttresses of the 14th century.

The cloister on the south of the nave is 140 feet square, and has in a corner a few bays of Norman arcading which opened on to the green. The 12th century range of the lay brothers lay on the western side of the cloister. On the eastern side are gravestones of some of the abbots, a coffin in which Abbot Ailred may have lain, and remains of a two-storeyed shrine believed to be of the first abbot St William, buried in 1148. He had been secretary to St Bernard of

Clairvaux. This eastern range was extended beyond the cloister till it reached a length of 320 feet from the south transept, and the whole of its upper floor served as the dormitory.

On the south of the cloister is the splendid refectory, raised on a vaulted basement. The finest fragment of the domestic buildings, it is 124 feet long and 38 wide, and stands between the kitchen and the warming house.

On the east side of the infirmary cloister is the infirmary itself, a fine 12th century building, 145 feet long, thought to have been adapted in the 16th century as the abbot's house, with his rooms at the north end and the kitchens at the south. It was then that the doorway from the infirmary cloister, with a battered sculpture of the Annunciation above it, was built.

In the museum is a rich collection of Norman and mediaeval fragments, including capitals, a niche with a panelled canopy, a fragment of moulding with a man and a woman who seem to be flying, and a winged demon looking at itself in a mirror. A fragment of a frieze shows a horse bringing sacks of corn to a windmill, a broken sculpture of Christ, and a fragment of Abbot William's shrine. Among bits of mediaeval glass are some with a very rare blue, and there are pieces of old timber, fragments of pottery, beads worn by the monks, and leather tanned in the vats we may still see among the domestic buildings.

Altogether it is a ruin which would be hard to match for its solitude and beauty; Rievaulx on the Rye and Tintern on the Wye are among the rarest treasures of our countryside.

Robin Hood's Bay. Shut in on the north by the promontory known as North Cheek (or Ness Point), the bay is fringed by low cliffs rising to 585 feet at the southern horn, South Cheek (or the Old Peak). From the cliffs the hills go on climbing to the moors. On nearby Fylingdales Moor are two extremes of old and new. On a high point stands Lilla Cross, erected in 626 as a memorial to Lilla, who shielded King Edwin with his own body from an attack by an assassin. It overlooks the three radomes of the Air Ministry Early Warning Station, built in 1961-2. Unhappily the very existence of much of the town is in jeopardy, owing to the alarming rate of coastal erosion hereabouts. Soft glacial clay, through which run many streams, provides the problem; a scheme is afoot to build a concrete wall to stabilise the clay, but it would be vastly expensive.

With its road from the sea very steep for cars, the town is one of the astonishing sights of the Yorkshire coast. The houses are built one above another, some seeming to overhang the cliff, others so near the sea (which at times comes roaring up the street) that a ship's bow-sprit once ran into the window of an inn. Narrow passages and sudden flights of steps thread among the houses. There are tiny gardens where the sun and the spray come together, arches giving us peeps of ships, and walls where we look down on chimneys and roofs. In the Methodist church the congregation sits above the choir. Fishing nets drying in the sun, lines and crab-pots, and rooms with the secret cupboards of old smugglers—all these we see at Bay Town.

Far up the long hill the old parish church stands solitary at 450 feet above the sea, looking out on the moors and down to the Bay from a churchyard packed with stout grey gravestones. A simple little building reminding us of a stone box, it has a quaint interior with galleries, and a three-decker pulpit rising in steps among the high pews. The Norman font, which was used here for many generations, and was then a drinking trough on a farm, is now a battered relic in the 70-year-old church of St Stephen at Fylingdales, where the new town has grown near the station.

Designed by G. E. Street, this striking and dignified church has a slender tower with a saddleback roof and a melodious peal of eight bells. A fine porch leads to the handsome interior. The chancel has an apse and a vaulted roof, and the arcade between the nave and its aisle has lovely capitals of natural foliage. On the altar shines a silver cross.

Two vicars here served from Trafalgar to the middle of the Great War. John Harrison, vicar for 55 years last century, has an inscription, and in memory of Robert Jermyn Cooper, whose ministry of 56 years ended in 1916, is a splendid bronze panel showing his portrait and a shepherd of the hills with his flock. The Te Deum window at the west end is in memory of Bishop Wilberforce, and a lancet in the tower has a blue-winged angel designed by Burne-Jones.

In the windows are pictures of Christ calling fishermen to be His

178

disciples, and the miraculous draught of fishes; and in memory of about 250 men of the Bay who have paid the toll of the sea is a striking bronze panel with sailing ships, a flight of seabirds, and six sailors carrying a dead comrade. A unique memorial is an inscription to Robin Hood Bay's first lifeboat, named after Ephraim and Hannah Fox. The lifeboatmen of Robin Hood's Bay are famous for their courage, and the story is remembered of a wreck in 1881 when, there being no lifeboat here and the seas being too rough to bring it from Whitby, they dragged the boat over the hills, let it down the cliff, and saved six men. The fishermen of the Bay were written of by Leo Walmsley, who lived here as a small child. The place has attracted many artists and we found Roger Murray working at one of his paintings of ships in his small studio, a converted bake-house.

Rokeby. The beauty of the scenery and the interesting things hereabouts are all described in Sir Walter Scott's *Rokeby*. The hall was the home of his friend John Bacon Morritt, traveller, scholar, and lover of beautiful things, and they spent days together walking and riding about this enchanting place.

Here comes the River Tees from a wooded gorge like a "mighty trench of living stone", and here comes the charming River Greta, both meeting at a corner of the glorious park, which they have bounded on two sides.

Above the Greta is the lovely Dairy Bridge of a single arch, and on the bank near by is the mediaeval Mortham Tower immortalised by Scott. The three rooks of the Rokeby shield are still on the weathered walls, and near the gateway to the small courtyard is a barn with a sundial of 1566.

In the park, with its noble sycamores, beeches, oaks, and magnificent silver firs, is the house Scott loved, built in the 18th century by Sir Thomas Robinson, who also built the beautiful Greta Bridge at the south gate of the park, painted by Turner and John Cotman. There are pictures collected by Scott's friend, and a series of fine tapestries worked by Miss Morritt, many of them copies of famous pictures. Hereabouts are some stones from a Roman camp.

Monuments of the Morritts, with their marble busts, are in the formal little church standing by the Roman road to Bowes; it is an

18th and 19th century building. Here are Scott's friend John Morritt, lying with his wife; William of a later day, of whom we read that he was upright, honourable, and unflinching in courage when bearing pain; and Robert who fell in South Africa. There is also a monument of Septimus Robinson, who is wearing a wig and a cravat as in the 18th century.

But for John Morritt it is not likely that Scott would have written *Rokeby*. Morritt had a fortune, enabling him to travel widely and to study the classics, for which he had a passion. At 22 he visited what he believed to be the scene of Homer's *Iliad*, and afterwards wrote a book about the Siege of Troy. His friendship with Scott began in 1808, and lasted till Scott died. The next year Scott spent a fortnight with Morritt, and, charmed with the loveliness of it all, he began writing his poem *Rokeby*.

Popular in Scott's day, the poem brought hundreds of travellers to see the woods and rivers it describes, and Morritt humorously threatened to punish his friend for bringing too many visitors to his house. It was a few months after the appearance of *Rokeby* that *Waverley* appeared, and for years only three men knew the secret of its authorship, Morritt being one of them.

Romaldkirk. One of the most charming villages hereabouts, it has a church worthy to be called the Cathedral of the Dales. The church and the inns, fine houses and humbler ones, gather round the wandering green. There are fragments of the old stone stocks, an old pound for stray sheep and cattle, a rectory in a delightful garden, fine trees, a stream flowing to the Tees near by, and beautiful almshouses by the road to Eggleston.

The noble old church has the shape of a cross, with mediaeval aisles and transepts, and a 15th century west tower with a vaulted roof. Through a graceful 13th century doorway, sheltered by a quaint old porch, we come to an interior even more charming than the outside—the old door opening on an arresting sight of grey walls of crazy stonework and majestic Norman arcades, whose great pillars and arches reach the lofty roofs of the aisles. Both transepts have unusual window tracery, the north side like rows of leaves.

The fine long chancel, down two steps and filled with light, comes from about 1370. Its double piscina has leafy arches with finials. A little barred window in the north wall is open to a priest's room over the mediaeval vestry. The rood stairs and part of the old three-decker pulpit are still here, and a Jacobean cover crowns the splendid font, which may be over 700 years old, its bowl carved with three rows of formal leaf pattern upside down. There are traces of old painting on the arcades.

A great stone set in a blocked doorway has a cross which was carved on it in Saxon days, and a stone under the tower has two crosses, a belt and horn, and a sword. A stone from which the brass has gone is in memory of John Newlyne, a 15th century rector who may have built Egglestone Bridge over the Tees. In the north transept lies the fine figure of Sir Henry Fitzhugh, a knight in chain mail, drawing his sword. He was buried here in 1304. The church also possesses a *Breeches Bible*.

Rosedale Abbey. The beautiful valley from which it takes the first part of its name is like a deep furrow ploughed across the moors by a giant of long ago. Nine miles long, it has the River Seven and a road running through, the steep sides flanking it rising to a height on which grow miles of heather.

By the village, which lies in the middle of the dale, the western slope is as steep as any hill in Yorkshire, and at the top are old iron-works with a chimney which is a landmark from afar. It is said that the monks of Byland had iron mines hereabouts.

The second half of the village's name reminds us of the nunnery founded here late in the 12th century by Robert de Stuteville. Some of its material was used in building the houses round about. A few of its stones lie by the church, and in a garden over the churchyard wall is a fragment of a turret stair.

The old church, which stood on one side of the cloisters, was re-built in 1894. Standing by the green, it is a plain little place shelter-ing a quaint old lectern which has an angel supporting the desk, and a stepped platform round which are cherub-heads and a panel carved with figures of a woman and children. There is a fine syca-more in the churchyard, and the road bringing us to the church has an avenue of them.

Roxby. From its steep slope this tiny place looks over the wooded glens through which the Roxby and Easington Becks are winding to their meeting before reaching Staithes and the sea. The Cholmleys had a great house here; now there are only cottages, a few farms, an inn, a forge of 1858 with a fine horseshoe doorway, and a dismal church with mouldering stone walls. It was made new last century, and has on a floorstone an inscription to Thomas Boynton, who built the older church and was buried in it in 1523. Another stone is to Lady Kathleen Fairfax of Gilling Castle, who died in the year of the Great Fire of London.

Runswick. Artists delight in this fishing village at one end of the lovely bay bearing its name, and the white houses with red roofs, perched one above another on the cliffs which hang between the purple moors and the sea, are a charming picture seen from Kettleness on the eastern horn of the bay. A steep road climbing to the cliff-top brings us to beautiful views. Looking up to the village from below we can well believe that in 1682 its houses began sliding into the sea. Landslips are still a serious problem here.

Runswick is famous for its lifeboat services, over 200 lives having been saved here within living memory. In 1901 the women of the village launched the lifeboat and went to the rescue of fishermen who had been caught in a sudden squall.

Ruswarp. In the beautiful valley of the Esk, where the river is nearing the sea, it has an iron bridge and a tall brick viaduct, many new houses among the trees on the hillside, and old houses at the foot of the steep winding hill where the modern church stands among flowers. Its tower and spire are 120 feet high. Inside is a bullet-scarred Crucifix picked up on the battle field at Ypres.

Not far from the church is the Old Hall, a dignified house built in Stuart times. Here lived Captain Bushell who, in the Civil War, was sometimes for Parliament and sometimes for the king. It was a sad day for him when he betrayed Scarborough Castle to the Royalists, for it cost him his head.

Saltburn-by-the-Sea. High above the waves, it is much loved by folk from the industrial towns near the River Tees, who come for the bracing air, the firm sands, and the charm of a lovely wooded glen where gardens are laid out by the Skelton Beck flowing to the

Snape Hall

Staithes

The abbey

Whitby

The harbour, the town and the church

sea. There is a delightful view of the glen from the iron girder bridge which crosses it, 800 feet long and 140 feet high. Higher up, the valley is crossed by a fine railway viaduct. Between the new holiday town and the bold height of Hunt Cliff "which had a Roman signal station" is the little village of Old Saltburn, so near the sea that the spray beats against the windows of the white cottages. The church in the town is of 1870.

Saltergate. It is the motorist's halt on the road from Pickering to Whitby, with magnificent views of moors and hills and a winding valley from Saltergate Brow. Near by is one of the astonishing sights of Yorkshire, the wonderful Hole of Horcum at the end of a deep glen through which runs the Levisham Beck. The road sweeps round the green parapet on the eastern side of this stupendous natural amphitheatre—a green bowl which seems to have been scooped out of the ground and is traditionally said to have been dug by a giant. At the bottom of the bowl is a single farm and surely no building in England has a more remarkable setting of its kind.

Salton. A small village in the Vale of Pickering, it lies off the beaten track, where the River Dove is nearing its meeting with the Rye. Standing near the green, which is shaded by a solitary tree with a seat round its trunk, the charming church has been well restored, but its story goes back to the Normans who built it early in the 12th century. Before the century closed fire swept through this little place, leaving its mark on much of the walling we see today. After the fire came the pointed lancets in place of some of the older windows, and the weatherworn tower with shafts to the belfry windows and a fine pointed arch on clustered shafts. The lead pyramid cap, the battlements, and the supporting buttress are modern. Worn stone heads are in the corbel table outside. Norman zigzag enriches the priest's doorway, and the fine chancel arch which has a hood of balls and grapes. The worn Norman south doorway (with renewed shafts) is carved with heads of men, and a double row of beak-heads gripping the inner moulding. The north doorway is a little later. The beautiful chancel has the east end made new, and a tiny modern firegrate under a Norman window. A splendid 13th century chest has original ironwork, and there are a dozen old coffin-lids by the porch.

Sand Hutton. It is the Sand Hutton near York, a small village hiding in trees and full of charm; its lanes are a delight to all who love woods and glades. On a green hill is a well that might belong to a fairy tale; another well is on the green facing the church, and by the green are the gates to the great house in a 100-acre park. Reached by an avenue of yews and chestnuts, and sheltered by the spreading arms of two cedars, the church of St Mary is almost a centenarian, with a chancel half as old. The small tower with a shingled spire serves as a porch, its doorway bowered in greenery. Outside the chancel is the grave of John Ancomb, a corporal at Waterloo.

In the churchyard is all that is left of the 12th century chapel of St Leonard, overgrown fragments of walling, a 15th century window with a niche below it, and a Norman doorway with a scratch dial. Here too is a Norman font.

Sandsend. It is well named, for here end the Whitby sands, and here is a sheltering arm of the rugged cliffs which rise till we come to Ravenscar. It lies where the stream from one of two richly wooded glens falls into the sea, with its neighbouring hamlet, East Row, at the end of the other stream which is crossed by a stone bridge of a single span. The two streams run parallel from the lovely Mulgrave Woods, and over them near the sea strides the great railway viaduct. Between the two little watering-places stretches a promenade. There are stone houses and black-and-white houses nestling charmingly among trees on the steep banks, houses sheltering in the valleys, and others so near the sea that we wonder they are not washed away. From Sandsend a very steep hill climbs to Lythe's magnificent church.

Scalby. It is on the Cut running from the River Derwent to the sea, and is now almost part of Scarborough, attractive with its beautiful gardens and trees, and a stream winding down a narrow glen. Naturalists come here for rare flowers, and geologists to study the glacial moraine. Antiquarians find the neighbourhood interesting for its flints and urns.

Looking its best outside, with its buttressed tower and its gabled aisle wider than the nave, the church stands on a knoll from where there is a fine view of the valley and the moors beyond. Much of it was rebuilt in the 17th century (the time of a sundial in the church-yard), and it has since been enlarged, but the chancel arch and the pillars of the nave arcade have stood since the close of the 12th century. The font may be Norman. There are two Jacobean chairs, and a Jacobean pulpit with an old hourglass stand. Above the old almsbox is the inscription cut in the stone of a pillar, *Pra Remember The Power.*

One of the vicars was James Sedgwick, brother of the famous Yorkshire geologist Adam Sedgwick. Another vicar preached here for 54 years, and Scalby is proud to remember that William Mompesson, the hero of Eyam in Derbyshire, was once vicar here.

Scarborough. It is Yorkshire's most famous holiday town, and Yorkshire's millions every peaceful summer crowd it in countless multitudes. A majestic piece of our English coast, with its Castle Rock looking down on two sweeping bays, it has the old town and the new, the old gathering round the mediaeval harbour, the new a pleasure-loving town with its fine promenades, its busy streets, and natural glory in abundance.

Some of the old narrow streets are as captivating as Chester's, and it has been said that the old houses and the red funnels of the ships below the grey castle are not unlike Gibraltar.

Romans, Saxons, and Normans have been here; pirates have raided the harbour; German shells have shattered its houses. Kings and rebels have pursued each other in the streets. Yet it is not for any historic interest that we come to Scarborough; we come to it as a place of sheer delight, one of the best gardens on England's 2000 miles of coast. Spring comes early to the Valley Gardens and the natural ravine spanned by two fine bridges—the Cliff Bridge which we cross on foot for about 400 feet, and the Valley Bridge about twice as long. The trees above the South Bay give us enchanting peeps of the sea among the leafy branches. Dominating the South Bay is the Grand Hotel completed in 1867 and designed by Brodrick, architect of Leeds Town Hall. The Northstead Manor Gardens, which, like the Chiltern Hundreds, provide a means for an M.P. to resign his seat, have a delightful miniature railway and a large open-air theatre. Peasholm Gardens have a Peter Pan island that all children love.

It is the North Bay that has the high cliffs and houses perched above the rocks and the South that has the harbour, the old town, and the Spa.

The first Spa buildings were set up at the close of the 17th century, following the discovery of "Spaw" water by Mrs Farrow, but were destroyed by landslips and high tides in 1836, and the fine group of buildings here today are from the end of last century. Near them are the town hall and the museum. In the museum collection is a ducking stool, a mediaeval stone crucifix, an old key of the castle, Roman pottery, a coffin hollowed out from the trunk of an oak, and the bones of a man who was buried in the coffin about the time Moses was buried in the valley of Moab. The town hall has grown out of a Tudor mansion; it has two turrets and a stone oriel in what is now the council chamber, a room furnished in old oak. There are five pictures in the hall, an old ironbound chest, and a bronze bust of one of Scarborough's famous sons, Lord Leighton, who was born at 13 Brunswick Terrace in 1830. Though he does not rank as one of our great painters, his pictures have a permanent place in our galleries as an artist typical of his day, and his name is linked with one of the best periods of the Royal Academy, of which he was President. He was the first artist to be made a peer, and died the next day. The Crescent contains the Art Gallery, formerly Broxholme, dating from 1845, and the Natural History Museum, housed in Woodend, the Scarborough house of the Sitwell family; one room is devoted to the family. The Library is near by, which has been associated for some time with the Theatre in the Round movement.

From the hill known as Oliver's Mount, a huge green platform 500 feet above the sea, is a wonderful view of the town and the ships below the Castle Rock; unlikely as it may seem, one can enjoy skiing on its slopes all year round, for an all-weather artificial ski-slope has been built here. Into its sweep come the Mere, Raincliffe Woods 3 miles away, and the coast on the way to Whitby. Crowning the hilltop is a stone obelisk 75 feet high, a memorial which can have few rivals for position in England. It is seen 10 miles away, and is a tribute to 750 who died in the Great War, among them not only men who fought but women and children who were killed by the

German bombardment of Scarborough. Four German cruisers shelled the town for half an hour, hardly a house escaping. The Grand Hotel had two storeys demolished. The lighthouse was shattered, and a great hole was torn in the town hall.

St Martin's is a fine 19th century building with a tower 100 feet high. It has a reredos by Burne-Jones (a triptych of the Annunciation, saints, and angels), a roof designed by William Morris, and an east wall with ornamental tracery as a setting for paintings by both artists, *The Adoration of the Magi* by Burne-Jones, and angels by Morris. Some of the windows have glass by both these artists and also by Ford Madox Brown, and here is an old painting of the Madonna with the Holy Child and St John. By the fine chancel screen is an unusual pulpit with printed panels under glass, showing the *Annunciation* (by Rossetti), the *Four Evangelists*, and the *Four Latin Doctors*. There are inscriptions to Charles Mackarness and to an officer who remained at his post when the *Titanic* went down.

Old Scarborough lies below the Castle Rock. A red-roofed little town, it was popular long before the Spa was fashionable. The harbour has four piers, one a huge breakwater with stones which have been buffeted through 700 winters, one with a lighthouse gleaming white in the sun. In St Nicholas Gardens is a huge anchor which is said to have belonged to Paul Jones's pirate ship, sunk near Flamborough Head after one of the most memorable of English sea-fights.

Some of the narrow streets of the old town are really long flights of steps, where nets, lines, boats, anchors, lie outside quaint houses with tiny windows and old beams. Scarborough fishermen come to worship in St Thomas's Church on a steep little hill by the harbour; it has a quaint pulpit, a curious screen decorated with painted holly leaves, and an east window of Christ walking on the waves.

In one of the oddest corners of the old-world town is a house known as the Three Mariners Inn, its foundations 600 years old. Believed to have been a smuggler's den, it has many secret cupboards and is now a show-place. Near it is one of Scarborough's notable houses, a stone building with bay windows and a gable, all that is left of a 14th century house in which Richard Crookback is said to have lodged. Known as Richard III's House, it has a heavy outer door turning on old iron hinges, and some queer stone figures. The king's bedchamber has a ceiling believed to be one of the oldest of its kind, made by Italian workmen about 1500, with painted ornament of curious symbols and a queer trio of rabbits, each rabbit having two ears though there are only three ears among them; we have seen this clever device in a few church roofs.

Above the red roofs of the old town are a church and a great fortress, both centuries old. Commanding the two bays and crowning with awe and majesty the great rock, the castle seems to have gathered half the history and romance of Scarborough within its precincts. An impregnable stronghold, it is built on a broad platform above natural walls, and has the sea to protect it, only a narrow ledge of rock linking it to the town. Over 3000 feet above the sea, and covering 19 acres, there is no finer site in all England for a castle, and in all its years it has never been taken by storm. Two half-round towers, grim and forbidding, guard the gate, and beyond the arch is a narrow roadway protected by massive stone walls. At either side the cliffs fall away steeply.

Above the walls stands the Norman keep. The mark of the Civil War and the German bombardment are on it, but in ruin it is magnificent. It is 55 feet square, has three storeys and a basement, and its walls, 11 feet thick, are from 70 to 90 feet high. Of the wing in which the original doorway was built there is little more to see than a few stones and the steps to the entrance, but a wooden bridge brings us to what was then the second doorway, a hole in the wall showing where the beam was drawn out to bar the door. Below are traces of the dungeons, and a curious bit of masonry like a walled-in doorway is a stone cupboard.

A strong wall rising above the moat protects the keep from the castle plain, and a wall still rises above the green slopes on the south of the rock. In the courtyard are the foundations of a tower where Richard III's queen stayed, and a little way off is one of the most astonishing things on the headland, a Norman well 170 feet deep, much of it hewn from the solid rock. It is a masterpiece of engineering, and still has water in it.

The outer wall is strengthened with towers, and if we climb one of them for its view we are abundantly rewarded. We see the castle to advantage here, and look down on the old town as Harold Hardrada looked down on it when he made bonfires up here and threw burning hay on to the roofs of the houses. The castle was built in Norman days, and was surrendered to Henry II, who rebuilt it as a fortress; much of what we see comes from his time, though the existing approach is 13th century. King John stayed here many times, and Edward I held Courts here. Piers Gaveston was starved out by the Earl of Pembroke. An attempt was made to capture it during the Pilgrimage of Grace, but the garrison laughed the pilgrims to scorn. It was the scene of a rebellion in Mary Tudor's day, and was twice besieged in the Civil War, when its surrender by the Royalists was of such national importance that Parliament appointed a thanks-giving day for it. At the close of this siege the keep was mined and partly destroyed. After that the castle has no history, but it was a prison for George Fox in 1665.

The coastguard station has been built over the foundations of a 16th century mill on the site of a church which was here in Norman times; and three sides of the Norman church had foundations of a Roman signal station, of which we can still trace the outline. The signal station would have a high tower, and would be built about the end of the 4th century, when the Saxons were beginning to steal out of their harbours to raid the east coast, known as the Saxon shore. Here, as in our own day, signals would be given when a fleet was approaching; and it is thrilling to reflect that the Saxon pirates of the 4th century and the German barbarians of the 20th were both signalled from this spot.

But this is not the end of the tale, for the Romans were not the first to stand on Castle Rock. Below the foundations of the Roman tower fragments of weapons and tools and pottery have been found, many of them now in the museum, all relics of Bronze Age folk who lived here 30 centuries ago.

At the foot of the castle is Scarborough's mother church, looking out to the bay over the piled-up housetops of the old town. It is the parish church of St Mary, which has seen many changes since it was built in the first half of the 12th century. Richard I gave it to monks who had a small cell here. About 1180 began the rebuilding which went on until, by the middle of the 15th century, it had given York-shire one of its noblest churches, a cross-shaped pile 200 feet long, with three high towers. It was in the 15th century choir that Sir John Meldrum set his cannon and stormed the castle in the Civil

War, the garrison replying with such heavy fire that the walls were destroyed and the central tower was so much weakened that it fell in the year after Cromwell died. The tower was rebuilt from the ground, and other parts of the church restored, but the choir was left in ruin, and only fragments now remain, the church having the odd appearance of an old central tower projecting at the east end.

Most of the nave arcades are from the 12th or 13th century. The west doorway was built in the 15th, and the rest of this front (together with the two towers which have lost their upper storeys) was refashioned last century. The tilting north arcade has sturdy round pillars, but on the other side some are round, one is octagonal, one is a cluster of four shafts, and another has round it a cluster of six shafts. There is a fine lancet clerestory.

Beyond the north aisle is the 14th century St Nicholas Aisle, known as the Fishermen's Aisle, of which the walls were rebuilt after the Civil War with the materials of St Thomas's Church, demolished in 1649; the 14th century pillars of its arcade are said to come from that last church. Very striking is the south side of the church, with its two-storeyed porch like a tunnel of stone, and the row of four chapels between the porch and the transept—porch, chapels, and transept all 14th century. Each of the three eastern chapels has its piscina, aumbry, and what may be a founder's recess, and all four have massive stone roofs reminding us of those of mediaeval bridges. One of them is now the Children's Corner. The south transept was used as a school for 200 years after the Civil War, and on the hood of its south window are old stone heads believed to be of Edward III and Archbishop Melton. The north transept has gone. The upper room of the porch has a piscina and a fireplace and is now used as a small museum, among the treasures being a copy of *Foxe's Book of Martyrs* and some drawings of the old church.

The three fine lancets and the wheel window at the west end shine with a mosaic of red and blue glass, and two of the eight 19th century bells won distinction at the Great Exhibition of 1851; they would ring out in the original Crystal Palace. There are about 200 small brass inscriptions (chiefly 18th century) brought into the church from gravestones outside, and a fine bronze plaque has the portrait of Bishop Blunt who was vicar of Scarborough for 40 years. On Elizabeth Craven's memorial is her portrait and the family arms, the work of Roubillac. There are stone coffins within and without the church, and an old sundial on the porch. Near the south transept lies Scarborough's historian, Thomas Hinderwell, who died in 1825 at 81. He founded the local museum and has a drinking fountain to his memory in the town.

There is one grave on this hillside which every pilgrim comes to see, the last resting-place of Anne Brontë. In the easternmost grave-yard, shut off from the road to the castle, is her white stone, carved with books and an urn.

In that dark year of revolution, 1848, death was knocking at the door of the unhappy parsonage at Haworth. Branwell Brontë had died in September, Emily in December, and now Anne was at the gate of death. She longed for a sight of the sea, and it was felt that Scarborough would do her good. She left Haworth on May 24, called at York and visited the minster, and arrived at Scarborough on May 25. On the 27th she was thrilled by the sunset on the castle cliff. On the 28th the doctor came, and she asked him how long she might live. "The Angel of Death has arrived", was all that he could say, and Anne sat back in her easy chair saying, "Take courage, Charlotte, take courage", and in a few hours her spirit had fled.

Scargill. A narrow, gated road threading the tumult of little hills brings us to this lonely spot, where a stream flowing to the River Greta chatters in a deep glen, and the ruins of a castle stand on the bank above. The castle was an important place in the 14th century, and Edward II is said to have been entertained here; but now there are only broken walls and a small gabled gatehouse, hobnobbing with farm buildings. Sir Walter Scott, who visited this little place with its spacious views of Teesdale, was so charmed with it that he made it the scene of an incident in *Rokeby*. Near by are remains of two Roman shrines.

Scawton. Far from the highway, it has Old Byland and Cold Kirby for neighbours on the foothills of the Hambleton range. If we come to it over Scawton Moor, from Sutton Bank, magnificent views of the Cleveland Hills are spread before us; from Rievaulx in the valley of the Rye the way is steep but enchanting. The base of an old cross is by the village pond, and standing neighbourly with the grey cottages is a small church whose rough walls are weathered by the storms of nearly 800 winters. It was built by the monks of Old Byland, and stands much as it stood in their day, singularly odd inside with its stout walls leaning, windows at all levels, and many recesses. We come in by a Norman doorway carved with zigzag, and at each side of the tilting Norman chancel arch is a big recess with a peephole cut in the back. Grouped with a window and a blocked doorway in the south wall of the chancel are a stone seat, a piscina, and a low window like a long narrow slit. On the opposite wall is another low window; and here too, at the foot of a Norman window, is a vessel which is thought to have served as a washing bowl. It is like a table-top on pillars, with a stone below it hollowed like a trough. An old cupboard has been fitted into it. There are old beams in the roof, and the Norman font has an odd cover like a hat with a tall crown; one of the bells is said to be 14th century, the gift of Abbot Roger of Byland. The Hare Inn here was said to be the smallest in England, before living accommodation was added.

Scorton. A neighbour of Bolton-on-Swale, it has a great walled green which is one of the biggest in the county. On it cricket is played, and round it are gathered in happy medley the old houses and shops, the inns and the forge, and the grammar school (founded in 1720) with a clock in its quaint turret. Here too is the imposing Hospital of St John, with a courtyard of lawn and flowers, and a Roman Catholic chapel attached. Built last century and made new in ours, it is a home for 200 sick and needy men.

Scruton. A tranquil place near the River Swale, it has cottages and farms and great trees, some making a fine avenue on the green and bringing us to the church. The church, dedicated to St Radegund, has much that is new, but the Normans built the fine nave arcades of mottled stone, and the chancel, built aslant, is partly 13th century. Capronnier's brilliant glass in the east window shows the Ascension. The tower is over 500 years old, and old gravestones serve as the lintel of the doorway to its stair. Another with a fine cross is in the churchyard. Under the east wall of the chancel, with nothing to mark his grave, sleeps one of Yorkshire's famous antiquarians, Roger Gale, who built the older part of the hall, which stood until recently demolished, by the church, a fine brick house with ivied walls, mantled in the trees of a lovely 140-acre park. He wrote learnedly about coins and medals. He is said to have chosen the wood for his coffin a few days before he died in 1744, and it was by his own instruction that no memorial was set up over his resting-place.

Seamer. Strung along a road crossing the Carrs, it has grey and white cottages with red roofs, a fine embattled church of weathered stone, and a fragment of what was once a magnificent home of the Percys, who knew this place from Norman to Tudor days. Not far away are entrenchments made on the Wolds before the Romans came. Mesolithic man built a camp here about 7500 B.C., and when excavations took place in the early nineteen-fifties, thousands of tools were uncovered. But older than all the other old things here-abouts is a great boulder at the station. It is a relic of the Ice Age, and is thought to have been brought here by glaciers.

Part of the church is as the Normans left it, but the 15th century builders extended the chancel eastward, and added the north aisle with its low arcade under the Norman windows. The tower was re-fashioned 100 years ago. The nave has Norman pilasters, and the sunken 15th century porch shelters a Norman doorway. The old door opening to the nave has hinges probably seven centuries old. The arresting feature of the church is the splendid Norman chancel arch, near which is the old rood stairway found when the church was restored last century. The head of a Norman window is set over a massive arch in the north wall of the chancel. There are two heads and a medley in old glass, several old piscinas, a sanctus bell, and a modern pulpit with Elizabethan panels. The arms of Napier are on the oak screen set up over 300 years ago, and a startling stone face peers from a capital in the nave.

On Richard Wilson's monument is a relief of the seamen's home he gave to Scarborough last century, and Susannah Boutflower's memorial has a realistic deathbed scene. Outside a sundial warns all who come that—*A day may ruin thee; improve this.*

Seamer. Its low stone church with a tiny tower was made new over a century ago, but its fine outlook over a wide countryside south of Middlesbrough, with the moors rising in the south, has not changed. From this hilltop village came a great scholar of Cromwell's day, Brian Walton, who spent years making a Polyglot Bible. Published in 1653, it was a monument of learning and is useful to students even now. To us it is interesting as one of the first books ever printed by subscription, £8000 being subscribed within a few months. Walton died in London in 1661, but his memorial in St Paul's perished in the Great Fire. A rare copy of the Bible is treasured in the library of Sir William Turner's hospital at Kirkleatham.

Sessay. A byway village with little to disturb its peace, it has a small stream flowing by the church and the school, close companions with stone roofs. There is Church Farm with stones said to have come from a great house built by William Darrell, a famous swordsman of Richard Lionheart's day.

The tall shaft of an old cross stands in the churchyard, but the church, with a tiled spire, was made new last century. It has an arcade without capitals, and a peace window with St George and Our Lord in rich mantles of purple and red. The step of the porch is a great stone in which a small figure was once set, and within the church is a single old possession in the chancel floor. It is the portrait of Thomas Magnus, exquisitely engraved in brass, showing him in rich vestments, his hands at prayer. On his breast is the word Jesus. Below him is a coat-of-arms with the motto "As God will", and at the four corners are two holy lambs and two sprays of columbine.

A learned man and the friend of Wolsey, Thomas was a successful ambassador. Henry VIII sent him on important missions, and as king's chaplain he was present at the Field of the Cloth of Gold. He died in this lonely village 30 years afterwards.

Sheriff Hutton. It is not possible to know the story of England and stand here unmoved, for this gaunt ruined castle has been at the heart of history and at the cradle of English literature; if its walls could speak they would tell romantic and melancholy tales.

Rising above the red roofs of this tranquil village of the old Forest of Galtres (so familiar in Shakespeare) are the impressive ruins of a castle which has lost its glory but can never lose its memory.

It is 800 years since the first castle was built on this hill by the man who gave the village its distinctive name, Bertram de Bulner, Sheriff of Yorkshire. With Sheriff Bulner's daughter's marriage the estate passed to the Nevilles, who held it till the Tudors came, and it was John Neville who rebuilt the castle in the 14th century and made it one of the noblest in the north. Today it is a grim ruin with the inner court enclosed by walls 6 feet thick, its four corner towers sadly broken except for one that still rises about 100 feet; the court has become a farmyard with a haystack in one corner. The deep moat can still be traced, and the 15th century gateway stands adorned with the proud arms of the Nevilles, who lived here for centuries when the crown of England was on the battle field or in the hands of evil men.

We may like to think of one of the truly noble men who spent some quiet years here, Anthony Woodville, brother of Edward IV's Elizabeth. Wearying of battles and treasons, he loved most of all to read religious books or to go on pilgrimage, and it was on one of his pilgrimages that he came upon a French translation of the *Latin Sayings of Philosophers*, which he called "a glorious fair mirror to all good Christian people to behold and understand". He brought it home with him to Sheriff Hutton and translated it for Caxton, and it was the first book to be printed in England. We like to remember the story that Woodville refused to translate a certain part of the book in which Socrates is sarcastic about women, and that Caxton did this for him. He became Earl Rivers and was made guardian of the Prince of Wales.

Here lived another poet in due season, our poet laureate John Skelton, whose patron Thomas Howard, Duke of Norfolk, was living at the castle after his victory on Flodden Field. It was here that Skelton wrote his *Garland of Laurel*, "a right delectable treatise upon a goodly garland of laurel studiously devised at Sheriff Hutton Castle". It celebrates his crowning with a laurel wreath by several noble ladies.

But it is not for libraries or poets that the castle is chiefly re-membered: it was to become the home of Warwick the Kingmaker, and therefore the scene of plotting and intriguing; and it is said that his daughter Anne, queen of Richard III, met here the funeral procession of her little child, her seven-year-old boy Edward, Prince of Wales, who had died at Middleham Castle while his parents were away. She died the year after him, and the year after that came Bosworth Field.

It was while his queen was dying that Richard was turning over in his mind the thought of marrying her niece, Elizabeth of York, daughter of that Elizabeth Woodville whose marriage with King Edward had shaken the throne. He had sent her to Sheriff Hutton as a captive, and it was within the walls of this ruined castle that she heard the news that if Anne should die she might be Queen of England. Her widowed mother sent the betrothal ring of the princess to Henry Richmond, exiled in France, and soon he was back to claim for himself the crown of England and his bride. He won the crown on Bosworth Field, and in a little while the lonely prisoner of Sheriff Hutton Castle heard church bells ringing, and was escorted up to London, where she became the wife of King Henry VII, the red and white roses being tied together at their wedding. The prisoner of the castle was the first of our Tudor queens, and she lies in the centre of more than 70 royal figures in the rarest little chapel in London.

It is said that the little Prince of Wales who died at Middleham was laid to rest in Sheriff Hutton church, and near a window is a small battered alabaster figure supposed to represent the prince, a cap on his head, his tunic falling to his feet, his hands at prayer. It is on what is believed to have been his tomb, the ends of it and the front of it, with carvings of God the Father and Our Lord, saints, and angels carrying shields. A picture shows us the tomb as it was.

Much of the church is 14th century, the south chapel is 15th, and the lower part of the tower is Norman, opening by striking mediaeval arches to the nave and aisles, and entered by a mediaeval doorway with an old door. Two old yews standing like guardians by the massive tower make a charming picture of the west end, throwing a green bower over the little gabled porch with its white gates. The south arcade of the nave has beautiful capitals carved with foliage. There are big box pews and an old chest, and two old doors in the vestry, a fine one with traceried panels coming from the 15th century. Among the fragments of original glass remaining in the windows of the north wall are arms, pinnacles, the head of a bishop, a red rose,

196

and a golden sun. In the south chapel are a helmet and gauntlet and a tattered banner of Charles I's day. On the chancel floor we see in brass Mary Hall of 1657 with her baby in her arms; and on the nave floor is a small brass of 1491 showing two babes, probably of the Fiennes family. Near the little Prince of Wales lies the stone figure of a knight in chain armour and surcoat, with a sword and shield, his feet on a lion, and two angels at his head. He is Sir Edmund Thweng, who fought against the Scots and died in 1344.

There is a fine view from the church of the low hills to the north and east, and not far away is the park with the big house started, as a country seat, in 1621, by Sir Arthur Ingram. In the middle of the village is a sloping green which has taken the place of the market square of the great days of Sheriff Hutton's story.

Sinnington. We see it best from the graceful little stone bridge over the River Seven, here flowing from Rosedale into the plain. With its houses by the long green where the maypole shows above the trees, and the wooded hill behind, it is all a scene for our delight. A new road cutting across the old loop has left the village its quiet ways.

An uphill lane brings us to an ancient church with a magnificent beech and other fine trees for company, and a building close by almost as old as the church. Used now as a barn, it has windows of the 13th and 15th centuries in walls of about 1200, built probably by the canons of Guisborough who had a house here. Later it was used as a private chapel by the Latimers. One Latimer fought at Falkirk and one at Bannockburn; and John was the second husband of Catherine Parr, who may have seen this village before she became the last wife of Henry VIII—and his lucky widow.

The church was built by the first of the Normans or the last of the Saxons, and there are many carved Saxon stones in its rough walls. The head of a Saxon cross with a Crucifixion, and another with knot-work, are in the nave wall outside, and the bottom stone at the north-east corner is a hogback on which is carved a bear. An old coffin-lid forms part of a window near by. There are two ancient sundials. The chancel arch is part of the original church, and the blocked north doorway (with a slit above it) may be as old. The 12th century Normans made the font, a piscina, the west doorway with a stoup beside it, and the south doorway over which is a stone carved with a horseman.

Skelton. Just off the highway from York to Easingwold, it has a gem in a perfect setting, a 13th century church among the loveliest of its size. It stands by the banked green, which is shaded by a fine sycamore, by houses and cottages keeping it company. The old manor house has windows enriched with old glass, doors with old ironwork, and a delightful room with 30 wooden gods and goddesses holding painted shields. A bower of beech and yew shelters the gateway to the creepered Skelton Hall standing in a small park with fine chestnut trees. The Grange is another substantial house among noble trees where we enter the village.

The church has its own mantle of trees, and a yew hedge borders the flagged path bringing us to the exquisite gabled doorway, its arch enriched with carving like strings of flowers, and its array of dainty shafts crowned with overhanging leaves. Though it is 13th century, it is later than the rest of the church, which was completed before 1247, and is only 44 feet long and 33 feet wide. Tradition says it was built of the stones left over from the transepts of York Minster, and that the masons who raised the greater splendour gave Skelton this modest treasure. Exceptionally lofty, it has a single steep roof crowned with an imposing bellcote, and adorned with gable crosses. The west end has three lancets divided by buttresses, the middle one framed by a rich arch on banded shafts; over it is a recessed round window in a carved frame. The east wall, more beautiful still, has a group of three lancets between two single ones, and an oval window above. The tall arcades have pillars with detached shafts, and specially lovely are those on which the chancel arch rests. The old piscinas and aumbries are still here, and the font with a carved and tapering bowl.

Skelton-in-Cleveland. Its fine things are an 18th century house and a 19th century church, but its memories are older than the Domesday Book.

The Norman castle, built by one of the Bruces and made new in 1330 by the Fauconbergs, who owned it from the time of Edward I till that of Henry VI, was one of the greatest strongholds in the north of England, but it is long since its splendour vanished. More than once it fell into decay, and it was in ruin when inherited by John Hall Stevenson, the original of Eugenius in Laurence Sterne's *Tristram Shandy* and *Sentimental Journey*. A few years after his death in 1785 the castle was pulled down, except for a small part surviving in the magnificent house which rose in its place.

Described by one historian as one of the grandest buildings he had ever seen, this Skelton Castle of 1794 stands in a park with beautiful gardens, great elms and beeches, a wonderful yew hedge, a fine cedar, and a stream running from the Skelton Beck. Near the trees which clothe the moat at the entrance to the park is the plain 18th century church, sheltering three ancient stone coffins.

On the hillside above the castle are the remains of an old well and the old village cross. At the east end of the long street on which the modern village lies is the fine church of 1884, built of Yorkshire stone. Much of it is in 14th century style, with a tower akin to the 15th century, a striking landmark from afar. Lofty arcades run from east to west, and the wagon roof has enormous coloured bosses of flowers. On the floor stands a bell from the older church; it is said to have a queer shrill tone, and is, like a sister bell now at South Kensington, 13th century. Another treasure from the old church is a fragment of a sundial fixed to the windowsill of the porch, believed to be 11th century. The broken dial seems to have divided the day into 12 hours, and the words of the incomplete inscription are said to be Old Norse, though the letters are Saxon.

A remarkable possession is the glass of the huge west window, amazing in its conception, its dramatic scenes, and its dazzling colour. It was given by Colonel Wharton of Skelton Castle in memory of Skelton's men who fell in the Great War, and the horrors of modern war are shown.

Sleights. Amid some of the most delightful scenery in Eskdale, it lies where the road from Pickering, known here as Blue Bank, drops steeply down to the river on its way to Whitby. There are many new houses on the hill, gay gardens at the foot, charming peeps of the river, and a shady lime avenue by the church of 1895. Built in 13th century style, it is dimmed by the rich glow of stained-glass showing scenes in Our Lord's life, John the Baptist preaching, and other saints. In a low field near the river are traces of an ancient chapel which was standing in the 18th century.

Slingsby. As we come along the Roman road from Malton the village is a charming picture of stone houses with red roofs, a church with a fine tower, a picturesque ruin known as the Castle, and great trees. A noble beech shades the garden of an old house near the green, and a maypole about 90 feet high replaced an older one in 1895.

Rebuilt in 1868, the beautiful church still treasures a few fragments of the old. A battered knight in chain mail, with a sword and shield and holding a heart, may be Sir William Wyville of the 14th century. Near him are a broken altar stone and a coffin-lid with a fleur-de-lys cross. Hanging in the nave like a great canopy is a candelabra holding 50 candles in its lacy network of brass.

Close to the church stands the castle, the house begun by Sir Charles Cavendish before he fought on the losing side at Marston Moor and had to run for his life. It is said that the great place was never completed, and that it has never been a home. Three centuries of time have left it a romantic ruin, with high walls, corner turrets, and mullioned windows, still with its vaulted cellars, and still with the surrounding moat which protected the mediaeval fortress.

On the south of the village are barrows where British urns have been found, a Roman entrenchment, and woods in which rare flowers grow.

Snainton. One of the string of villages on the busy road from Pickering to Malton, it shows its finest possession to all who pass by. It is a fine Norman arch enriched with zigzag and beak-heads, now resting on modern shafts and forming part of a gabled stone lychgate from which a shady avenue of cypress trees leads to the church. The arch belonged to the doorway of an earlier church. The modern one shelters the Norman font which has long been used as a drinking trough on a farm.

A narrow road from the village climbs towards the great earthworks known as Scamridge Dikes, some of them high enough to hide a man on horseback. Many of the dikes hereabouts are miles long, and are thought to have been made by the Ancient Britons.

Snape. Lying off the highway near Bedale, its great possession is a castle standing proudly by the village road, reached by a fine lime avenue, its embattled walls and towers gleaming against a background of trees. There is an old dovecote among its buildings, and beyond it the red-roofed cottages straggle along by the green.

The estate belonged to the Nevilles, and the memory of one of the family (Catherine Parr) clings to this fine old place, which is now partly in ruin, though one side is still inhabited, and the old chapel is much as it was when she worshipped here before she became Queen of England. A flight of stairs brings us to its single room, with rich panelling, a ceiling Verrio may have painted, and windows with ancient portraits of nine of the Apostles, all in rich robes. There are old choir seats and old altar-rails, two great oak figures by the west doorway, and Peter and Paul under canopies by the east window. The striking feature of the woodwork is the carving telling the story of Our Lord's life, a Crucifixion with women weeping and the sky crowded with cherubs, a startling Resurrection in which Christ is leaping from the tomb, and the Ascension.

When Catherine Parr's second husband, Lord John Latimer, died, his widow attracted the attention of Henry VIII, who had lost or beheaded five wives, and Catherine, knowing well how dangerous it was to be Queen of England, went from the quiet of this village to the pageantry of the Court. A great scholar, she looked after the education of Henry's children, is believed to have corrected Edward's exercises and to have taught him to write a beautiful hand, and is known to have interceded on behalf of Elizabeth, who wrote her a grateful letter. It is a long way from this small place to London, but this Yorkshire village sent a lady there who helped to shape our history and is remembered as Henry's lucky wife; she had the good fortune to become his widow.

Sneaton. Here we look down on the River Esk and out to the moors and the sea. From the hill where a beacon flamed years ago is a splendid view of Whitby, the abbey and church crowning the red-roofed old town. A lovely lane brings us to Rigg Mill with its old waterwheel, in a setting of woods and rocks and waterfall.

With a few white cottages and sheltering trees stands the church, a stout stone building of 1823. Its tower is oddly crowned by a lantern and a stumpy spire, and between the spacious nave and the short chancel are three arches, the middle one of oak having its head filled with tracery. The lectern is a pillared canopy of St Hilda with a book and a crook. The treasure here is the wonderfully preserved font, which was hewn from a great block of stone by the Normans; it has pillars at the four corners, and carved on the sides are zigzag, star pattern, spirals, and crosses in circles. Dyer Bond's memorial tells us that he fought under Nelson and sleeps in Middlesex.

South Cowton. More scattered than its neighbours North and East Cowton, it has a surprisingly attractive church in the fields, with a red-roofed farmhouse near by. Above it on the hillside is the embattled 15th century tower known as Cowton Castle, and higher still is the great house called Pepper Arden, in a deeply wooded park of 235 acres.

It is thought that Richard Conyers built the tower on the hill, and that he and his wife built the striking church in the meadows. The massive tower has a pointed arch without capitals, and the vaulted porch has an upper room with a fireplace, reached by steps in the church. A fine old studded door opens to the nave, which is divided from the chancel by an extraordinarily crude arch looking older than the rest; it is all askew, its capitals are like shelves, and traces of painting still remain. The old font has a cover with old carving, a piscina has a worn face on its projecting bowl, and a smiling man and a bishop adorn the crude hood of the vestry doorway. The old oak roof has great pegged beams, the screen and a few poppyheads in the chancel are 15th century, and glass of that time shows the Madonna and the shield of the Conyers.

On the south side of the sanctuary lies an alabaster knight in armour, his hair long, his hands at prayer. He has a long sword and a collar, and by his helmet is a shield of arms. Lying one above another on an iron rack on the opposite wall are figures of two women, who, like the knight, may be of the Conyers family. Both have mantles with flower clasps, dainty dresses with girdles dotted

with flowers, and necklaces with pendants, and both have angels at
their head. One has a quaint headdress, the other has long hair and
a rich band round her head, and is remarkable for her tiny ears,
which are not as big as her eyes. A gauntlet and a helmet hang on
the wall.

South Kilvington. The rectory was the home of an astonishing
parson, William Towler Kingsley, a cousin of Charles Kingsley, who
came to stay with him in this place on the busy road from Thirsk to
Yarm. The rector, who seems to have been a Jack of All Trades, as
handy with a chisel as with a pen, entertained Ruskin and Turner,
yet was eccentric enough to put a notice in his garden warning
people to beware of mantraps. When anyone wished to see the traps
he pointed to his three housemaids. Born in Waterloo year, he lived
to see the Great War, dying at 101, humorist to the last, and known
as England's oldest parson.

Some of his woodcarving is in the church, where he preached for
over 50 years. An odd building within and without, it has a wooden
turret and a humble mediaeval porch shaded by a great laburnum;
it shelters an old lattice-framed door. The Norman nave has one of
its original windows, and the chancel, made new 600 years ago, has
a curious 15th century entrance with short pillars placed on the top
of taller ones to support the arch; it may have been altered at a
later time.

The interior of the chancel is truly amazing. Except for a narrow
aisle down the middle, it is almost filled by the richly-carved modern
woodwork and the organ, with its fine case and pipes reaching
almost from the floor to the roof. The low ceiling is recessed to take
the top of the east window. There are old hat-pegs on the nave walls,
half a dozen simple old benches, and big modern poppyhead benches
elaborately carved with tracery and flowers; they are all different.
The 15th century marble font has a great display of heraldry and an
inscription to Thomas le Scrope and his wife. Near the pulpit is the
old hourglass in its stand, one of the few left in Yorkshire; the sand
runs through in six minutes, apparently for short sermons.

South Otterington. Among the woods and meadows, with the
River Wiske dividing it from Newby, it has a big sycamore on a

small green, and a stone church of 1846 on an older site. The tower with a pyramid cap and the doorway enriched with zigzag proclaim its Norman style. The bowl of an ancient font, massive and battered, lies within. On the list of rectors, which begins in 1254, is the name of John Darnbrough, who served this new church for its first half-century.

Sowerby. It joins hands with Thirsk, but keeps its own identity. On its long road, lined with trees like an avenue, are an old timbered house and a church of old and new; and over the Cod Beck at its southern end is an old packhorse bridge. The 19th century work in the church is in the style of the old. Remains of the Norman church are in the tower, with a stout arch opening to the nave, and in most of the wall of the south aisle with its fine little doorway enriched with zigzag and beak-heads. The old door has studs making up the date 1680, but its ironwork looks old enough to be Norman. A rare feature is the tiny peephole in the corner between the tower and aisle, through which the altar is seen. In the window near it is beautiful glass in memory of a chorister of 15, showing him kneeling before Our Lord and holding a cross.

Spennithorne. From a delightful green setting above the Ure it sees the towers of Middleham Castle over the river, and has a glorious view up the dale. In a lovely churchyard of lawn and trees stands the fine old church, with a massive 14th century tower, its stair turret climbing to big battlements guarded by worn figures, others sitting on the corbel table below. Most of the windows are as old as the tower, and some are adorned with fine heads. There are faces on each side of the beautiful 13th century doorway within the buttressed porch, and others peep from the foliaged capitals of its shafts. Queer heads hold up the tower arch, and a man and a woman in square headdress support the chancel arch. Between the nave and aisles are leaning arcades, the north chiefly Norman, the south 13th century. In the north chapel (over 300 years old) is a tomb with 14 shields, thought to be that of John Fitzrandall of 1517, grandson of Lord Scrope of Masham, last of his line at Spennithorne.

There is a stone bench with arm-rests in the chancel, and a painting of Father Time (perhaps 17th century) is fading away on a wall.

The vestry has an old stone altar with five crosses, and a stout beam said to have come from Jervaulx Abbey, its two bosses carved with foliage, a lamb, and a dove. Built into the vestry is a splendid Saxon stone carved with knotwork and two crosses, and a Saxon fragment with knotwork is in an outside wall.

In the churchyard stands a Russian cross from the military chapel at Sebastopol, brought to England by Sir Van Straubenzee, who sleeps in this secluded spot. At the embattled rectory, in a garden with cedars, larches, and great yew hedges, John Hutchinson was born at the end of the 17th century. He was described as a fanciful man of boundless vanity, and, not knowing how little he knew, took upon himself the hopeless task of informing the world that Sir Isaac Newton was wrong. He has long been forgotten, but he made a stir in his day, doing his best to rid the world of the theory of gravitation, and maintaining to the end of his days that the earth was a cube.

Sproxton. A small neighbour of Helmsley, it crowns a little hill-top in a big bend of the River Rye, which flows by Duncombe Park. The tiny church of St Chad is a gem of the 17th century, charming and complete, standing invitingly at a corner of the road. It has had an adventure, for it was the private chapel of a great house at West Newton Grange near by, and after being used as a barn was rebuilt at Sproxton in 1879. Its one room is divided into nave and chancel by a dignified modern oak screen (designed by Mr Temple Moore), with arcaded bays and entrance gates, and figures of Mary and John by the Cross in the broken pediment. The old screen at the west end makes, with the carved balcony above it, a vestibule through which we enter. The barrel roof has borders carved in classical style, and ribs painted black-and-white and green. The oak panelling is high in the chancel and low in the nave. There are only nine benches, and their ends are neatly carved. The east window has the Crucifixion, and in the 14th century glass of a small north window are fragments, pinnacles, and a figure of Our Lord crucified.

Stainton. Though the chimneys and cranes and great bridges of Middlesbrough come into the view from its little hill, Stainton is a quiet village just withdrawn from the highway, and shaded by elms and poplars. From a bank the church looks over the Beck to

Thornton Wood, where one of the finest cedars in Yorkshire has oaks and yews for company.

The tower (rising from the west gable of the nave) is mainly 15th century, but the nave is later and the chancel new. The mediaeval arches still lead to the chancel and the transept, and an old iron-bound chest is high enough to serve as a reading-desk. Within the church are the stone figure of a man with long curling hair, an ancient stone carved with looped ornament, and the small head of a man. Built into the north wall outside are fragments of Saxon crosses, and part of a hogback on which a bear is carved.

Staintondale. A moorland village between Cloughton and Ravenscar, it is a mile or so from the sea, and has a church in a windswept churchyard with a few Christmas trees. In the tower are one or two stones from Bell Farm, where centuries ago a bell rang out to guide travellers across the moors. It is strange that, although King Stephen gave this lonely spot to the Knights Hospitallers on condition that services should be held here, the condition remained unfulfilled till this church was built in our own day.

Staithes. One of Yorkshire's surprising places is this small fishing-town, where the older women still wear the characteristic "Staithes bonnet", hidden till we are right upon it, for it lies on the banks of a deep creek through which the Roxby Beck runs between precipitous cliffs to the sea. On the east side of the little bay is Penny Nab. From Colburn Nab on the western side the cliffs rise till they reach Boulby Cliff with its disused alum quarries and fine views from 666 feet above the sea. It is the highest point along the English coast.

A turn in the road brings us above the cluster of cottages built one on to the other in the queerest way. We look over the wall of a garden and see the smoke curling up from a chimney below. There are narrow passages, small alleys, amazing streets running to the road which goes down to the water's edge, and a small stone pier where fishermen land their cargoes. Under Penny Nab is a ledge of rock where stood 16 houses till they were all swept away in one night, an unkindly outrage by the ocean waves, for one of them was the little grocer's shop where James Cook began his life, the boy who ran away from it to Whitby to sail the seas and find a continent, and to make life so safe at sea that the British Fleet and the British Empire could come into being. He had come here from Great Ayton, where his father, a mason, had told him to find the shop of Mr Sanderson, who was to train him to be a grocer and draper. He was a poor apprentice, and his master flogged him because he was idle when he should have been weighing sugar and measuring cloth, or because when he should have been busy in the shop he would be looking through the window at a ship with its sails set to the wind.

One morning he was up before the sun, packed up his belongings (a shirt and a knife) in his handkerchief, took a last look at the counter, and began the tramp to Whitby. In the early part of this century the village held a regular artists' colony—including Dame Laura Knight.

Stanwick. Two miles from the Roman road running as straight as an arrow, Stanwick is notable for its amazing earthworks, huge ramparts high and strong, standing like walls about this beautiful spot. There is a great mound, and ridges stretching away into the fields. It is thought they may have been linked with the great Scots Dike which stretched from the Swale to the Tees.

The fine hall and most of the park which was one of the glories of Yorkshire, for generations the home of the Dukes of Northumberland, has gone, and with it the gardens which thousands came miles to see. By the little green (with an ever-flowing well at its side) are two lonely companions, the church made almost new last century, and an old gabled house with a cluster of buildings looking like a hamlet in themselves.

An avenue of sombre Irish yews leads to the very long church, a surprisingly attractive building to find in this out-of-the-way place. It still has remains of the 13th century in the tower, the nave arcade, several windows, the sedilia and two piscinas, and the south doorway, sheltered by a porch which has lost the roof once supporting an upper storey. The font cover, like a pinnacled spire, may be Jacobean.

Among many old stones in the porch, and built into the south aisle wall, are coffin-lids with crosses, swords, shears, and a horseshoe; the fine shaft of a Danish cross carved with interlacing work and two animals; and the wheel-head of a Saxon cross with worn ornament.

On the windowsills of the aisle and in a chancel recess lie four battered stone figures of mediaeval days, probably ancestors of Sir Hugo Smithson, who has a monument showing him with Cavalier curls and rich armour, his jewelled sword having a tiny face engraved on the handle. He reclines on his elbow, and with him is his wife in elaborate costume and high-heeled shoes, holding an open book. Above them hang gauntlets, a helmet, and a sword. A wall-monument with the figure of a woman lying with her arm over three urns is in memory of three daughters of a Duke of Northumberland, and a brass tablet with a portrait of St George is to nine men who gave their lives for us in the Great War.

Startforth. A handsome stone bridge across the River Tees links this old place with Barnard Castle in Durham. The gaunt ruins of the castle rise on the other bank, and grim forsaken mills are about the bridge. From Startforth's church, standing finely in the trees on the brow of a hill, the neighbouring town is seen as a piled-up mass of roofs climbing to the church.

The 19th century saw Startforth's ancient church rebuilt. The pleasing tower has the symbols of the Evangelists round the base of the spire, and in the porch are four fragments of old coffin-lids. There is a 15th century font, and the worn figure of a woman with a long neck and a tiny face, probably representing Helen de Hastings, who gave lands to Egglestone Abbey. Not far from the church is the old gabled hall.

Hereabouts are some of the sombre houses where there was much wretchedness in the bad days of Yorkshire schools. It was to these cheerless places that unwanted boys were sent from the south of England, and it was here that Dickens found Mr Kirkbride's Academy, with such cruelty as saddened his heart. He was here in 1838, and the publication of *Nicholas Nickleby* raised such a storm of protest against these Dotheboys schools that soon not one was left.

Stillington. A pretty patchwork on the hillside, it has the quiet charm of red roofs shining in the sun, guarded by a quaint low church with grey and amber walls. The broad street dips in delightful fashion between green banks on which perch the old houses.

In the 100-acre park going down to the River Fosse was the Hall, now demolished to make room for a housing estate. One afternoon in 1758 a country parson hurried up the drive. He was one of many guests entertained by the squire, and after dinner was asked to read a few pages of a book he had written. But before long the guests were asleep, and in a temper the parson flung the pages on the fire. Jumping up, the squire rescued them from the flames and gave them back to the author, Laurence Sterne, who had been reading *Tristram Shandy*.

The church in which Sterne preached for about 25 years comes chiefly from the 15th century, though the small tower has an older lancet arch and modern battlements, and the spacious chancel has a priest's doorway (with a mass dial beside it) of the 12th century. The font is believed to be Norman. The cream-walled interior gleams with light, the only colour in the 15th century windows being in one or two old fragments. Some of the stones in the chancel walls have grooves worn with the sharpening of tools or weapons.

Stokesley. We think of it as one of the most gracious old towns in Cleveland. There is an interesting group of old houses, some in sad disrepair, a green, and a great market-place to which people come from miles round to see fairs and shows. The River Leven flowing along a quaint street is crossed by many bridges, one a graceful stone footbridge with a single arch.

Tucked in a corner near the river, the church has for company a fine old stone house and some cottages. The great nave is 18th century rebuilding, but the tower and the small chancel are still partly mediaeval. There are old carved stones, a broken piscina, a 600-year-old door to the vestry, and part of a curious coffin-lid showing a leafy shaft at each side of the stem of a cross, and also a pair of shears. Lady Anne Balliol, whose brother founded Balliol College, was laid to rest 700 years ago in the chancel.

Stonegrave. A small place with a notable church, Stonegrave shelters under the wooded slope of Caukleys Bank, which juts into the Vale of Pickering. Though the church has been made to look almost new, except for the tower, its story is very old. The bulk of the tower is Norman or Saxon; its west doorway (now blocked), the tall narrow arch to the nave, and a window on the south are original, but the rest of the windows and the battlements are 15th century.

The fine Norman arcades have three bays on the north and two on the south, their capitals carved with scallop, stiff leaves, and nail-head ornament. One has carving in circles above the scallop. The great possession is a splendid Saxon cross with a damaged wheel-head. About 6 feet high, it is covered with rich plaitwork, and has on the shaft two quaint little men with a cross between them, one with his arms uplifted, the other with arms akimbo. It is 1000 years old, and stands on a coffin-lid on which is a pair of shears. Many carved Saxon fragments lie by the cross, and one fragment is carved with a bird perched on what looks like a lamb.

The figures of a 15th century man and wife lie in a recess in the north aisle, both wearing pleated gowns with belts. The hawthorn leaves on the shield hanging from the man's arm proclaim him one of the Thornton family. In the next recess lies Sir John Stonegrave of 1295, a quiet smile on his worn face.

There is beautiful woodwork, both old and new. The old is 17th century—a lovely pulpit and a remarkable chancel screen, the screen having four slender pillars, canopies with pendant acorns, and rich cornices. The screen between the chancel and its chapel has pillars crowned with heads of men and women, and a cornice carved with pomegranates. Similar carving is in the panelling behind the stalls, and on the solid screen across the north aisle.

One of the rectors was Richard Talbot, Archbishop of Dublin 500 years ago; and another was Richard Barnes, Bishop of Durham in Elizabeth I's day. The church also gave a dean to Durham—Thomas Comber, who was rector here and lies here. He was a champion of Protestantism in its perilous days at the end of the Stuart dynasty, and at the accession of William and Mary he preached to a crowded congregation in York Minster. He wrote about 20 books.

Sutton-on-the-Forest. It was the birthplace of *Tristram Shandy*. Here, for over 20 years of the time he was vicar of Sutton and Stillington, lived one of the greatest of all English humorists, Laurence Sterne, who laughed away his melancholy. It was in 1759, the year before he went to live at Coxwold, that he wrote the first two volumes of *Tristram Shandy*, waking up at the vicarage one morning to find himself famous, for all the world was reading his book. It is said that a letter addressed to Tristram Shandy, Europe, was promptly delivered to the vicarage here.

Part of the old Forest of Galtres, Sutton has a gracious air with its wide green verges and cottages in bright gardens. The church stands behind old elms, and coming up to the chancel wall is the cobbled yard of the old vicarage with a steep pantiled roof. Facing the church is Sutton Hall, a fine house sheltered by great trees.

We see Laurence Sterne in the picture gallery of vicars in the church where he preached, rebuilt since his day except for the 15th century tower with its weird company of gargoyles, and the south wall of the nave with 15th century windows. Its best feature is the spacious chancel, bright as day, keeping a 14th century east window. The poor box is 1673, and the pulpit where the humorist was seen in serious mood is still here. In a little medley of old glass is the head of a saint, and in the outside walls of the vestry are fragments of coffin-lids, one with a fine leafy cross. An inscription tells of Richard Harland who fought at Marston Moor, and the churchyard has a wheel-head cross to those who fell in the Great War, its carvings showing a battleship with an aeroplane above it, and soldiers on horseback.

Sutton-under-Whitestone-Cliffe. Houses with gay gardens line the road which runs through the village on its way from Thirsk to Sutton Bank, the famous climb so well known to Yorkshire motorists. From the top, 960 feet above the sea, is one of England's superb views, with York and Ripon among the towns and villages in the great Vale, and in the distance the long line of the Pennines and even the peaks of the Cumberland mountains. Near by the Yorks. Gliding Club can often be seen launching their craft.

Rising like a precipitous wall beyond the fields, the cliff (a steep scarp of the Hambleton Hills) has at the foot huge masses of rock which fell with a roar like thunder one day in 1755. John Wesley wrote about it in his Journal. On the slope is the lovely Gormire Lake, a pool as blue as a sapphire when seen from above.

It was from Whitestone Cliff that Wordsworth watched the sun go down on his wedding day.

Terrington. It has beautiful trees shading the banked road which climbs the hill. The Hall (now a school) and a grand company of beeches are near the church, which has remains of faraway days. The tower is chiefly 15th century, but its arch is older still, and two stones in its west wall may have been the triangular head of a Saxon doorway. The wide and lofty nave has a curious 12th century arcade of two bays, with one of the biggest Norman arches we have seen. By a 14th century arch to the south chapel is a Norman slit, and within the chapel is a fine mass of herringbone masonry in what was once an outside wall. The font and some windows are mediaeval, and a bell found seven feet under the tower is believed to be 500 years old. By the lovely road to Hovingham is Wigganthorpe Hall in a park surrounded by woods.

Thimbleby. A hamlet below the moors, it is almost lost in trees. Oaks and sycamores make an arch over the road by the pretty lodges at the entrance to the park, where the hall hides in trees, and on the wooded slope between Thimbleby and Over Silton is Nun House, a farm said to be on the foundations of a mediaeval nunnery. On the moor above it is Hanging Stone, a great mass of rock 931 feet above the sea.

Thirkleby. It is High and Low Thirkleby, with the stream flowing between them on its way through green pastures. There are charming houses with quaint porches and chimneys, and from the 19th century church at High Thirkleby we have fine views of the spacious Vale of York and the White Horse of Kilburn on the Hambleton Hills. Here too is the hall (designed by James Wyatt) where the Franklands lived, in a park of 164 acres stretching to the old North Road; but the old glory of house and park is gone.

One of the Franklands memorials in the church was sculptured by Flaxman, showing the father and mother bowed with grief for four children who died young. An inscription to Sir Thomas Frankland tells us that he died in 1722 of a long and painful distemper; he was a Governor of the Post Office, and we read that he considerably improved that branch of revenue. It was one of these Franklands who married Agnes Surriage, the remarkable woman who rescued him from death in the Lisbon earthquake of 1755 and lies in a

Chichester graveyard. It is a romantic story which is told in our Somerset volume; Oliver Wendell Holmes wrote a famous ballad about it.

The Frankland chapel here is an octagon. The base of the church tower (crowned with a spire) serves as the baptistery. The nave has a hammerbeam roof of oak.

It is a fine neighbourhood for rare flowers, and its stream is a haunt of the kingfisher. Years ago the drumming of the bittern was sometimes heard here. By the road to Thirsk is a mighty sycamore with a trunk over 20 feet round. It is about 120 feet high and probably about 300 years old. On it is an inscription telling us that it is the *finest tree growing inside the fences on any highroad between London and Edinburgh*. We can well believe this to be true, even though the tree has lost one of its limbs.

Thirsk. Old and New, Thirsk is an old-fashioned market town in the fruitful Vale of Mowbray, with the Cod Beck flowing between the two highways on which it lies. Few towns of its size have more old inns than Thirsk, once a famous posting station. There are narrow streets, old houses with roughly shaped beams, and black-and-white cottages. In the beautiful grounds of Thirsk Hall, a solemn 18th century house near the church, is the ancient cross which once stood in the cobbled market square. Here, too, is an old lime with a huge spread of branches.

There are still traces of the bull-ring in the square, and of the site of the Norman castle Roger de Mowbray built. On the failure of the rebellion against Henry II (in which he joined) the castle was surrendered to the king and demolished. It stood by the Cod Beck, which is notable here for its network of waterways, known as The Holmes and shaded by veteran willows whose gnarled trunks and massive limbs are a rare sight to see, their foliage reflected in the quiet pools. There are many wooden bridges, and two stone ones linking the Old town with the New.

Thirsk has nothing to compare with its splendid church of St Mary, which has probably no equal for its time in the North Riding. Set on the green bank of one of the willow-bordered streams, it is a magnificent tribute to those who built it in the first half of the 15th century. Nobly yet simply planned, it has a lofty clerestoried nave with aisles, a lower chancel built over a crypt, a west tower, and a two-storeyed porch. A lovely feature of the exterior is the openwork parapet of traceried battlements edging all the walls, as well as the tower and the porch, as with delicate embroidery. There are slender and leafy pinnacles, weird gargoyles, and a glorious array of windows which make the interior a veritable lantern of light.

The tower has unusual buttresses, stepped and sloping, and a niche with a battered sculpture, probably a Madonna. The porch has an oak roof with bosses, but we still see the springers which were meant to support a vault. The richly moulded inner doorway has its worn 15th century door, still magnificent with its studs, tracery, and wicket. It is an introduction to much beautiful old woodwork within. The finest of the 500-year-old roofs is that of the nave, a barrel of open timbering with rich beams and bosses, and spandrels with tracery. In the carving of the one or two bench-ends that remain we see the asses of Askwith and the lion of Mowbray. There are 15th century screens in the aisles, a mediaeval door in the chancel, an old chest, and an exceptionally fine altar-table said to have come from Byland Abbey; it has a border enriched with heads of men and women, and is supported by seated lions. Some old wood is worked into the pinnacled cover of the font.

Beautiful arcades soar to the great clerestory, where, between the windows, are traces of 17th century paintings of saints. The chancel has a trefoiled niche at each side of the east window, and three handsome sedilia. An oil painting of *Doubting Thomas* is thought to be 16th century, and one of the bells is believed to have been ringing at Fountains Abbey 500 years ago. In the 15th century glass filling the east window of the south aisle with a rich medley of red, blue, and silver light are many little heads and many complete figures, among them Anna, Cleopas, St Leonard, St Giles kneeling, and angels with shields. On two of the shields are three asses and the lion to match those carved in wood. St Catherine and angels are recognisable in glass fragments in the other aisle. The window above Sir Robert Lister Bower's bronze portrait plaque has rich glass in his memory. He had a thrilling adventure in his army days, for as a young man he was in the regiment which went up the Nile to try to relieve Gordon at Khartoum. There is a small brass to Robert Thirsk who founded a chantry here, and died in 1419.

Thormanby. There are wonderful views from this hilltop village between Easingwold and Thirsk. Over the rolling countryside to the north is Hood Hill with its diadem of trees, and Roulston Scar with Kilburn's great white horse; and westward are the Pennine fells beyond the Vale of York. In a little lane leading to nowhere is the neat and simple church with a Norman story, though its chancel arch is modern, and its odd-looking tower is brick. The nave has a Norman window, and another is blocked in the chancel. Under a blocked arch in the north wall is a gravestone with a cross and a sword, and a stone with a chalice forms the step of the porch. There are rough old beams in the roof.

Thornaby. Time was when Thornaby had only a few houses round a green; today it is an industrial town by the Tees, its streets crowded between Middlesbrough and Stockton. It has a town hall, a bridge taking us over the river to Durham, and a group of modern churches and chapels. The spacious St Paul's is now the parish church, taking the place of the lowly little chapel of St Peter with its pantiled roof and bellcote, standing with one or two old cottages by the green, aloof from the busy road. Built in Norman days and re-fashioned in the 14th century, it has a blocked Norman doorway, a Norman font, and old stones with carving of battered figures and a little man looking out of a window. The chancel has vanished, but its arch, with rich capitals, is a frame for the altar.

Thornton Dale. The first of the string of villages along the marvellous road from Pickering to Scarborough, it has much to enchant us. Here the highway is embowered with trees and crossed by a road running from the moors to the Vale. On the green at their meeting are the old stocks and the older market cross. A lusty stream from the hills flows under the highway near the hall gates, and is crossed by many little bridges as it winds along the street, passing flowered banks and cottage gardens.

The hall was begun in Tudor days, and its chestnuts and copper beeches are a fine sight to see. Links with the 17th century are the almshouses and the grammar school, the school used by the scholars till the new school was built at Pickering. The church, looking proudly down from a high bank, has an older story than its 14th century rebuilding, and a mile nearer Pickering are green mounds telling of Roxby Castle, where the Cholmleys lived. Sir Richard Cholmley of Elizabeth I's day, known as the Great Black Knight of the North, was famous for his hospitality. Sir Hugh Cholmley, the most famous of them all, was born at the castle.

He lived through the whole life of Charles I, coming round to his cause after first fighting as a Cromwellian. He sat for Scarborough in the Long and Short Parliaments, and first appeared in affairs of great moment in giving his support to John Hampden's protest against Ship Money. Cholmley remained faithful to Parliament until Henrietta Maria landed at Bridlington, when he paid homage to her and kissed her hand. He held a command at Marston Moor, but was forced to surrender when the battle was lost and managed to escape into exile. He spent some years in Rouen, but returned to England after the execution of the king, being then imprisoned for a few weeks. He was set free, however, and lived for eight more years, during which he wrote his memoirs.

The church has a wide nave and narrow aisles, separated by arches on clustered shafts. The chancel, wider and loftier than the nave, mounts in six steps to the altar and has a stone figure of a mediaeval woman lying in a recess. There is a fine old almsbox with three locks, and the font was shaped about 1200. The clock in the tower was set going in 1920 as a thankoffering for peace after four years of war.

In the churchyard is the gravestone of Matthew Grimes, who was 96 when he died in 1875, a grand old soldier who fought in India and in the Peninsular War, his proudest boast being that he stood guard over Napoleon at St Helena, and helped to carry to his grave the man who had shaken Europe to its foundations.

Thornton-le-Moor. It looks over cornfields and meadows, and has a modern bellcote church with its houses new and old in long gardens. There are yews which have stood for centuries, some so old that they must have been here when the Scots invaded Yorkshire in 1318, destroying every house in the village.

Thornton-le-Street. Its name reminds us that the Romans came this way. The cluster of red-roofed cottages and the small church are by the road from Thirsk to Northallerton, with the Cod Beck close by and the hall in a spacious park. The narrow nave and chancel are chiefly 14th century, with a modern west end and turret with a spire. The plain doorway blocked in the north wall is Norman, and the south doorway is only a little later. The font looks mediaeval, and two chairs are Jacobean.

One of the memorials to the Talbots who lived here is an inscription to Roger of 1680, who fought for Charles I. Among those to the Cathcarts we read of one who was killed at the Relief of Ladysmith. Other Cathcarts fought at the Battle of Copenhagen, in the Peninsular War, and at the Crimea. The 3rd earl restored this church last century.

From the churchyard is a fine view of the Vale of York, with the Hambleton Hills like a great barrier a few miles away.

Thornton Steward. The few cottages, the carpenter's shop, the smithy, and the village pump are by the sloping green, perched on the hillside above the Ure. The road from Thornton Watlass skirts the village and runs by the beautiful park of Danby Hall. The village's own little road goes through the courtyard of the pleasant Danby Grange (a farmhouse now), and ends at the church a good half mile away which sees the river gleaming in the meadows as it flows towards the fine old Kilgram Bridge. Here the impetuous stream flows under wooded banks, dashes against the bridge piers and through its four ribbed arches.

There are wonderful views from the windows of Danby Hall, a charming house with some remains of the 14th century from which it has grown. Much of it is Elizabethan, and part is 19th century, and it has its magnificent old oak staircase. It is the home of the Scropes, the only descendants today of the family which gave England men who came into Shakespeare and into history.

The neat and bare little church is as old as the early days of the Conqueror, and may have been here when he came to our shores. Many traces of Saxon days are seen in the lofty old walls—parts of windows and doorways, and long and short work here and there. Part of the original chancel arch is above the one we see today, and the ancient doorway of the west porch has a new tympanum with the names of five who fell in the Great War. Two of the fragments of Saxon crosses on a window sill are carved with the Crucifixion.

The mediaeval bellcote may be as old as the 13th century stone seats, and the font, its bowl resting on a pillar and a cluster of shafts with carved capitals, is also 13th century. Its cover is Jacobean. From the 14th century comes a richly moulded recess with a head at the top, and there are parts of old coffin-lids in the porch and two stone coffins in the churchyard.

Sir Edward Banks, the builder of Waterloo Bridge and London Bridge, is said to have been born near by.

Thornton Watlass. There is room and to spare in this delightful village between Bedale and the River Ure. The spacious green is shaded by lofty trees, the fine grey hall is in a park of 100 acres, and the ivied church stands on a little hill by the duck-pond, with magnificent views of the fells in the west and the Wolds beyond the Plain of York.

Rebuilding last century left the church its 14th century tower, which has heavy vaulting, an upper room with a fireplace, and a ring of 12 trefoiled windows. There are fragments of ancient stones (one showing the outline of a figure on a cross), a battered piscina, and an old reading-desk with a curious wooden figure of a boy angel, looking like the figurehead of a ship. On the wall is a tribute to a hero of the war, Henry Cowell, who saved his guns but lost his life, and was buried at sea off Gallipoli. Lying among the daffodils out-of-doors is a stone with the brass of George Ferrars, a 17th century rector, showing his shrouded figure on a mattress. A touching sight is the mounted wooden cross, a temporary memorial erected by the men of his regiment to Lieutenant-Colonel Tom Hussey, killed on D-Day 1944.

Tollerton. Near the little River Kyle, this village old and new is on the edge of the vanished Forest of Galtres which lives in Shakespeare. At the crossroads is a small green with a young sycamore, and gleaming white in the meadows is a great windmill.

Topcliffe. A tranquil place set finely on a little hill, it has the shaft and steps of a mediaeval village cross, and a church looking down over the housetops to the graceful two-arched bridge where the Swale comes swinging round one of its many bends. It has come from an old water mill, where it foams over a weir after flowing by the richly-wooded Baldersby Park, in which the great house is now a school.

The church is imposing outside with its fine pinnacled tower, and a wide north aisle as long as the lofty nave and chancel. The rebuilding of last century has left only a few fragments of the 14th century church, the east window and another in the chancel, the sedilia, and two piscinas. The oak altar table is 300 years old, and in the porch are fragments of ancient stones with lettering on them, and the perfect wheel-head of a Saxon cross.

The great possession here is the magnificent brass with portraits of Thomas Topcliffe and his wife. A superb example of Flemish craftsmanship of the 14th century, it is nearly 6 feet long and half as wide, and is wonderfully preserved, showing Thomas in a fur-lined mantle and leather boots, his sword at his side and a lion at his feet; and his wife in draped headdress, her gown, with long buttoned sleeves, falling to her feet, where a dog is gnawing a bone. The exquisite canopies are enriched with foliage, and angels with musical instruments and censers; and over each of the portraits is a Deity holding a soul in a winding sheet. The brass is a palimpsest, the hidden side having what is believed to be *the oldest known engraving of a ship on any brass in England.*

An ornate wall-monument of 1688 shows Sir Metcalfe Robinson with long curling hair reminding us of shavings, but his rich cravat is arresting for its truly wonderful carving of lace, perfect in detail.

At Maiden Bower, the ancient earthworks in a loop of the river a mile from the village, William de Percy, who fought for the Conqueror at Hastings, built his timber castle, the first home in England of this great family who were to help to shape our history. Their mediaeval manor house stood close by, one of their three Yorkshire homes. Topcliffe saw many generations of this famous line—one who fought in Palestine, the proud earls of Northumberland who come into Shakespeare and the *Ballad of Chevy Chase,* and the bishops, soldiers, and conspirators who belong to the story of our land. Here lived Richard Percy who saw King John seal Magna Carta, Henry who fought at Crecy and another Henry who fought at Towton, William the poet, Thomas who was executed at York, and Shakespeare's melancholy Northumberland, who was butchered not far from his great house here.

Ugglebarnby. Its few houses are on the green hillside where we look far up the Esk valley, and its church, rebuilt last century, looks across to that of Sleights. A reminder of the older church are the shafts and capitals of a Norman doorway in the porch. A simple place outside, it is richly furnished within. The benches filling the nave have low traceried doors and big fleur-de-lys poppyheads finely carved. Angels with outspread wings support the beautiful hammerbeam roof of the nave, and others are under the wagon roof of the chancel. Eight angels seem to be flying from the curious font cover, which is a sturdy affair with gables and a dome. The font itself, like the stone pulpit and the lectern, is elaborately carved. The reredos of alabaster and marble has a beautiful sculpture by Matthew Noble of the Last Supper, Judas crouching in the background.

Ugthorpe. There are miles of moorland round this bleak spot between Whitby and Guisborough, and there can be few days in the year, we think, when the wind here fails to turn the sails of the old windmill. Facing each other across the road are two churches of last century, Christ Church shaped like a cross, and the Roman Catholic church of St Anne with an east window to its founder, Father Rigby.

Down in a hollow is a relic of Elizabethan England. A farmhouse now, but once the hall, it has uneven corridors panelled with oak before the Armada came, a winding stair to a quaint bedroom with painted woodwork. In a stable is a chimney which more than one priest knew as a hiding-place in days gone by.

In a small Roman Catholic chapel which stood not far away Father Postgate said mass at the risk of his life. He visited the local houses in secret in the days of the Popish Plots, living here in a cottage till he was dragged to York and condemned to death for baptising a child. He was over 80 when he walked firmly to the scaffold and died smiling. His chalice is still in the village.

Upleatham. Its stone houses are on the hillside above the deep wooded valley of the Skelton Beck, and higher still, sheltering below a fine coppice, is a neat little 19th century church in Norman style, with remains of an old cross for company. Its treasure is a font 800 years old.

The Norman font belonged to Upleatham's older church, still standing in the old churchyard half a mile away on the Saltburn road. Its situation is delightful, looking over the valley to the battlements of Skelton Castle peeping above the trees, and to Skelton village dominated by its fine church tower. Of the old church only part of the nave is left, with the tiny tower at its west end looking rather like a buttress, but it makes a quaint picture, and is not forsaken.

Much of what we see is 17th century, though the gargoyles seem older, and traces of an old arcade are in the south wall. The nave roof has ancient beams, and through it we see the solitary bell hanging in the belfry. Under a niche from the vanished chancel is a mitred figure of the 14th century, probably representing Walter de Thorpe, prior of Guisborough. There are coffin-lids whole and in fragments, the finest having a sword by a cross enriched with oak leaves, and a carved border with a man's head peeping from foliage.

Upsall. Near the great house on the steep hillside is the fine forge of 1859, with the words Upsall Town carved over its horseshoe archway. Higher still climb the few cottages, to where an opening in the road suddenly reveals a magnificent view to the west, over the great Plain to the long low lines of the fells.

Built by the Turtons who have lived here for nearly two centuries, the 19th century Upsall Castle was destroyed by fire in 1918. The first castle was from the 14th century a home of the Scropes, though their story belongs to Masham and Bolton Castle. A tale of their association with Upsall concerns a Scrope who found the first castle in ruins, and dreamt that if he stood on London Bridge he would find enough money to build it again. We are told that, dressed as a beggar, he stood there for three days till a tinker said, "I see you are as poor as I am, but if only I could get to Yorkshire, I would soon be rich."

"What would you do?" Scrope asked. "I would find gold under an elder tree near Upsall Castle," replied the tinker. The tale goes on to say that Scrope hurried back to Yorkshire, found the gold, and rebuilt the castle.

Nearer Felixkirk is Nevison House, said to have been one of the hiding-places of Nevison, the highwayman whom Charles II nick-named Swift Nick.

Wath. In a lovely setting of woods and meadows near Ripon, its wide road with trees and cobbled pavements comes to the gates of the Norton Conyers park which lies between the village and the River Ure. Here, among noble old trees and lawns with spacious views, is the Tudor home of the Grahams, made only more beautiful by the hand of Time.

Charlotte Brontë loved Norton Conyers, and Wordsworth knew its tragic memories and made them the theme of *The White Doe of Rylstone*. Here in Elizabeth I's day lived the Nortons, ardent Roman Catholics who wished to see their old faith restored in England. From this house Richard Norton, last of his line at Wath, rode off to join the Rising of the North, and with him went six sons and his brother Thomas. Their rebellion came to nothing, and two of them were executed.

The Nortons and the Grahams sleep in the church, at the end of the long street with many old creepered cottages and the 17th century schoolhouse. Some of the church is new, but the walls of the nave may have been here when the Battle of Hastings was fought, though its windows are 15th century. The chancel (made new in the 13th century) has remains of a stringcourse carved with nail-head, windows from the 14th century, three sedilia, a double piscina, two aumbries, and a diamond of glass believed to have been made within a generation of Magna Carta. Old glass in the south chapel shows a 14th century Crucifixion and a brilliant 15th century shield.

This big chapel was built for a chantry about 1328 by John Appleby, a rector; and a huge battered canopy which may have belonged to his tomb now shelters a stone with a sword and a cross, perhaps a memorial to John's brother. Near the canopy is a big piscina, and in the east wall is one of the biggest aumbries we have seen. A Flaxman monument of a man with his head bowed is a tribute to Thomas Brand, a rector who died in the year before Waterloo, and a brass inscription to a rector of 1706 has the words, *God send us all a happy meeting*. A striking alabaster monument of the tragic year of Charles I shows Catherine Graham and her husband kneeling on a ledge above the worn figures of two sons and four daughters. Brass portraits of the Nortons show Sir John of 1489 in armour, and Sir Richard of 1420 and his wife, who both died of the plague. Sir Richard was Chief Justice of the Common Pleas, and we see him in his robes, his wife wearing a rich robe and mantle and a draped headdress.

The 15th century vestry on the north side of the chancel has lost its upper room but keeps its spiral stair, a peephole to the chancel, and the lintel made from an old coffin-lid with a cross over the mediaeval door. By the door is a stone with crude carving of two little men arm in arm. In the vestry are the head of a mediaeval coffin-lid with a cross, part of the head of a Saxon cross, and a splendid chest about 600 years old, carved with tracery and a hound springing on a deer. On the base of an old cross in the churchyard is what is thought to be a 13th century font.

Welbury. Here are magnificent views of the Hambleton Hills and a lowly church reached by a path embowered with sycamores, yews, and laburnums. The chancel is made new, but the nave has its old walls and a massive double bellcote over the west gable. The modern porch has a sundial, and shelters an old door with 1690 patterned in studs. The old doorway in which it hangs is worn with sharpening of tools or knives, and its lintel is a coffin stone engraved with a cross, a book, and a chalice. In the north wall is a fragment of Norman zigzag.

Well. An old-fashioned village between Ripon and Bedale, it shelters under a hill from which we see a score of churches in a magnificent view of the Vale of York, ending in the bold lines of the Wolds. The little red-roofed houses are set in gay gardens; and behind the long line of almshouses coming to the lychgate is Well Hall, with a high wall between its garden and the churchyard, where one of the tallest old crosses in Yorkshire raises its headless shaft as high as the chancel. The almshouses were founded 600 years ago by Ralph Neville, Lord of Middleham, and the priests in charge were the builders of what is now the dining-room of the hall, a beautiful 14th century stone-vaulted chamber with great round pillars down the middle of it.

The well which gave the place its name was known to travellers before the Romans built a villa here. It has been excavated, and a fragment of tessellated pavement dug up last century is treasured in the church. It is believed that the church itself has in its walls much stone from the Roman house.

With a story old enough to have brought it into Domesday Book, the church is chiefly mediaeval, though the rough masonry of the lower part of the high tower is believed to be Norman. The south chapel was the burial place of the Latimers, descendants of the powerful Nevilles. Here is 14th century glass showing four knights and shields; and on a big tomb lies the stone figure of a knight in armour with a creature like a harpy at his feet. He was Sir John Neville, the last Lord Latimer, who went with Henry VIII on his last journey to France. There is a tomb with a brass inscription to his mother, Lady Dorothea. Another of his father's three wives was Catherine Parr, who became Henry VIII's sixth wife and his lucky widow. One of the old gravestones here is probably to the wife of a 14th century Neville; another has shears carved on it, and a third has a sword, a hammer, and a horseshoe.

The north chapel has a piscina set in a peephole, an old altar table, and a reredos with fine old carving showing Adam and Eve, Abraham and Isaac, the Annunciation, the Nativity and shepherds, and a quaint Resurrection. The mediaeval sacristy has corbels which once supported the floor of an upper room; there is a window looking to the chancel, and the top stone of a tomb is carved with a cross and a chalice. There are old roof beams, old hinges on the modern door, and a font with a fine cover dated 1352. The exquisite embroidered altar frontal was the gift of a kinswoman of the Lady Margaret Milbank whose marble monument by Westmacott shows a girl in the arms of an angel.

Wensley. Fortune has smiled on Wensley, for the small village is as delightful as its setting. It has given its name to Wensleydale, where the River Ure flows for 20 miles of its journey to the Swale. It is the biggest of the Yorkshire dales, and, many think, the loveliest.

The village is on the sunny side of a hill dropping sharply to the river, here broad and deep as it comes by the park of Bolton Hall, under the four arches of a mediaeval bridge widened for modern traffic. The Preston Beck, running through the village, joins the river below the bridge. The houses, the church, and the gates to the park are by sloping greens, one shaded by the mingling foliage of two oaks and a beech, another by a magnificent elm with a trunk over 20 feet round. A footpath runs through the park, and a long drive with beeches, limes, and yews leads to Bolton Hall, the handsome 17th century house which comes into the *Ingoldsby Legends* and has been partly rebuilt after a fire. There are fine gardens and a terrace 692 feet long, the length of the Great Eastern, which was the talk of the day when the terrace was being made. A fragment of glass from Bolton Castle has on it the signature of Mary Queen of Scots, and there are portraits of the famous Scropes.

The builder of the hall was Charles Paulet, 1st Duke of Bolton, a strange man who travelled about England in the 17th century with four coaches and 100 horsemen, sleeping by day and entertaining at night. It is said that he would not speak till late in the day, when he thought the air was pure.

The church is a fine old building with a rich store of treasure. The massive tower was rebuilt in the 18th century, but the chancel has stood since 1245, when the church was built on the site of one of Saxon days. Its east window is curious for the plate tracery over the two shortest of its five trefoiled lights, and the lancets in its south wall are enriched with ornament. The same ornament is a delightful openwork edging for the three sedilia, but the plainer trefoiled piscina beside them is a century later. The nave and aisles are 14th and 15th century; the porches, and the two-storeyed sacristy on the north of the chancel, are 15th century. The north porch shelters a beautiful doorway of about 1300, and the south porch has a sundial with the words, *As a shadow, such is life.*

There is much here to remind us of the famous Scropes, whose castle is a few miles up the dale. Their shields are carved on buttresses and on the north porch, and shine in the east window in old glass. Round the extraordinary Bolton pew (looking like a box at the theatre in a bay of the north aisle), is magnificent screenwork 400 years old, once surrounding the Scrope chantry in Easby Abbey and brought here after the Dissolution. Above and below its bays of leafy arches, finials, and pinnacled buttresses, runs an inscription in memory of many Scropes, and on panels below are brilliantly painted shields. The pew itself has a panelled roof with pendant bosses. Set in the wall of this aisle is a black stone of about 1514, with the portraits (carved in relief) of two boys of the Scrope family, their eyes sad, their tiny heads under rich canopies.

The arms of the Scropes are on the shields adorning the lovely stalls, which were made for Henry Richardson, rector, in 1527. Said to be the work of the Ripon school of carvers, they have poppyhead ends, and curious little tabernacles enclosing the pillars, which support a fine array of heraldic beasts, among them a hound with a collar and chain, a wyvern, a crowned leopard, a lion, a bear, and a hare ready to leap. The altar-rails are Jacobean; the nave has some mediaeval benches and box-pews of 1820, and the pulpit is part of an 18th century three-decker. A rare treasure is a wooden reliquary from Easby Abbey, where it is thought to have held the relics of the abbey's patron, St Agatha. Made in the 15th century, it has an embattled top and is carved on the front.

The 17th century font has a crude inscription with some letters upside down, and a carved cover surmounted by an acorn looking like a pineapple. In the traces of mediaeval painting on the east pillars of the arcades are the Archangels Gabriel and Michael, Satan being cast out of Heaven, and two figures who may be Adam and Eve; on the north wall are Jacob and Esau with the head of a horse, and a gruesome fragment of the legend of the Three Living and the Three Dead. Carved on one of several Saxon stones in the wall are curious animals and birds, and others commemorate three 8th century priests, Donfrid, Eadbrecht, and Aruini. Two brother rectors centuries later, Richard and John Clederow, lie in the nave, their huge gravestone now doing service at marriages and funerals.

One thing more has to be added to the list of treasures, for the church has in its keeping a brass which claims to be the finest in Yorkshire, rarely surpassed in any village church in the land. The work of a Flemish engraver, it is the portrait of a rector, Simon de Wenslawe, who died in 1395, showing him in robes adorned with weird animals in medallions, with two dogs at his feet, two angels by his head, and his crossed hands falling gracefully below a chalice; the brass is over 5 feet long. Above the portrait is a brass inscription to Oswald Dykes, a rector of 1607.

The churchyard has a fine view, the shaft of an old cross, and quaint gravestones. There lies in one of these graves Thomas Maude, a poet born in Downing Street in 1718 and therefore born, one would have thought, to fame. But he had no fame, though he wrote six volumes of verses and essays, and of the last of his volumes (which was cut short abruptly at page 100) only two copies were printed, one of which we may see in the British Museum.

West Acklam. It is the Acklam near Middlesbrough, once a lonely spot with a hall and an ancient church in a green and pleasant land. Today there are many new houses, the hall is a school, and the church has been made new, but they are still companions in a quiet spot by the fields, with a moat close by filled with water. New buildings have been given to the old hall, which is attractive with gables, a baluster parapet, and tall chimneys. The church is a neat little place with a charming bellcote resting on an angel, a south chapel with two arches to the nave, and a chancel arch with angels above capitals enriched with foliage. One of the windows has lovely glass showing St Luke and St Hilda, with pictures below them of an artist painting the Madonna, and Caedmon singing the first English song in the Saxon monastery at Whitby. Above the saints are angels working as carpenters and artists.

Two stone figures of mediaeval women (one very battered) are believed to belong to the Boynton family who had land here seven centuries ago. A third figure is a very dainty lady with drapery on her netted hair, and a string of flowers down the front of her dress which has buttoned sleeves. She is thought to be Margaret Conyers, wife of Sir Thomas Boynton, who died in 1402. The arms of both families are on the cushion under her head.

West Ayton. A handsome stone bridge carries the road from Pickering to Scarborough across the Derwent, separating West Ayton from East Ayton, which has the old church. Looking down on the river and the cottages and gardens from a bank in a field are the ruins of a castle, said to have been built in the 14th century to defend the narrow opening of the richly-wooded Forge Valley through which the Derwent has come. Here lived Lord Evers in 1500, and Sir Ralph Evers, who had a strong garrison here in the days of the Pilgrimage of Grace. Now only the broken shell of the castle is left, with some windows and archways, and the vaulted basement of a tower where cattle come for shade and shelter.

West Burton. A mile and a half from Aysgarth, it is near the meeting of two lovely dales whose wild moorland streams unite before falling into the River Ure—Bishopdale running from Kidstones Bank, and Walden Dale, deep and secluded, from the slopes of Buckden Pike. Impetuous and enchanting is the Walden Beck as this village knows it. The music of the stream reaches the great hillside green which is another proud heritage of the village, a fascinating picture with horses grazing, children playing, and an unusual stone cross, like a church spire, on a flight of steps. There is a cottage by the cross which was once an inn, and other houses on and round the green, a big happy family sharing in the beauty of this countryside of mighty hills and lovely dales. Above the village rises the ridge of Penhill, nearly 1800 feet at its highest point.

Westerdale. The River Esk running through the dale is only 4 miles on its journey to Castleton when it flows by Westerdale Hall, now a Youth Hostel, whose embattled tower peeps above the trees. The church, standing on the hillside above the hall, was made new last century, but has in its porch half a dozen fragments of old crosses and coffin-lids, one of them rare for having carved on it a bow and arrow and a dagger. Near by is a fine mediaeval packhorse bridge.

To the west of this valley other streams unite to flow through the narrow and secluded Baysdale, which cuts through the Cleveland Hills on its way to Castleton. The house known as Baysdale Abbey is on the site of a Cistercian nunnery. At the very head of Westerdale, at the junction of several ancient ways is Ralph Cross, with, near by, the charming Fat Betty and a memorial to the Cleveland naturalist Frank Elgee.

West Rounton. It lies among the little hills, its houses in gay gardens, the green shaded by five chestnut trees, and the small church perched on a pretty slope, looking down on the trees where the bridge crosses the River Wiske. A simple nave and chancel with a double bellcote, it has been made partly new, but has something to show of the Norman church. The south doorway is carved with zigzag, and rich zigzag adorns the low and massive chancel arch. The fine though battered font is a Norman treasure, carved with foliage and zigzag, a grotesque with the face of a grinning man and the bodies of two animals, and Sagittarius shooting an arrow at the head of a giant. A scratch dial is probably Norman, and a small stoup is made of fossil marble.

West Tanfield. It has almost all we could wish to find in an English village. Wooded hills rise above it, and the broad River Ure, fresh cascading over the rocks in the delightful Hackfall Woods, comes grandly to an old bridge of three arches, and grouped near the bridge are the church, the lovely Chantry Cottage (its stone porch a gem), and a noble 15th century gatehouse with an oriel window above the great arch. A peep from the oriel gives us one of the most enchanting bits of river scenery.

There is much to remind us of the Marmions, who came here in 1215 and lost the last man of the house 600 years ago. Their monuments are in the church, where they sleep. The gatehouse was probably built by Elizabeth Marmion's husband, Henry Fitzhugh, but of the manor house itself nothing is left.

Though the south side is partly new, most of the church is mediaeval. The nave and chancel and the low arcade are about 1350, and the spacious north aisle and its chapel are a century later. The tower comes from early and late in the 15th century; from the 14th century come the two most curious features of the building. One is a small bay projecting from the nave into the churchyard, probably serving as a shelter for the ringer of the sanctus bell; the other is a tiny chamber built in the thickness of the wall by the chancel arch, and projecting into the chancel like a lean-to. This fascinating room, 5 feet by 4, has small trefoiled windows, and may have been a chantry. The font is 14th century.

Beautiful woodwork of our time (some of it signed with Robert Thompson's little mouse) adds greatly to the charm of the church. A lovely oak figure of St Michael is in memory of one who fell in the Great War. There are rich altar-rails, and the reredos (carved and coloured) has the Nativity scene, and golden figures of St George and St Michael under canopies. On the reading-desks are four monks playing the harp, the fiddle, the horn, and the flute; and the poppyhead stalls have linenfold and a fine array of animals, birds, and grotesques, among them a hen with a chick on her back, and a serpent catching a big fly. The pulpit also has fine linenfold, and on its stairway is St Nicholas with three children in a tub.

We see St Nicholas again in modern glass, together with the Madonna and St Hilda. In a window filled with old glass are the Madonna, St Gregory, and the Crucifixion, and above them St John, St James, and John the Baptist; in the top of the window are figures of St Michael (weighing a demon and a soul), St Ambrose, and St William. At the foot are the shields of Marmion and John of Gaunt, and in the borders are black eagles and golden butterflies.

Lying on a 14th century alabaster tomb are a knight and his lady, he wearing armour with a rich helmet and collar, she with the arms of St Quintin on her mantle, held by a cord and clasps. The knight is probably either John Marmion or his brother Robert, each of whom married a St Quintin. The striking feature of the tomb is the fine original iron hearse above it, with uprights like the frame for a tent, and an embattled bar above the sleeping figures. Here would hang a rich pall, and candles would be placed on the seven spikes.

Under a 14th century recess enriched with a lofty canopy are two battered figures, believed to be Maude Marmion (who died about 1360) and the husband she outlived. A worn figure with feet on a lion is supposed to be a woman. Another battered lady of the 14th century, lying on a tomb, is probably Avice Marmion. The knight lying in chain mail, his legs crossed, is either Sir William or Sir Robert Marmion of the 13th century, and is interesting to antiquarians because the monument shows the old method of attaching the shield to the left arm by two straps.

On the floor of the chancel we see Thomas Sutton in an elaborate cope; he died about the time America was discovered, and his brass portrait shines like new. Cut in the base of the porch (which has a stone roof and a quaint gable) is an inscription to Ralph Bourn, who came into the world a year before Shakespeare went out. He lived through the turbulent days of Charles I, saw the Puritan hour of triumph give place to the dissolute days of Charles II, escaped the Great Plague, heard the news of the Fire of London, lived through

WHENBY

Queen Anne's reign and into the reign of George I, and died in 1728 after well over a century of life.

West Witton. Its long street is a wavy line on the northern slope of Penhill, and from its splendid perch behind the old grey houses the church looks far up Wensleydale, seeing the river shining below limestone crags rising like battlements above the village. Silver birches shade the path in the churchyard, the last resting-place of John James, a poet and scholar who was born here in 1812, wrote a monumental history of Bradford, and came to lie in the village he had loved as a child. Educating himself, he began life by working at a lime-kiln and then as a clerk in a lawyer's office, eventually turning to journalism and antiquarian research. He edited books of poems and wrote a *History of Worsted*. The church was made almost new last century, but it has old glass showing a shield with three shells, and bells that were ringing before the Reformation have found shelter in the nave. One is an alphabet bell, the other, queerly shaped and highly pitched, is said to be one of the oldest in Yorkshire. Older still is a fragment of a cross with carving thought to have been done long before the Normans came.

An annual event here is a bonfire known as "the Burning of Owd Bartle". Bartle, it appears, was a thief of many years ago who was threatened that if he extended his activities to West Witton he would be severely dealt with by the inhabitants, who then included many tinkers and suchlike people. He did arrive in West Witton, was duly spotted and chased round the Penhill area, run to ground in the village, and burned. Every year now his effigy is publicly burned with due ceremony—presumably as a warning to those who think they can take liberties with the inhabitants of this village.

Whenby. Aloof from the world, it has a handful of farms and cottages, and a fine little 15th century church sheltered by trees which almost hug its walls. Its charming porch has stone seats, four windows, a gable cross, and stones worn with the sharpening of tools or weapons. An old door opens to a spacious interior. The arcade has three heads, the chancel screen and some pews are 15th century, and a Jacobean screen divides the aisle and chapel. The old font is one of the lowest we have seen.

Whitby. It stands superb and masterly above the sea, looking out to the rolling ocean over which a Yorkshire boy was to sail away to find a continent. It was Captain Cook who sailed from here to win immortal fame.

And it was here that there began another immortality, our English literature. For both these things the world owes much to Whitby, for it was the inspiration of the intrepid seaman who made our sea-power possible, and the inspiration of Caedmon who started our English poetry on the spot where we stand in the ruins of Whitby Abbey.

It will seem to most of us an adequate distinction for any town, and yet we must be deeply moved by one more impressive fact concerning Whitby. Captain Cook's dust lies far across the world and he has no grave at which we can pay homage, but here in the abbey ruins is not only the dust of Caedmon our first poet but also the dust of that King Oswy who fought and won the last great fight against paganism in this land. For centuries Christianity had been struggling for existence, and had been beaten again and again. It seemed that it was finally established by King Edwin after the Council of Goodmanham and the founding of York Minster, but it fell from its high place, and the pagan King Penda, who fought King Edwin and slew him, rose supreme again. King Oswy gave his daughter to King Penda's son, and offered the king all his rich treasures; but Penda had nothing but scorn for peace with Oswy, and led him to a battle-field in which the forces of paganism were heavily against him. Penda was slain and his troops scattered. Then it was that Christianity was at last established, and it was Oswy who made peace between its warring factions at the Council of Whitby in the year 664. In Oswy's day the burning question between the rival forces of Christianity in these islands were when we should celebrate Easter, and whether a priest should shave his head in the shape of a crescent or a ring. Oswy decided in favour of the Roman way.

It is good to find that Whitby, with such a thrilling tale, is so superb a place. And yet there are two Whitbys, or perhaps there are four—old and new, up and down. The thing we come for is up at the top of 199 steps, the crowds that throng the streets are down below, with the beach still farther down. Its houses crowd themselves between the Eastcliff where nearly everything is old and the

Westcliff where nearly everything is new. There are stone piers with lighthouses; narrow passages that lead us to little colonies of cottages; peeps of the harbour through houses centuries old; a street too steep for cars, with the mounting-stone for the horsemen who rode up and down it long ago; the wooden carving of a smuggler on an inn; an old chapel John Wesley opened with a sermon; the odd little town hall; and Bagdale Hall, the oldest house in the town, full of beautiful things, with a Venetian lamp outside it, great ship's beams inside, and a garden of enchantment.

The new Library by the station is a striking building, and the Pannett Art Gallery and Museum are set in a pleasant garden. The museum has fossils telling the story of the Earth, monsters like huge crocodiles, ammonites extraordinary (Whitby has them on its shield), model lifeboats, a stone with a Roman inscription and a bronze comb with a Saxon one, and a tiny head of St Hilda carved in a chestnut. Most precious of all are the little group of things concerning Captain Cook: a bone club he brought home, a plan of a harbour he drew, and part of a quadrant he used. In a little fleet of model ships is one of Cook's *Resolution*, on which he made his last voyage; it shows the cabin in which he would write the last entry in his journal.

There is a model of the *Resolution* as a weathervane on Westcliff, close by the bronze statue of Captain Cook himself—a noble figure, showing him with a chart under his arm and compasses in his hand, his coat thrown open as if by the wind, his hair drawn back and tied with a ribbon, his eyes looking out to the North Sea in the direction he took when he ran away and sailed from Whitby harbour. The inscription tells us that his lasting memorial is in Whitby's keeping because the town was the birthplace of those good ships which bore him on his enterprises, brought him home to glory, and left him at rest.

A boy with all the world before him (a tremendous part of it waiting for him to discover), he was to make three voyages in Whitby-built ships, the first of them owned by two Quaker brothers whose house still stands in Grape Lane. The house was old in Cook's day, for part of it is 15th century. We climbed up to the attic where little James would sling his hammock and teach himself mathematics and astronomy and the principles of seamanship. From this room he would look down on the harbour and see the beauty of the River Esk as we see it from his window, but he would not dream that people would come from the ends of the earth to see his statue and the place where he was born.

Whitby's shipbuilding days have gone, but the town may well be proud of the fine ships launched here, and of the captains who sailed them to the Greenland whaling ground. Among them were the two William Scoresbys. Old William, one of the pioneers of whaling, sailed from Whitby every year for 30 years, bringing home oil worth about £100,000. Said to have captured more whales than any other man, he reached the Farthest North of his day, and it was he who devised what is known as the crow's-nest, the look-out at a ship's mast-head. His son was one of the chief authorities on the Arctic regions.

A pathetic figure would be seen wandering by the wharves here in the 17th century, Luke Fox. He had done a great thing and had gone unrewarded. It was he who revived interest in the search for the North-West Passage, and made an expedition from London to the Far North in an unusually small ship; but he came home, disappointed at his failure to find a way through, and was neglected and forgotten for his pains. He sleeps in the churchyard on the cliff, the sea thundering below his grave.

Whitby is not famous for its churches, but one good church there is to see—the 19th century St Hilda. It has a handsome stone pulpit on which are carved tiny demons and angels carrying a shield with three ammonites, the badge of the town. Two churchwarden staffs have lovely little figures. There are beautiful oak screens, a chair like a bishop's throne rich with angels and shields, and a canopied reredos with a host of angels and a Crucifixion on a gilded background. The roof is painted. Up the hill also is the queer church not unlike a house outside and very much like a ship inside, one of the most amazing and astonishing churches in Britain, at present desperately in need of money for its upkeep. It has a massive west tower, a Norman window, a striking south doorway, and a splendid chancel arch; Georgian porches, sash windows, a roof on iron pillars lit by skylights, galleries like the decks of a ship, and box-pews of all shapes and sizes, some low down and some high up, all with little doors.

We imagine that the parson here must feel like the captain of a very strange ship. He preaches in the oddest three-decker pulpit we remember, with a square lower deck, and a many-sided top deck. There is one stirring monument, a marble dome set on eight pillars in memory of 13 lifeboatmen who five times in one day went out, and then went out a sixth time, which smashed the boat and drowned 12 of the 13, the odd man swimming to shore. With many old sailors in the churchyard lies poor Luke Fox, and among the gravestones near him we found one of a man and his wife who were born on the same day and died on the same day, the anniversary of their wedding.

We come from this queer place to one of our most sacred shrines, the cradle of English literature. If we have climbed the 199 steps from the streets above the leaning houses, above the ships and shops, we are rewarded abundantly at last, for here is this magnificent view of hills and moor and sea, the old cross on its broken steps, and the ruins of the Abbey of St Hilda.

The abbey church is almost all that has come through the long centuries of storm; this is the very place where Caedmon dreamed his dream and wrote his *Song of Creation*. For most of our ruins we must look in deep green valleys and lonely corners, but here we stand a stone's throw from the cliff, beaten by high winds. For situation, Yorkshire has no other abbey to compare with it.

These Saxon stones we find here and there among the 13th century ruins are thrilling things. It is all from the days when Caedmon was looking after the swine for the Abbess Hilda, unlettered and all afraid when they called on him to sing a song, yet finding such inspiration in a dream that in the morning he brought them his *Song of Creation*, the first poet and the first poem known in our literature.

It was in those days of the birth of Poetry that our Easter holidays were fixed for us at Whitby, where the Saxon leaders of the Church met to settle the date of Easter. King Oswy of Northumbria had to decide between the way of the Britons and the way of the Romans, and the Romans had a powerful champion in Wilfrid of York, who declared that his authority came from St Peter, who held the keys of Heaven. The Britons were bound to confess that they had no such authority, and Oswy answered, "Then I will obey St Peter, lest when I come to the Gate of Heaven there be none to open to me". So we take our Easter holidays when we do—often wishing we did not, but doing it because the Saxon bishops and the Saxon saints decided it at Whitby in 664.

Of their old abbey only the stones are left, but of the 13th century church there are spacious and noble ruins. The west end has a beautiful doorway and a noble lancet under a delightful little diamond window. There are 14th century windows with their tracery intact, clustered pillars in the nave (one complete with its capital), a stone seat from the old porch, and enough of the chancel to show that it must have been a majestic structure. The triforium has great arches which once framed lancet windows, each pair with a central clustered column, and above the triforium is an arcaded clerestory from which stone faces still look into the chancel. There is a broken roof in the choir aisle, with stone vaulting and bosses on which are holy lambs.

The great north transept is the supreme glory of the ruined abbey. It has panelled buttresses, niches with old faces looking out to sea, and stone enrichments on the windows. It has a pillar with traces of an inscription recording the dedication of the transept in the 14th century. It has a glorious triforium and clerestory, arcading round the walls, windows with deep moulding and marvellously perfect foliage, and a wall with nine superb lancets below a rose window.

On this green hillside Caedmon looked after his cattle. Here it was, when the harp was passed round the great hall, that he had no song to sing, though he dreamed a song that night that should live for all time. Captain Cook below at the foot of these steps, Caedmon on the hill—it is a famous place. There is a memorial to Caedmon, a stone cross carved in Saxon style unveiled to our first poet by Alfred Austin, poet laureate, in 1898. It is 20 feet high, and is carved with panels showing Christ giving blessing, St Hilda treading snakes, which she is said to have banished from Whitby (so giving rise to a picturesque explanation of the many ammonite fossils found near by), under her feet, David the Psalmist, and Caedmon with his harp. The cross has animals and birds carved in its foliage, and on it are the first lines of the first great English song:

Now must we praise the Guardian of heaven's realm,
The Creator's might and his mind's thought.

The imagery of Caedmon's song has been simply put in this way:

As yet was nought save shadows of darkness; the spacious Earth lay hidden, deep and dim, alien to God, unpeopled and unused.

Thereon the Steadfast King looked down and beheld it, a place empty of joy. He saw dim chaos hanging in eternal night, obscure beneath the heavens. Here first with mighty power the Everlasting Lord, the Helm of all created things, Almighty King, made Earth and Heaven, raised up the sky, and founded the spacious land. The Earth was not yet green with grass; the dark waves of the sea flowed over it; midnight darkness was upon it, far and wide.

This is nearer to the way Caedmon wrote it; these are the first lines of his first poem, on the first day of Creation:

There had not here as yet,	*Here first shaped*
Some cavern-shade,	*The Lord Eternal*
Aught been;	*Chief of all creatures,*
But this wide abyss	*Heaven and Earth,*
Stood deep and dim,	*The firmament upreared,*
Strange to its Lord,	*And this spacious land*
Idle and useless;	*Established,*
On which looked with his eyes	*By his strong powers,*
The King firm of mind,	*The Lord Almighty.*
And beheld those places	*The Earth as yet was*
Void of joys;	*Not green with grass;*
Saw the dark cloud	*Ocean covered*
Lower in eternal night,	*Swart in eternal night,*
Swart under heaven,	*Far and wide,*
Dark and waste . . .	*The dusky ways.*

Whitby is no longer the important fishing and shipbuilding centre it was—indeed unemployment here is high. Recently a scheme to mine potash on the outskirts of the town and near by has provoked much controversy; it would provide much-needed employment, but would damage Whitby as a tourist centre.

Whorlton. Detached from the Clevelands, the conspicuous Whorl Hill gives a name to this place, which has the remains of an old castle, an ancient church partly in ruins, and a church (with a tower and spire rising above the trees) which took the place of the old one in 1875. The new church is down in the valley at Swainby, where the moorland stream, flowing by old houses and under many bridges, has come its charming three-mile journey through Scugdale.

Robert de Meynell is thought to have built the first Norman castle here. The crumbling mass of masonry we see on the mound is of the tower-house which followed. There is a deep fosse shaded by trees, and a fine gatehouse of about 1400 which has over its archway the carved shields of Meynell, Darcy, and Grey. Among those who once lived here was the Earl of Lennox whose son Darnley married Mary Queen of Scots, tradition linking this grim place with the intrigues which brought about the unhappy marriage.

In a churchyard with a yew tunnel 50 yards long, the church has a story as old as that of the castle. The old nave is roofless now. Its aisles vanished long ago, but here are still the old arcades through which we can walk—the north arcade Norman, the south a generation after them, though its arches are round, except for the pointed western arch of a later time. The tower is about 1400 and has a mediaeval bell, and the massive font is Norman work.

Used now as a burial chapel, the chancel is chiefly Norman and 14th century, with a 15th century east window showing an angel and a shield in old glass. On its west gable is a mediaeval bellcote. The Norman chancel arch, with three shafts at each side, is curiously blocked and has a door with a tiny wicket gate through which we peep. Its great possession is a beautiful canopied tomb, probably of about 1400, adorned with figures of two bishops. On it lies one of the rare wooden figures still left in our churches, with his legs crossed and a dog at his feet. He is thought to represent Nicholas, 2nd Lord Maynell, who died in 1322, and to have been carved by the craftsman who made the wonderful monument to Edmund Plantagenet in Westminster Abbey.

Wilton. Below Easton Nab, one of the most striking landmarks hereabouts, Wilton has a glorious background of woods and a great company of trees hiding it from the Redcar road. Only 6 miles from Middlesbrough, which is fast encroaching on it, it has small houses in the splendid park of Wilton Castle, a house with creepered walls, battlements, and a great array of turrets, of which we get a fine peep

from the churchyard. It was built early last century on the site of
the old home of the Bulmers, who lost their estates through their
share in the Pilgrimage of Grace in Tudor days.

The church is quaint and charming with its walls of amber-
coloured stone and a turret crowned with an odd wooden spire,
resting inside on a triple arch. The Norman nave and the 13th
century chancel are very well restored, but some of their original
windows remain, and the tall doorway through which we come and
go has the zigzag carving of the Normans. In the sheltering porch
are the stone figures of a knight and lady who are probably of the
Bulmer family, the knight's armour interesting to antiquarians for
the ailette worn on the shoulder. Round his stone is a border of
flowers.

Wilton. Four miles along the road from Pickering to Scarborough, it has a small gathering of stone-built houses and farms,
and a fine little church rebuilt in 1922 by the Hothams. It is full of
light, and through its windows we see the land rising to the moors
on the north side, and the great Vale spread out on the south. An
arch in the west wall suggests that some day there will be a tower.
One old bell rings in the gabled bellcote, and another stands in the
nave which has on its walls the panelling of 17th century pews. The
font is Norman. Some of the pillars and arches on the south side of
the nave are mediaeval, and have set the pattern for the rest in both
arcades. There are black-and-white roofs, with kingposts in the
nave.

Wycliffe. It is the home of the Wycliffes who gave the world the
Morning Star of the Reformation, and claims to have been his birthplace, but it is believed that that distinction belongs to Hipswell not
far away. Here, however, still live folk using the words Wycliffe used
in his translation of the Bible, and here for centuries the Wycliffes
lived. In the rectory is what is claimed to be the only authentic
portrait of the reformer, showing him with a fine strong face and
kindly eyes; a reproduction of it hangs in the church. At the risk of
his life he gave us the Bible in our common speech, and sent out his
Lollards as sheep among wolves. He brought a storm of indignation

over his head, and had priests and bishops thundering about him; but he went on quietly with his work, finished it, and died in his bed before his enemies could drag him to the stake.

Though there may be doubt about its being Wycliffe's birthplace, there is none about its right to be called one of the most fascinating and delightful villages in Yorkshire. The handful of dwellings in lovely gardens are with the church where the steep lane drops down to the Tees—here a broad river rushing over a rocky bed, with the wooded cliffs of Durham on the other side. The old mill, now a children's hospital, has the waterwheel for the entrance to the garden through which the mill-race flows, and the axle stands on the lawn. From the road above the village the hall is seen among lovely trees, a splendid cedar on its lawn.

The high ivied walls of the nave and chancel seem to be roofless as we stand by the small 13th century church which was made partly new in the 14th. The chancel is aslant from the long nave, which is crowned with an old bellcote and entered through an old porch with the ancient studded door still swinging. There are three windows from the close of the 13th century, and a fine row with the flowing tracery of the 14th, of which the east window is a modern copy. Their beauty is enhanced by the rich mediaeval glass filling two of them and half-filling others, a collection unsurpassed in the North Riding; there are shields of arms, minstrel angels, two Madonnas, a Trinity, and many saints, as well as much canopy work and medleys of fragments.

There are fragments of Saxon stones with knotwork, and part of a hogback with carving of scales and the head of a bear. A stone figure has long hair and praying hands, and a black stone on the chancel floor has one of the quaintest portraits of a priest we have seen, showing him under a canopy above which are a chalice and a book. He is like a Chinese Mandarin, his face sour, his tiny feet with toes turned out, his portly body in a bundle of vestments.

In the chancel sleep many Wycliffes. Ralph, who was only 14 when he died in 1606, has his portrait in shining brass, and there is an inscription to William of 1611, and another to Roger, who died four years before the Reformer. Oak choir-stalls by Thompson of Kilburn commemorate those from the village who fell in the two world wars; and there is more woodwork by Thompson in the church. Other treasures include a 13th century altar top and an Elizabethan chalice.

Wykeham. It lies by the great trees of the beautiful 160-acre park, and has a stream flowing behind a 19th century church with a lychgate which must surely be unique. It is the tower of the vanished chapel of St Mary and St Helen, said to have been founded by John de Wykeham in the 14th century; and was thoroughly restored in 1855 and given its spire. The rich woodcarving within the church (in the seats, the altar-rails, the candlesticks, and the Litany desk) is proclaimed by his little mouse to be the work of the well-known craftsman of Kilburn.

The old parish church of All Saints was pulled down when the new one was built. It stood in the park near Wykeham Abbey, a modern house on part of the site of a priory of which a broken wall is almost all that is left. It was founded for Cistercian nuns in the 12th century, by Paganus de Wykeham.

Yarm. Its busy days are over. All the bustle and stir of Yarm came to an end with the rise of Stockton and Middlesbrough, and today it is a quiet little town with its mills deserted and its warehouses empty. Running through a long narrow loop of the Tees, the spacious main street has a few trees, and cobbled verges where the grass tends to grow now. There are old inns and old houses, a school grown up from one founded in Elizabethan days, and a house known as the Friarage, said to be on the site of a monastery founded for the Black Friars by a 13th century Bruce. A curious octagonal chapel of 1760 where John Wesley preached is down an alley near the market hall, an 18th century building with arcades supporting an upper floor with a turret for a clock and bells.

On the market hall is a plaque showing an old engine described as Locomotion Number One, and below it are the names of the five men who founded the first railway in the world. They were Thomas Meynell, Benjamin Flounders, Jeremiah Cairns, Richard Mills, and Thomas Miles, whose meeting here, at the George and Dragon inn, was destined to have astounding results. The meeting, which took place on February 12, 1820, is recorded by a plaque on the wall of the inn. They had no idea that they were going to change the world, for all they were to do was to ask Parliament to help them to build a railway, but it was the first of all public railways, the famous line from Stockton to Darlington. Their meeting at Yarm was the beginning of the hundreds of thousands of miles of railways now covering the earth. The railways are never forgotten here, for, striding above the housetops on its way through the town, is a splendid viaduct on which the trains run over 40 arches spanning together about half a mile. One of the biggest of its kind in England, it was built of brick and stone in the middle of last century at a cost of over £80,000.

The river which makes Yarm almost an island has many times brought calamity in the shape of floods, which have risen in the market-place to a height of more than 4 feet. One flood height is recorded on the side of a house in Church Wynd. The dredging of the river bed below the town has lessened the danger. The stone bridge carrying the road across the end of the loop was first built about 1400 by Walter Skirlaw, Bishop of Durham, but it has been restored and widened since his day. Egglescliffe's church crowns a grassy bank on the Durham side.

What is known as Tom Brown's House was once an inn where lived a hero of Dettingen who rode into the thickest of the fight there, rescued the British flag, and came back to talk of his exploit to the end of his days. Every boy knows the namesake of Rugby, but this Tom Brown, bearing the same name, is little known. He died here with 20 bullets in his body, and sleeps in the churchyard on the river brink.

The church was much rebuilt in formal style in 1730, but part of the church the Normans left survives in the surprising west end, with the tower growing from the gable, low flanking turrets, plain and carved stringcourses, and three round-headed windows. One of these windows, and an oval above it, are cut in a huge flat buttress. The top of the tower may be 15th century, and the font with plain shields is probably as old. A mediaeval stone has small figures of a man and his wife, their hands at prayer, and a window of 1768 shows Moses with the Tables of the Law and a picture of him among the bulrushes. The oak pews lending distinction to the interior have panelled ends with scrolled tops.

Yarm's curiosity is its castle. Built over half a century ago on a garden wall facing the church, it is a fine little model with a keep and bastion towers, and with it is a model of the market hall.

APPENDIX

Places of interest open to the Public

(* Indicates National Trust Property)

(† Indicates Ministry of Public Building and Works Property)

Bainbridge: Roman fort.
Beningborough, near Newton-on-Ouse: *Beningborough Hall.
Bowes: †Bowes Castle.
Byland Abbey†.
Castle Bolton.
Castle Howard.
Coverham Abbey.
†**Easby Abbey.**
†**Egglestone Abbey.**
Glaisdale: Byre Art Gallery.
†**Guisborough Priory.**
†**Helmsley Castle.**
Jervaulx Abbey.

Kiplin Hall.
Middleham: †Castle.
  *Braithwaite Hall.
Middlesbrough: Art Gallery.
†**Mount Grace Priory.**
***Nunnington Hall.**
***Ormesby Hall.**
†**Pickering Castle.**
Richmond: †Castle.
  †Georgian Theatre.
  †Green Howards Museum.
†**Rievaulx Abbey.**
Scarborough: †Castle.
  †Art Gallery.
Whitby: Pannett Art Gallery.

Some Museums

1. **Hutton-le-Hole:** Ryedale Folk Museum.
2. **Malton:** Roman Museum.
3. **Middlesbrough:** Dorman Memorial Museum.

4. **Scarborough:** Museum; Natural History Museum, Wood End.
5. **Whitby:** Pannett Museum.

NORTH RIDING TOWNS AND VILLAGES

In this key to our map of Yorkshire are all the towns and villages treated in this book. If a place is not on the map by name, its square is given here, so that the way to it is easily found, each square being five miles.

Ainderby Steeple	K6	Burneston	K7	Egglestone Abbey	G3	Hornby	J5
Aislaby	R3	Buttercrambe	P10			Hovingham	O8
Aldwark	M9	Byland Abbey	N7	Egton	Q4	Hudswell	H5
Allerston	R7			Ellerburn	Q6	Huntington	O10
Alne	M9	Carlton Hus-		Ellerton Abbey	G5	Hurst	G4
Amotherby	P8	thwaite	M8	Eryholme	K4	Husthwaite	N8
Ampleforth	N7	Carlton-in-		Eston	N2	Hutton Buscel	S6
Appleton-le-Moors		Cleveland	M4			Hutton-le-Hole	P6
	P6	Carperby	F6	Faceby	M4	Hutton Lowcross	
Appleton-le-Street		Castle Bolton	G6	Farlington	O9		O3
	P8	Castle Howard	P8	Felixkirk	M7	Hutton Rudby	M4
Appleton Wiske		Castleton	P3	Finghall	H6	Huttons Ambo	Q8
	L4	Catterick	J5	Forcett	H3		
Aske	H4	Cayton	T7	Foston	P9	Ingleby Arncliffe	
Askrigg	F6	Cleasby	J3				M4
Aysgarth	F6	Cloughton	S5	Gate Helmsley	P10	Ingleby Greenhow	
		Cold Kirby	N6	Gayle	E6		N4
Bainbridge	E6	Constable Burton		Gillamoor	O6		
Baldersby	L7		H6	Gilling	H4	Jervaulx Abbey	
Barningham	G3	Cotherstone	F2	Glaisdale	Q4		H6
Barton	J4	Coverham	G6	Goathland	Q4		
Barton-le-Street		Coxwold	N7	Great Ayton	N3	Keld	E5
	P8	Crambe	P9	Great Crakehall		Kettleness	Q3
Bedale	J6	Crathorne	M4		J6	Kilburn	M7
Bellerby	G5	Crayke	N8	Great Edstone	P7	Kildale	O3
Bilsdale	N4	Croft	K3	Great Langton	K5	Kiplin	K5
Bilsdale Midcable		Cropton	P6	Great Smeaton	K4	Kirby Hill	
	N5	Cundall	L8	Greta Bridge	G3	(Borough-	
Birdforth	M8			Grinton	G5	bridge)	L9
Birkby	K4	Dalby	O8	Gristhorpe	T7	Kirby Hill (Rich-	
Boltby	M6	Danby-in-Cleve-		Grosmont	Q4	mond)	H4
Bolton-on-Swale		land	P3	Guisborough	O3	Kirby Knowle	M6
	J5	Danby Wiske	K5			Kirby Misperton	
Borrowby	L6	Downholme	H5	Hackness	S6		Q7
Bossall	P9			Hardrow	E6	Kirbymoorside	P6
Bowes	F3	Easby	H5	Hart Leap Well		Kirby Sigston	L5
Brafferton	M8	Easington	P2		H5	Kirby Wiske	L6
Brandsby	N8	Easingwold	N8	Hauxwell	H5	Kirkby Fleetham	
Brignall	G3	East Ayton	S6	Hawes	E6		K5
Brompton (North-		East Cowton	K4	Hawnby	N6	Kirkby-in-Cleve-	
allerton)	L5	East Gilling	O7	Hawsker	R4	land	N4
Brompton (Scar-		East Harsley	L5	Haxby	O10	Kirkdale	O6
borough)	S7	East Layton	H3	Helmsley	O7	Kirkleatham	N2
Brotton	O2	East Rounton	L4	Hilton	M3	Kirk Leavington	
Brough	H5	East Witton	H6	Hinderwell	Q2		L3
Bulmer	P9	Ebberston	R7	Hipswell	H5	Kirklington	K7
				Holwick	E1		

245